CONTEMPLATION AND FREEDOM

Contemplation and Freedom

The Liberating Power of Spiritual Practice

Edited by
BENEDICT R. SHOUP
and
MARY FROHLICH

PICKWICK *Publications* · Eugene, Oregon

CONTEMPLATION AND FREEDOM
The Liberating Power of Spiritual Practice

Copyright © 2025 Wipf and Stock Publishers. All rights reserved. Except for brief quotations in critical publications or reviews, no part of this book may be reproduced in any manner without prior written permission from the publisher. Write: Permissions, Wipf and Stock Publishers, 199 W. 8th Ave., Suite 3, Eugene, OR 97401.

Pickwick Publications
An Imprint of Wipf and Stock Publishers
199 W. 8th Ave., Suite 3
Eugene, OR 97401

www.wipfandstock.com

PAPERBACK ISBN: 979-8-3852-1602-4
HARDCOVER ISBN: 979-8-3852-1603-1
EBOOK ISBN: 979-8-3852-1604-8

Cataloguing-in-Publication data:

Names: Shoup, Benedict R., editor. | Frohlich, Mary, editor.

Title: Contemplation and freedom: the liberating power of spiritual practice / edited by Benedict R. Shoup and Mary Frohlich.

Description: Eugene, OR : Pickwick Publications, 2025 | Includes bibliographical references.

Identifiers: ISBN 979-8-3852-1602-4 (paperback) | ISBN 979-8-3852-1603-1 (hardcover) | ISBN 979-8-3852-1604-8 (ebook)

Subjects: LCSH: Spiritual life. | Spirituality. | Freedom (Theology). | Liberty—Religious aspects—Christianity.

Classification: BT83.57 .C675 2025 (paperback) | BT83.57 .C675 (ebook)

VERSION NUMBER 04/21/25

Scripture quotations marked NABRE are taken from the New American Bible, revised edition © 2010, 1991, 1986, 1970 Confraternity of Christian Doctrine, Washington, DC, and are used by permission of the copyright owner. All Rights Reserved. No part of the New American Bible may be reproduced in any form without permission in writing from the copyright owner.

Scripture quotations marked NRSVue are taken from the New Revised Standard Version Updated Edition. Copyright © 2021 National Council of Churches of Christ in the United States of America. Used by permission. All rights reserved worldwide. Scripture quotations marked NIV are taken from the Holy Bible, New International Version®, NIV®. Copyright © 1973, 1978, 1984, 2011 by Biblica, Inc.™ Used by permission of Zondervan. All rights reserved worldwide. www.zondervan.com. The "NIV" and "New International Version" are trademarks registered in the United States Patent and Trademark Office by Biblica, Inc.™

Contents

Contributors | vii

Introduction | 1
BENEDICT R. SHOUP

LIFE

1   Christian de Chergé: Freedom, Community, and the Martyrdom of Love | 17
    CHRISTIAN KROKUS

2   The Freedom of the Contemplative: Thérèse of Lisieux in Dialogue with Louis Lavelle | 30
    MARY FROHLICH

3   Fire's Triptych: Rimbaud, Virgil, and Annie Dillard's Contemplative Transformation | 48
    KRISTEN DRAHOS

THEORY

4   Kenosis and Freedom | 65
    JACOB W. TORBECK

5   Interiority as Freedom: Arendt and Stein | 81
    PETER NGUYEN

6   The Freedom of Being Before God: The Sanjuanist Paradigm of Freedom in Edith Stein and Jean-Yves Lacoste | 99
    BENEDICT R. SHOUP

7   Divine Desire, Divine Freedom: Coakley and Lonergan on Prayer in Trinitarian Theology | 118
    JONATHAN HEAPS

PRACTICE

8   The Liberating Transformation of Mystical Eros | 139
   AMY MAXEY

9   Reclaiming Silence as a Spiritual and Political Practice of Freedom | 156
   MIN-AH CHO

10   On Care for Our Common *Gnome:* Eco-Spirituality and Freedom in Maximus the Confessor | 172
   KATHLEEN MCNUTT

11   *Lectio Divina* and Freedom: The Prayerful, Poetic Witness of Christophe Lebreton | 186
   MICHAEL RUBBELKE

Contributors

MIN-AH CHO, Assistant Teaching Professor of Theology and Religious Studies at Georgetown University.

KRISTEN DRAHOS, Assistant Professor of Great Texts and Theology at Baylor University.

MARY FROHLICH, RSCJ, Professor Emerita at the Catholic Theological Union; Visiting Scholar at the Clough School of Theology and Ministry, Boston College.

JONATHAN HEAPS, Director of the Bernard J. Lonergan Institute at Seton Hall University.

CHRISTIAN KROKUS, Professor of Theology/Religious Studies at the University of Scranton.

AMY MAXEY, Assistant Professor of Spirituality and Rolheiser Chair in Spirituality at the Oblate School of Theology.

KATHLEEN MCNUTT, Teaching Assistant Professor of Theology at Marquette University.

PETER NGUYEN, SJ, Associate Professor of Religious Studies at the College of the Holy Cross.

MICHAEL RUBBELKE, Assistant Professor of Spirituality and Monastic Studies at the College of Saint Benedict and Saint John's University.

BENEDICT R. SHOUP, Doctoral Candidate in Systematic Theology at the University of Notre Dame.

JACOB W. TORBECK, Sisters of St. Francis Endowed Professor in Theology at Briar Cliff University.

Introduction

Benedict R. Shoup[1]

CONTEMPLATION AND THEOLOGY

In the 1990s, Christophe Lebreton, a Frenchman by birth, lived near a small Muslim community that was increasingly threatened by the out-of-control violence of the Algerian civil war.[2] A peaceful man who farmed with his neighbors and served their needs, he nonetheless became a target of Islamic militants. Two years before he was murdered by terrorists, he wrote in his journal that while he felt more and more like a hostage in his own home, he identified this experience "with the little people, with a view to LIBERATION and with the very FREEDOM of Jesus Christ."[3] It is easy enough to believe that these are the words of a radical Christian committed to interreligious dialogue and loving tolerance in the face of lawless hate. That this radical was a Trappist monk, equally committed to a fifteen-hundred-year-old way of life dominated by contemplative prayer, might strike the contemporary mind as strange. It is precisely the sense of wonder at the paradoxical collision of silent prayer and liberating freedom that this book takes as its point of departure.

This volume asks how Christian contemplation and freedom relate to each other. Each essay adopts some facet of contemplative prayer as a methodological point of departure or linchpin. With these methodological tools, the authors probe different dimensions of freedom, both in itself and in terms of its individual and communal realization. What emerges from

---

1. Special thanks to Mary Frohlich and Amy Maxey for comments and bibliographical recommendations.

2. For a brief biographical introduction to Lebreton, see Kiser, *Monks of Tibhirine*, 64–66, 79–82.

3. Lebreton, *Born from the Gaze*, 82, cited by Rubbelke in chapter 11 of this volume.

these studies is a common set of insights born from a shared contemplative methodology: that prayer opens new horizons of personal and communal self-understanding and responsibility; that prayer and loving service are inseparably linked; that the solitude of contemplative prayer is not a retreat from the human family, but a privileged foundation for solidarity with the forgotten and oppressed.

Linking prayer and theological reflection has deep roots in twentieth-century theology. Karl Rahner and Hans Urs von Balthasar were two of the greatest systematic minds of their age. But they were also two of the greatest champions of Christian mysticism.[4] This combination of systematics and mysticism was no accident. Both figures, in fact, worked to reintegrate theology with the life of Christian prayer.[5] And if Balthasar and Rahner concerned themselves more directly with the speculative domain, the pioneers of liberation and political theology were no less interested in the synthesis of theology and prayer. Gustavo Gutiérrez, James Cone, and Johann Baptist Metz all insisted on the fundamental importance of prayer for liberative action.[6] In the wake of these seminal contributions, a growing number of studies have taken up the question of how to integrate prayer and theology.[7] Along with this methodological work, an even wider array of theologians have increasingly appealed to prayer as a means of addressing a panoply of theoretical and practical problems, ranging from racism and the environmental crisis to the presumptuousness of philosophical rationalism.[8]

4. McGinn, "Role of Mysticism," 380, 383–89; *Foundations of Mysticism*, 285–90.

5. McGinn, "Role of Mysticism," 380; Balthasar, "Theology and Sanctity." On Rahner's integration of theology and spirituality throughout his corpus, see Egan, "Theology and Spirituality," 13–28. For important examples of this integration, see Rahner, *Dynamic Element in the Church*; *Experience of the Spirit*.

6. Gutiérrez, *On Job*; Cone, *Spirituals and the Blues*; Metz, *Passion for God*. Concerning Cone, Andrew Prevot argues for the strong hermeneutical priority of prayer across his work, especially as drawn from black spirituals. See Prevot, *Thinking Prayer*, 288–94. On Gutiérrez and Metz, see Ashley, *Take Lord, Receive*.

7. A notable event in this trajectory came when Constance Fitzgerald became the first contemplative nun to address the Catholic Theological Society of America (CTSA) in 2009. For a collection of Fitzgerald's essays (including her address to the CTSA, published as "From Impasse to Prophetic Hope") coupled with the work of other scholars engaging with her thought, see Cassidy and Copeland, *Desire, Darkness, and Hope*. For other examples with a specifically methodological edge, see Sheldrake, *Spirituality and Theology*; McIntosh, *Mystical Theology*; Sölle, *Silent Cry*; Hughes, *Beloved Dust*; Coakley, *God, Sexuality, and the Self*; Lacoste, *Theological Thinking*; Cocksworth, *Prayer*; Robinette, *Difference Nothing Makes*; Prevot, *Thinking Prayer*.

8. The literature is extensive. For a sampling, see Coakley, "Spiritual Perception and the Racist Gaze"; Williams, "Deflections of Desire"; Frohlich, "John of the Cross"; Robinette, *Difference Nothing Makes*; Laird, "Open Country"; Christie, *Blue Sapphire of the Mind*; *Insurmountable Darkness of Love*; Copeland; *Knowing Christ Crucified*; Holmes, *Joy Unspeakable*.

INTRODUCTION

The topic of freedom has not been absent from this contemplative-theological tapestry, running like a golden thread throughout its development. Yet, the present volume aims to bring this line of thought to the foreground. While contemporary theologians intent on reintegrating prayer and theology have taken the relationship between prayer and freedom seriously,[9] this volume consciously and directly brings freedom to the center of the conversation. To this end, the following essays both unveil the (at times subtle) presence of this theme in the study of theology and spirituality over the past century, while also developing it by offering constructive proposals about how contemplation can continue to foster freedom in the face of the powers that oppose it.

The history of contemplation, for its part, is so complex that it makes the term difficult to define or encapsulate.[10] In late antiquity, contemplation entered Christian life and discourse through the patristic integration of Greek and Latin philosophical terms (*theoria* and *contemplatio*) with a certain set of episodes and concepts from the Bible (Moses's vision of God's back, the parable of Martha and Mary, John's language of trinitarian indwelling, etc.).[11] Patristic approaches to the meaning and gradations of contemplation varied. In the *Life of Moses*, for example, Gregory of Nyssa distinguished between "intellectual *theoria*" and "mystical *theoria*."[12] Augustine, for his part, understood contemplation of the Trinity as the eschatological goal of Christian life.[13] With the rise of monasticism in late antiquity and then the mendicant revolution in the high Middle Ages, the "contemplative life" and the "active life" became increasingly reified as distinct modes of Christian living. The "contemplative life" of the monastery focused on prayer,

---

9. Prevot draws out the thread of freedom running through many important authors in *Thinking Prayer*, including Hans Urs von Balthasar (70–110), Jean-Louis Chrétien (140–59), Metz (165–217), Gutiérrez (235–41), Ignacio Ellacuría (249–74), and Cone (280–325). For examples of other contemporary voices, see Holmes, *Joy Unspeakable*, 111–62; Sheldrake, *Spirituality and Theology*, 129–64. Robinette talks about freedom in a number of places, but explicitly ties it to contemplation in *Difference Nothing Makes*, 49–50.

10. For brief introductions to the Christian history and meaning of contemplation, see Frohlich, "Contemplation"; Nef, "Contemplation," 353–61. McGinn's *Presence of God* series, one of the great works of historical theology in the last half-century, is in effect a history of the "mystical" valence of contemplation in Western Christianity (*Growth of Mysticism*, ix–xv). For McGinn's understanding of "mysticism," see *Foundations of Mysticism*, xiii–xx; 265–343; "Mystical Consciousness."

11. Nef, "Contemplation," 353–4. See, for example, Exod 33:18–23; Luke 10:38–42; John 14:23; 17:20–23.

12. Nef, "Contemplation," 354.

13. Augustine, *Trinity* 1.17; 15.44. On the meaning and significance of contemplation in *De Trinitate*, see Cavadini, "Structure and Intention of De Trinitate."

and the "active life" of the mendicants prioritized apostolic ministry.[14] But theologians also worked to develop the sense in which the contemplative and active dimensions of Christian living depended upon and mutually enriched each other.[15]

In the early modern period, the Carmelites Teresa of Avila and John of the Cross pushed the notion of contemplation to new heights, exploring the transformation of consciousness that takes place in union with God.[16] At the same time, Ignatius of Loyola and others continued to develop more quotidian forms of contemplative prayer involving, for example, richly imaginative reconstructions of Biblical scenes.[17] Reflection on contemplation from the seventeenth century to the twentieth included both greater systematization of different states of contemplation, and a debate over the distinction between "acquired" and "infused" contemplation that reached its climax in the early twentieth-century Catholic controversy on the nature of mysticism.[18] Thus, from its patristic origins, contemplation has evolved and developed in multiple directions, describing a wide range of Christian practices, although with a consistent orientation towards the connotative domains of silence, solitude, and mysticism.

This volume adopts the term contemplation (rather than using another term for prayer, or simply speaking of "prayer" in general) in order to pick up several of the resonances that have emerged from contemplation's history. First, contemplation's connection with the notion of the "contemplative life" allows us to speak about prayer as a pervasive set of activities that orient the whole Christian life towards union with God. In other words, the exploration of contemplation lends itself to the consideration of the whole Christian experience from the perspective of prayer. Second, theologians have long compared and contrasted prayer and service using the duality of "contemplation and action." Therefore, the term contemplation lends itself to the probing of this binary. One of the primary thrusts of this volume has

---

14. For Aquinas's theology of these two states of life, see *ST* II-II.179–82.

15. See, for example Bernard, *Sermons for the Autumn Season*, 41–52; Eckhardt, *Meister Eckhart*, 177–81.

16. Nef, "Contemplation," 357–59. McGinn favors the language of "mystical consciousness," using John of the Cross as an important historical justification of this move. See McGinn, "Mystical Consciousness," 57–59.

17. On Ignatius, see the discussion in Gans, *Spiritual Exercises*, 162. On other notions of contemplation developing around this time, see Nef, "Contemplation," 359.

18. Nef, "Contemplation," 359. The two seminal figures in the twentieth-century debate were Augustin Poulain and Auguste Saudreau. See esp. Poulain, *Graces of Interior Prayer*; Saudreau, *Mystical State*. See also Nef, "Contemplation," 359; McGinn, *Foundations of Mysticism*, 278–79. For a helpful and broad history of the early twentieth-century debate, see Rubbelke, "Constant Closeness," 11–59.

been to elucidate the deep-seated interdependence of contemplation and action, precisely by examining the relationship between prayer and freedom, from which ethical action itself emerges.

Thus, contemplation provides this volume's methodological lens for approaching the topic of freedom. When it comes to defining freedom and excavating its history, our authors bring together a wide sweep of historical and contemporary resources, ranging from Maximus the Confessor and Thérèse of Lisieux to Jean-Yves Lacoste and M. Shawn Copeland. Therefore, each study speaks about freedom and liberation in its own voice.[19] But several motifs run through the volume, adding a distinctive harmony to the collection. Three stand out. The first establishes a kind of negative boundary, while the second two frame the positive content of much of the conversation that unfolds throughout the book. Concerning the first, explicitly or implicitly, the following essays distance themselves from the modern notion of freedom as autonomous, individual choice made possible by the absence of constraint.[20] Certainly, autonomy and lack of constraint are not irrelevant to the study of freedom. But our authors propose that they do not encapsulate either its essence or its purpose.

And if we leave the work of elucidating this essence and purpose to the chapters themselves, we would nonetheless like to frame the ensuing discussions with two more points based on a well-known distinction, memorably enriched by Gustavo Gutiérrez. The classic move that Gutiérrez picks up is the differentiation between "freedom from" and "freedom for." But he translates this notion into his own idiom of liberation in a way that speaks to the concern with oppressions and violence that runs throughout this volume. Gutiérrez explains that "freedom from" means "Liberation from sin . . . selfishness, injustice, need, and situations calling for deliverance."[21] Many of our essays concentrate on this dimension of freedom or liberation: the active overcoming of the multi-layered nexus of powers that entrap, intimidate, and dominate. "Freedom for," on the other hand, stands for "the final phase of liberation . . . namely, love and communion . . . with God and others."[22] In concert with this notion of "freedom from," our authors develop communal conceptions of freedom that locate its possibility and its end in relations of love with God and neighbor. These two mutually implicated

---

19. One might reasonably draw distinctions between "freedom" and "liberation." For the purposes of our introduction, we have used both terms fairly interchangeably in order to leave space for our authors to establish more precise delineations.

20. For an examination this modern conception of freedom, see Torbeck's "Context and Critiques of Kenotic Freedom" in chapter 4 of this volume.

21. Gutiérrez, *Truth*, 152, 29.

22. Gutiérrez, *Truth*, 29, 152.

ways of thinking about freedom thus provide some initial context concerning the communal and justice-oriented explorations of freedom that follow.

CHAPTER SUMMARIES

We derive the structure of this volume from the delineation of three different ways that contemplation and freedom intersect. Although most of the essays deal with multiple intersections, we have organized them according to the relationship between contemplation and freedom that stands out in each. The first section focuses on the "contemplative life" taken in its broadest sense, that is, as a prayerful journey of transformation in Christ. These essays offer examples of how this way of life opens new possibilities for human freedom, especially under the pressures of suffering and/or violence. The second section takes a more speculative turn, concentrating on how theories of contemplation and freedom can mutually enrich each other. The third section focuses more directly on contemplative practices and their liberative power.

Life

Our volume begins with Christian Krokus's essay on the Trappist monk Christian de Chergé, who, along with Christophe Lebreton and five of their monastic brothers, was martyred during the Algerian civil war in 1996. Krokus shows how De Chergé's practices of prayerful vulnerability gave him extraordinary freedom to share life and discernment with his Muslim neighbors. Krokus focuses especially on de Cherge's freedom to dialogue, to let the Muslim community shape his discernment, and in the end, to commit to the kind of incarnational being-with that transformed his murder into a sign of Christ's unfailing love. Krokus thereby investigates the yield for interreligious dialogue of one of the contemplative life's most elemental forms, that is, the vow of stability, and the life of prayer that then unfolds in the context of a very specific community. This community, for de Chergé, extended beyond his Catholic monastery and into his primarily Muslim environment. In the end, then, De Chergé's vulnerability to learn, discern, and devote his life to his Muslim friends and neighbors offers insights into the way that contemplative freedom can shape and enhance interreligious dialogue.

Mary Frohlich explores another aspect of contemplative life, this time focusing not so much on the contemplative's literal place in the world, but on the more interior process of transformation in Christ. For her analysis of transformation and freedom, she turns to Thérèse of Lisieux. The fact that Thérèse wrote very little explicitly about freedom complicates this task. Therefore, Frohlich enlists the philosophy of Louis Lavelle, a contemporary of Thérèse, who provides resources that can help us to translate key moments from Thérèse's life and writings into the idiom of freedom. What Frohlich shows is that Thérèse's confrontations with life's quotidian challenges demonstrate the gradual emergence of freedom for love and solidarity. In this way, Thérèse's witness discloses the way that seemingly mundane struggles can figure into a profound story of co-creation through cooperation with divine grace.

Completing our opening triptych, Kristen Drahos uses the motif of fire from Annie Dillard's *Holy the Firm* to shift our attention from classical forms of Christian contemplative life to the wilderness of prayer and suffering in the heart of the world. For Dillard, what was meant to be a writing retreat on Lummi Island turned upside down when a plane crashed on the island, resulting in the horrific burning of a child. Dillard cannot contemplate pain from afar. Rather, she lets the agony before her wrap her into a drama of solidarity, a drama that speculative theodicy fails to manage or contain. Under the pressure of this tragedy, the image of the flame forces itself across the distinction between viewer and viewed, contemplative and victim. Pain becomes the catalyst that frees those who pray to enlace their lives with those who suffer. In this way, Drahos introduces several themes that will characterize many of the ensuing essays: the translation of insights from traditional modes of Christian contemplation into a diverse set of analogous practices, the unification of contemplation and action, and the relationship between contemplation and solidarity with the suffering other.

Theory

Jacob Torbeck begins our second section by taking the collision between mystical and both modern and postmodern theories of freedom head on. The Christian mystical tradition has consistently held up self-emptying humility and obedience to Christ, that is, *kenosis*, as a constitutive element of freedom. Modern liberal thought, on the other hand, proposes autonomous choice without constraint as the essence of freedom. Postmodern thinkers, in their turn, have criticized *kenotic* freedom precisely for the way that it buoys up modern notions of indulgent individualism, while also supporting submissiveness to domination. Against this modern/postmodern pincer movement, Torbeck responds by developing kenotic freedom across three twentieth-century thinkers: Hans Urs von Balthasar, Simone Weil, and

Howard Thurman. Against the charge of individualism, Balthasar underscores the way that kenotic readings of mystical freedom make room in the self for both God and every human other. Responding to concerns about submissive passivity, Weil reveals that this kenotic "making room" for the other begins with the activity of attentiveness to God and neighbor. And against concerns that mystical freedom is self-centered, Thurman shows that the mystic has an obligation to work in history for the justice that she has tasted in prayer. By weaving together these three thinkers, then, Torbeck demonstrates that kenotic freedom means neither solipsism nor subservience, but the attentive integration of the good of the other into the self's core dispositions and endeavors.

Peter Nguyen enacts a conversation between Hannah Arendt and Edith Stein in order to address a specific question: how do we find freedom when faced with pervasive evil? Arendt's analysis of totalitarianism provides a starting point for considering the effects of wide-spread injustice and its capacity to normalize appalling violence. Arendt hypothesizes that personal interiority might protect against this normalization. But she wonders what in fact has the power to break through the psychological buffers that already rubble over communities trapped in totalitarian systems. Nguyen turns to Stein to propose a two-fold solution. First, Stein develops a theory of interiority that builds out the integral reciprocity between contemplative solitude and freedom to love one's neighbor. Second, Stein's martyrdom in solidarity with the victims of totalitarianism gives an example of the kind of manifestation of freedom that might succeed at breaking through evil's shell of banality. Contemplation thus becomes a resource for reimagining both the self in the community and the possibilities of liberative resistance.

Benedict Shoup also takes up Edith Stein, but this time in conversation with Jean-Yves Lacoste and one of their great common influences: St. John of the Cross. Specifically, he explores the influence of John's contemplative "dark night" on Stein's and Lacoste's philosophies of freedom. These two theorists deal with freedom in different contexts, and they have yet to be brought into sustained conversation. But Shoup argues that their common reliance on John's theology of darkness causes them to structure their conceptions of freedom in similar ways. For Stein and Lacoste, the sanjuanist night stands for a disorienting confrontation between divine freedom and human limitation. This confrontation proves generative, leading to a transformation of the self that extends human freedom beyond the confines of finite human experience and into a horizon defined by a relation with the divine. Although both thinkers concentrate especially on freedom in a more theoretical vein, Shoup illustrates how Stein and Lacoste ultimately offer positions on freedom that can guide ethical action in the face of evil.

Jonathan Heaps shifts our attention to Bernard Lonergan's understanding of freedom, using it to explore the yield of contemplation for theological methodology. To do so, he brings Lonergan into conversation with Sarah Coakley, one of the most influential contemporary pioneers of the use of contemplative prayer in systematic theology. Coakley suggests that focusing on contemplation brings desire to the center of theological methodology in general, and to the analysis of the identity of the Holy Spirit in particular. Heaps draws out the connection between Coakley on desire and Lonergan's identification of the free unfolding of the eros of the human spirit as the driver of human authenticity. What Coakley adds to Lonergan's methodology is a kind of contemplative practice that makes the personal appropriation and nourishment of the (Lonerganian) unrestricted desire to know possible. What this Coaklian twist on Lonerganian psychology further suggests is that the free impulse of the desiring mind might itself form a new way of thinking about the procession of the Spirit. That is, this free impulse might serve as a kind of supplement to the psychological analogy, one that enriches our understanding of the Spirit's place in the Trinity in particular. For Heaps, then, contemplative practice not only contributes to theological methodology broadly construed, but may in fact open up quite specific perspectives on classical theological themes.

Practice

Amy Maxey continues our discussion of Bernard Lonergan, while shifting the focus of the volume more squarely into the domain of praxis. Capitalizing on the dominant connotation of contemplation in its Christian history, Maxey addresses mysticism directly. She demonstrates that the right conceptualization of mystical consciousness makes it possible to think through the kinds of contemplative practices that can transform mystical eros for God into freedom to imitate Christ. She begins by enriching Bernard McGinn's theory of mystical consciousness with M. Shawn Copeland's understanding of eros in order to flesh out the relation between contemplation and the embodied exigencies of communal life. She then employs Lonergan's model of authenticity to explore the ways that specific prayer practices, like the daily examen, can translate growth in mystical eros into new horizons of responsible action. Thus, for Maxey, contemplative prayer does not end in detached abstraction, but instead integrates the Christian more fully into Christ's solidarity with, and loving regard for, marginalized others.

Min-Ah Cho opens an interrogation of silence itself. Cho questions the unthinking vociferousness of modern political life, which so often lionizes speech and autonomy over and against silence and communal listening. Cho then uses Paul W. Gooch's reflection on Christ's silence to propose a substantive model of contemplative silence, one that emphasizes its possibilities as a practice of both trust in God and resistance. She goes on to explore the concrete exercise of christoform silence in Christian liturgy, discerning how what we learn from liturgical silence can extend into our daily lives. For Cho, contemplative silence becomes not the opposite of autonomous speech, but rather a practice that makes room for the speech of the other, divine and human, a practice that buys time and perspective for redirecting freedom towards the good of these beloved others.

Shifting from the social to the environmental, Kathleen McNutt draws on resources from Maximus the Confessor to fill out the axial lineaments of an ecological spirituality. She proposes that capitalist consumerism funds a simplistic notion of freedom that reduces freedom to lack of constraint coupled with sufficiently plentiful options. But understanding freedom as the unconstrained selection among alternatives does not open any clear avenues for integrally linking freedom to ecological action. In response, McNutt lifts up Maximus, who argues that real freedom (arising from the "natural will") means participation in divine desire for the common good, a good which, for McNutt, must include the flourishing of the environment. Furthermore, Maximus's contemplation of nature (*theoria physike*) represents a practice that cultivates the kind of goodwill towards the created order that promotes care for our common home. Thus, McNutt's Maximian coupling of freedom and prayer suggests a way to link freedom itself to the healing of the environment.

Michael Rubbelke brings the volume to a close with a return to the Tibhirine martyrs. Rubbelke takes up Christophe Lebreton's spiritual journal, written in the three years leading up to his death, as a study in the way that the practice of *lectio divina* (sacred reading) can foster freedom in opposition to fear and violence. Rubbelke introduces *lectio divina* through Guigo II's classic text, *The Ladder of Monks*, before turning to the record of Lebreton's own lectio, focusing especially on his re-reading of John 6:67–68. Lebreton's prayer with this text became a decisive event in his discernment to stay in Algeria for the sake of "the little people," the villagers and neighbors with whom he lived and worked, and with whom he suffered the effects of the war. Ultimately, Lebreton's careful listening in prayer empowered him to participate in Christ's freedom to live and to suffer with the victims of violence. Rubbelke's essay thus serves as a fitting close to the book, summarizing in concrete form the way that contemplative practices free us from the coercion of violence, and for solidarity with our brothers and sisters.

REFERENCES

Aquinas, Thomas. *The Summa Theologica*. Translated by the Fathers of the English Dominican Province. New York: Benziger Bros., 1947.

Ashley, J. Matthew. *Take Lord and Receive All My Memory: Toward an Anamnestic Mysticism*. Milwaukee, WI: Marquette University Press, 2015.

Augustine. *The Trinity*. Translated by Edmund Hill. New York: New City, 1991.

Balthasar, Hans Urs von. "Theology and Sanctity." In *The Word Made Flesh*, 181–210. Translated by A. V. Littledale with Alexander Dru. Vol. 1 of *Explorations in Theology*. San Francisco: Ignatius, 1989.

Bernard of Clairvaux. *Sermons for the Autumn Season*. Translated by Irene Edmonds et al. Collegeville, MN: Liturgical, 2016.

Cassidy, Laurie, and M. Shawn Copeland, eds. *Desire, Darkness, and Hope: Theology in a Time of Impasse: Engaging the Thought of Constance FitzGerald, OCD*. Collegeville, MN: Liturgical, 2021.

Cavadini, John. "The Structure and Intention of Augustine's De Trinitate." *Augustinian Studies* 23 (1992) 103–23.

Christie, Douglas E. *The Blue Sapphire of the Mind: Notes for a Contemplative Ecology*. New York: Oxford University Press, 2012.

———. *The Insurmountable Darkness of Love: Mysticism, Loss, and the Common Life*. Oxford: Oxford University Press, 2022.

Coakley, Sarah. *God, Sexuality, and the Self: An Essay "On the Trinity."* New York: Cambridge University Press, 2013.

———. "Spiritual Perception and the Racist Gaze: Can Contemplation Shift Racism?" In *Perceiving Things Divine: Towards a Constructive Account of Spiritual Perception*, edited by Frederick D. Aquino and Paul Gavrilyuk, 153–76. Oxford: Oxford University Press, 2022.

Cocksworth, Ashley. *Prayer: A Guide for the Perplexed*. New York: Bloomsbury Academic, 2018.

Cone, James H. *The Spirituals and the Blues: An Interpretation*. New York: Seabury, 1972.

Copeland, M. Shawn. *Knowing Christ Crucified: The Witness of African American Religious Experience*. Maryknoll, NY: Orbis, 2018.

Eckhart. *Meister Eckhart: The Essential Sermons, Commentaries, Treatises, and Defense*. Translated by Edmund Colledge and Bernard McGinn. Mahwah, NJ: Paulist, 1981.

Egan, Harvey D. "Theology and Spirituality." In *The Cambridge Companion to Karl Rahner*, edited by Declan Marmion and Mary E. Himes, 13–28. Cambridge: Cambridge University Press, 2005.

FitzGerald, Constance. "From Impasse to Prophetic Hope: Crisis of Memory." *Proceedings of the Catholic Theological Society of America* 64 (2013) 21–42.

Frohlich, Mary. "Contemplation." In *Prayer in the Catholic Tradition: A Handbook of Practical Approaches*, edited by Robert J. Wicks, 65–76. Cincinnati, OH: Franciscan, 2016.

———. "'O Sweet Cautery': John of the Cross and the Healing of the Natural World." *Horizons* 43.2 (2016) 308–31.

Gutiérrez, Gustavo. *On Job: God-Talk and the Suffering of the Innocent*. Translated by Matthew J. O'Connell. Maryknoll, NY: Orbis, 1987.

Holmes, Barbara A. *Joy Unspeakable: Contemplative Practices of the Black Church*. Minneapolis, MN: Fortress, 2017.

Hughes, Robert Davis. *Beloved Dust: Tides of the Spirit in the Christian Life*. New York: Continuum, 2008.

Ignatius of Loyola. *The Spiritual Exercises of Saint Ignatius*. Translated by George E. Ganss. St. Louis, MO: The Institute of Jesuit Sources, 1992.

Kiser, John W. *The Monks of Tibhirine: Faith, Love, and Terror in Algeria*. New York: St. Martin's, 2002.

Lacoste, Jean-Yves. *From Theology to Theological Thinking*. Translated by W. Chris Hackett. Charlottesville: University of Virginia Press, 2014.

Laird, Martin. "The Open Country Whose Name is Prayer: Apophasis, Deconstruction, and Contemplative Practice." *Modern Theology* 21.1 (2005) 141–55.

Lebreton, Christophe. *Born from the Gaze of God: The Tibhirine Journal of a Martyr Monk (1993–1996)*. Collegeville, MN: Cistercian/Liturgical, 2014.

McGinn, Bernard. *The Foundations of Mysticism: Origins to the Fifth Century*. Vol. 1 of *The Presence of God*. New York: Crossroad, 1991.

———. *The Growth of Mysticism: Gregory the Great through the Twelfth Century*. Vol. 2 of *The Presence of God*. New York: Crossroad, 1994.

———. "Mystical Consciousness: A Modest Proposal." *Spiritus* 8.1 (2008) 44–63.

———. "The Role of Mysticism in Modern Theology." *Annali di scienze religiose* 7 (2014) 373–400.

McIntosh, Mark Allen. *Mystical Theology: The Integrity of Spirituality and Theology*. Malden, MA: Blackwell, 1998.

Metz, Johann Baptist. *A Passion for God: The Mystical-Political Dimension of Christianity*. Translated by J. Matthew Ashley. New York: Paulist, 1998.

Nef, Frédéric. "Contemplation." In Vol. 1 of *Encyclopedia of Christian Theology*, edited by Jean-Yves Lacoste, 353–61. London: Routledge, 2019.

Poulin, Augustin. *The Graces of Interior Prayer: A Treatise on Mystical Theology*. Translated by Leonora L. Jeffersonville IN: Caritas, 2016.

Prevot, Andrew L. *The Mysticism of Ordinary Life: Theology, Philosophy, and Feminism*. Oxford: Oxford University Press, 2023.

———. *Thinking Prayer: Theology and Spirituality Amid the Crises of Modernity*. Notre Dame, IN: University of Notre Dame Press, 2015.

Rahner, Karl. *The Dynamic Element in the Church*. Translated by W. J. O'Hara. New York: Herder and Herder, 1964.

———. *Experience of the Spirit: Source of Theology*. Translated by David Morland. Theological Investigations 16. New York: Herder and Herder, 1979.

Robinette, Brian D. *The Difference Nothing Makes: Creation, Christ, Contemplation*. Notre Dame, IN: University of Notre Dame Press, 2023.

Rubbelke, Michael. "'A Constant Closeness to This God': Reconsidering Karl Rahner's Mystical Theology." PhD diss., University of Notre Dame, 2018.

Saudreau, Auguste. *The Mystical State: Its Nature and Phases*. Translated by D. M. B. New York: Benzinger Bros., 1924.

Sheldrake, Philip. *Spirituality and Theology: Christian Living and the Doctrine of God*. London: Darton, Longman & Todd, 1998.

Sölle, Dorothee. *The Silent Cry: Mysticism and Resistance*. Translated by Barbara Rumscheidt and Martin Rumscheidt. Minneapolis, MN: Fortress, 2001.

Williams, Rowan. "The Deflections of Desire: Negative Theology in Trinitarian Disclosure." In *Silence and the Word: Negative Theology and Incarnation*, edited by Oliver Davies and Denys Turner, 115–35. Cambridge: Cambridge University Press, 2002.

LIFE

1

Christian de Chergé
Freedom, Community, and the Martyrdom of Love

CHRISTIAN KROKUS

During the Algerian civil war of the 1990s, the nine monks of Notre Dame de l'Atlas, the Trappist monastery in Tibhirine, found themselves increasingly surrounded by danger. They were encouraged either to leave Algeria or to accept government protection, but through a period of discernment they decided to remain as they were, knowing full well the risks involved. And in fact, in the early hours of March 27, 1996, armed rebels arrived at the monastery gate. They kidnapped seven of the monks, and although there remains some mystery about the final circumstances, the seven were murdered nearly two months later, on May 21, 1996. In 2018 Pope Francis beatified the seven monks along with twelve other Catholic martyrs of the civil war.

    The film *Des hommes et des dieux* [*Of Gods and Men*] depicts the monks's final days, and it includes a scene in which the leader of a local militia threatens the community. This is not the moment when the monks will be taken, but it is their first intimate brush with mortal danger. It's Christmas Eve 1993 and the monks are preparing to celebrate the vigil Mass. The emir, Sayah Attiyah, armed and accompanied by an armed entourage, demands money and medicines as well as Frère Luc, an elderly monk, who was not only the monastery physician, but who also ran a free medical clinic for the village. The prior of the Trappist community, Père Christian, refuses the demands, one after the other, until the emir finally and frustratedly threatens: "No. You have no choice." Christian pauses, collects himself, and responds: "Yes, I do have a choice."

The event is historical, and the dialogue closely follows the actual exchange.¹ Christian de Chergé (1937–1996) recalls it in several places, and although the word *freedom* does not appear, the episode evokes the tension between freedom and safety that pervades De Chergé's writing and preaching in the months leading up to the monks' capture. As another Trappist, Thomas Merton (1915–1968), observed, there's a freedom that can emerge from our deepest center when we are "brought to the edge."² Sensitive to the legitimate needs for physical, psychological, and religious security, Christian de Chergé, in his final homilies and chapter talks, was developing, for himself and for his brothers, the capacity not to be overwhelmed by those concerns at the expense of freely embracing the witness and values of the Gospel. After a brief biographical introduction, I focus on three nodes of De Chergé's cultivation of freedom-through-vulnerability, namely his dialogue with Muslims, his understanding of Church and discernment, and his commitment to a martyrdom of love.

BIOGRAPHY

Christian de Chergé was born in 1937 in Colmar, France, but he spent his early childhood in Algeria, where his father was stationed as a military officer. He himself served as a French officer during the Algerian war of Independence, and during that stint a Muslim friend (Mohamed) sacrificed his own life to protect De Chergé's when it was threatened by members of the Algerian resistance. That episode, which Christian Salenson has identified as the foundational experience for Christian de Chergé's later spiritual reflections on Catholic-Muslim encounter, convinced De Chergé that Muslims too were living and mediating Gospel values, as his comrade had laid down his life for a friend.³ It also clarified his vocation to return to Algeria and engage in dialogue with Muslims. In 1964 De Chergé was ordained a priest for the Archdiocese of Paris, but in 1969 he entered the Cistercian-Trappist Abbey of Notre Dame d'Aiguebelle. In 1971 he fulfilled his desire to return to Algeria by transferring to Notre Dame de l'Atlas in Tibhirine, which would remain his community for the rest of his life. From 1972–1974

---

1. Ray, *Christian*, 180–81.
2. Merton, "Ascetic Life," 64.
3. Salenson, *Theology of Hope*, 23–25.

CHRISTIAN DE CHERGÉ

he studied in Rome at the Pontifical Institute for the Study of Arabic and Islam (PISAI), and from 1984 until his death in 1996, he served as prior of the monastery.

CHRISTIAN-MUSLIM DIALOGUE

The article "L'échelle mystique du dialogue" is Christian de Chergé's major treatise on Christian-Muslim engagement. It opens by situating his experience at Tibhirine, where dialogue was usually between the monks and their neighbors, ordinary Muslims who by-and-large were not religious specialists. De Chergé refers to the monks' encounters as a form of "existential dialogue," an "essential characteristic of which is the fact that we never take the initiative."[4] A few pages later, in response to the complaints of fellow Christians that "it is always we who take the lead," perhaps by accommodating Muslim prayer in Christian spaces or by organizing dialogues, he writes: "Now, stop! As if we were not already beholden, first and foremost, to the awesome initiative of the One who 'loved us to the end'? [John 13:1]. We must abandon at all costs this tit-for-tat retaliation, which still haunts us in a thousand ways. Going towards the other and going towards God, it's all one, and I can't live without it. Each requires the same gratuity."[5] Gratuity, *gratuité*, here has the sense of *freedom of spirit*. As long as we cling to an attitude either of superiority or resentment vis-à-vis our Muslim interlocutors, we remain trapped in a pattern of keeping score, whereas we are invited to respond freely to Christ's gift of Himself in and through our Muslim neighbors. In his final *Testament*—to be read in the event of his death as a result of escalating violence—De Chergé imagines a critic mocking his supposedly naïve conviction that he could live in friendship with his Algerian-Muslim neighbors: "Let him tell us now what he thinks of [Islam]."[6] However, that is the point. In making ourselves available for dialogue, we may be rejected, exploited, or even abused. Our gesture may not be reciprocated. But is that not precisely the free gesture that God has made toward us in the Incarnation?

De Chergé's "existential dialogue" included experimentation with common Christian-Muslim prayer. As part of his profession of final vows, for example, De Chergé referred to a particularly dramatic example in which he had spent a night in prayer with a Muslim guest of the monastery. At times they prayed in concert, at other times in succession; at times they

---

4. Chergé, "L'échelle" 2. Unless otherwise noted, the translations of Christian de Chergé are by Christian Krokus and Habib Zanzana.

5. Chergé, "L'échelle," 7.

6. Salenson, *Theology of Hope*, 200.

used formal prayers, at other times they improvised.[7] He was aware of the hesitation that the Church's hierarchy expressed about such interreligious prayer. In "L'échelle mystique," he highlights the discussions that preceded the Day of Prayer for Peace in 1986, when Pope John Paul II invited the world's religious leaders to join him at Assisi. The question was whether the participants would be "together while praying" or "praying together." Although he understood the Vatican's need for careful planning, De Chergé suggests that it was a non-issue among the monks and Muslims gathered at Tibhirine in solidarity with the Assisi events: "Praying together, or together while praying? The question was irrelevant. We were a single community prostrated in the attitude of the publican."[8] Those gathered had agreed to adopt the humble attitude of the tax collector's prayer in Jesus's parable: "have mercy on me, a sinner!" (Luke 18:9–14 NIV). There is a pedigree of connecting humility and freedom in Cistercian spirituality. Commenting on a sermon of Bernard of Clairvaux (1090–1153), for example, Jane Foulcher notes: "Humility is . . . experienced as free, spontaneous, fervent, warm, fruitful, and enduring."[9] By recognizing themselves as sinners before God and thus centering the role of humility, the monks of Tibhirine and their Muslim friends seem to have been freed from the concerns expressed by others about the technical management of common prayer.

The humility-freedom nexus also informed Christian de Chergé's practice of meditative reading, *lectio divina*, with the Qur'an. Following the lead of Louis Massignon (1883–1962) and other Catholics engaged with Islam before him, De Chergé was convinced that it was possible and necessary to penetrate beyond a surface reading of the Qur'an and thus to glimpse the power it exercises in Muslim lives. He reports, for example, discovering "shortcuts of the Gospel" in the Qur'an, and he frames his practice as a participation in mutual hospitality: "Our Sufi friends like to quote the Gospel, which they are committed to reading, and we know how many parables and words of Jesus find a vibrant echo in the Muslim environment. Couldn't we let the Book of Islam resonate, in the peace of an interior listening, with the desire and respect of these same brothers who draw their taste for God from it?"[10] He was convinced that "the Christ of Easter would have something to tell us about Himself through [the Qur'an], if we would allow Him to meet us there as on a new road to Emmaus."[11] In other words, just as the resur-

---

7. Salenson, *Theology of Hope*, 27–30.
8. Chergé, "L'échelle," 20.
9. Foulcher, *Reclaiming Humility*, 203.
10. Chergé, "L'échelle," 10–11.
11. Chergé, "L'échelle," 11.

rected Jesus illuminated the Jewish scriptures in fresh and surprising ways for his companions on the road to Emmaus, so too he may illuminate the Qur'an for a Christian reader. However, he concludes: "It will be impossible . . . if we do not approach the Qur'anic text with a poor and disarmed heart, ready to listen to any Word that comes from the mouth of the Most High."[12] We must be "disarmed" in our approach to the Qur'an, stripped not only of our pre-judgments about its status vis-à-vis Christian revelation but also of our fears around its potential to persuade. We may discover Truth among our Muslim brothers and sisters. What then? What will that mean for our self-understanding as Catholics? For our understanding of Jesus? It is only an attitude of humility, a lowering of defenses, that allows us freely to listen for the word of God in the Qur'an.

CHURCH AND DISCERNMENT

In the Benedictine family of religious orders, the leader (abbot, abbess, prior, prioress) of the community is charged with regularly teaching his or her fellow monks or nuns, usually about some aspect of the *Rule* of St. Benedict. De Chergé typically gave three chapter talks per week, and he grouped them under themes that he would explore across several weeks. In the months leading up to the abduction of the monks, in light of how precarious their circumstances had become, he gave the brothers a series of talks under the headings of "The Situation of the Church *hic et nunc*" and "The Charism of Martyrdom."[13] Under the first heading—the situation of the Church here and now—De Chergé reflects on a cluster of interrelated virtues that include constancy and the monastic vow of stability as well as the importance of community, a topic that arises in the Cistercian Constitutions. Although all three are essential, I will focus on the term *community*. It is the one that appears most often in these talks, and it captures De Chergé's understanding of how the monks must respond to a call, a vocation, that is mediated by concentric circles of input, a process for which I am substituting the shorthand *discernment*. As he did in relation to Christian-Muslim dialogue and prayer, here too De Chergé was navigating the tension between safety and freedom.

Discernment begins, for De Chergé, with the individual, and across several talks he highlights the importance of individual vocations, noting, for example, St. Benedict's advice that even the newest or youngest novice's desires or concerns must be taken seriously. But he also turns to the Pentecost narrative in the Acts of the Apostles, suggesting that individual

12. Chergé, "L'échelle," 11.
13. Chergé, *Dieu*, 511–50.

experiences of conversion, though important in and of themselves, are in service of a "slower, more secret, but very real transformation of an entire environment."[14] So too in the monastery, individual vocations and individual discernment are in service of determining the character and the direction of the community as a whole, and that's where De Chergé focuses. At one point, he tells the brothers: "The pope is not going to say to our bishops: 'You must leave Algeria.'" Neither is the "Abbot General going to say to us: 'It is necessary to leave.'" What may happen, however, is that the Abbot General or his representative will come to "test everyone's will," investigating the degree to which the community is united in its resolve to remain. So, somewhat prosaically, De Chergé places a lot of weight on a series of votes that the community takes and which reveal "a unanimous desire for a communitarian destiny."[15] In other words, whatever decision the monks make, they will make as a whole. They will decide and act together. They also eventually agree, unanimously, that they will remain in Algeria as long as circumstances allow. This, De Chergé says, "is the logic of our vow of STABILITY," both the staying and the communal discernment.[16] Although Christian de Chergé insists that leaving must remain an option, especially if it becomes clear that "we are getting in the way," an important interpreter, Christian Salenson, is convinced that he always intended to stay.[17]

As essential as that level is, for De Chergé discernment cannot be limited to the monastery itself. The monastery at Tibhirine is part of the international Order of Cistercians of the Strict Observance; it is also part of the local Algerian Church, and between those two authorities the monks experienced some tension. De Chergé refers several times to a call, probably in 1994, from the Algerian bishops for a "core" of Christians to remain in the country despite the rising danger.[18] He affirms the correctness of that call, since in isolation the bishop's witness is impotent. When he asked his friend Léon-Étienne Cardinal Duval (1903–1996), the former archbishop of Algiers, for advice, Duval counseled "constancy" even describing the monastery as the "lungs" of the diocese.[19] On the other hand, when De Chergé asked advice of the abbot general of the Trappists, Dom Bernardo Olivera, he was told: "The Order has more need of monks than it does of martyrs."[20]

---

14. Chergé, *Dieu*, 515.
15. Chergé, *Dieu*, 513.
16. Chergé, *Dieu*, 514.
17. Chergé, *Dieu*, 530; Salenson, "Un chrétien face," 210.
18. Chergé, *Dieu*, 514.
19. Salension, *Theology of Hope*, 160.
20. Chergé, *Dieu*, 532.

That is a line to which De Chergé often returns. It becomes something of a foil for his own thinking, and in fact he spends a couple chapters exploring the Cistercian Constitutions on the relationship between a monastery and its local bishop. After the Second Vatican Council the Constitutions emphasize that Trappists ought to be "in communion with the whole people of God," and, especially in "mission" territories, they ought to see themselves as "participating monastically in the contemplative presence of the [local] Church."[21] So while he never rejects or ignores his abbot's hesitancy, he is certainly more sensitive and receptive to the call of his local Church, which is not totally out of monastic character. Jean Leclercq, for instance, has described Benedictine monasticism as a "school of freedom" that leaves a lot of room for various applications of the rule in light of particular contexts.[22]

There is yet another circle of community in conversation with which De Chergé thinks the monks ought to be discerning, and that is, so to speak, the local neighborhood. He tells a story of a Trappist who visited Tibhirine from the Abbey of Timadeuc in Bretagne, France. This brother remarked on the reassurance he experienced, knowing that 99 percent of Trappist life was identical no matter the location of the monastery. De Chergé impishly responded that he was interested "precisely in the 1 percent . . . where the difference seems to lie, because that is where we find our own personality," and that is where we hear a more specific call from God.[23] The French Catholic monks of Tibhirine lived almost exclusively among Algerian Muslims, and that context gave them a particular identity, as the monks put it, as "those who pray among others who pray."[24] The aforementioned Cardinal Duval argued that Trappist life was "the best way to make the religious instinct of the Church understood in a Muslim environment."[25]

De Chergé was deeply involved in reflection on the relationship between the Church and Islam, and the monks participated in formal Christian-Muslim dialogue with a local Sufi order as well as informal dialogue through myriad friendships with neighbors and associates. De Chergé wrote that, if the monks were to leave, not only "would the local Church be harmed" but also the slow, laborious, difficult work of cultivating Christian-Muslim trust would be upended.[26] There is a story in which Père Christian describes to some neighbors the monks' situation as being like birds on a

21. Chergé, *Dieu*, 525.
22. Leclercq, "Benedictine Freedom," 276.
23. Chergé, *Dieu*, 519.
24. Salenson, *Theology of Hope*, 181.
25. Chergé, *Dieu*, 520.
26. Chergé, *Dieu*, 520.

branch, between staying and taking flight. His neighbor responds: "But we are the birds, and you are the branch. If you depart, we have nowhere to go."[27] We must be careful not to interpret the story paternalistically. Rather it is an invitation to solidarity. As De Chergé put it: "We must not pretend to bring Jesus to people without also receiving JESUS from them. That is the condition of the Incarnation. It is a situation of mutual interdependence."[28] Just to mention one dimension of that interdependence, De Chergé observes how to that point the local community was protecting the monastery, placing itself at some risk, because increasingly foreigners were being targeted for violence. That act of hospitality has to be seen, he says, as a witness among the local Muslims to an adherence and a desire for an Islam and an Algeria not only tolerant but even appreciative of religious and cultural difference.[29] Hence, when his friend Maurice Borrmans (1925–2017), the White Father and longtime director of PISAI, cautioned Christian against moving too quickly on some point of Christian-Muslim dialogue and admonished him to "listen to your brothers," De Chergé responded: "Which ones?"[30]

For De Chergé the rich and prophetic web of relationships with the local Church and the local Muslim community was an important factor in discerning how the monks were going to live a vow of stability. To extract and relocate the monastery would be to preserve safety at the expense of meaning and mission. It would be, he says, like "keeping river fish in a bowl."[31] You might keep them alive but at what cost and for what purpose? As Hedwig Vrensen put it: "Cenobitic life is a life of availability."[32] That availability to each other, to the church of Algeria, and to their local Muslim neighbors, though frightening and potentially dangerous, was both the ground and the result of the monks' free decision to remain, unarmed, at Tibhirine. As De Chergé says to his brothers: "We made the decision to STAY . . ." That "choice was confirmed by the authorities of our Church, but also and above all, by the calls from our environment. There is, in this decision, something like a renewal of the GIFT that we made of our lives to the people, to these men and to these women. This choice must remain free. That's the Gospel . . . coming through the threat we are facing."[33] Whether, as we saw, by trusting that Christ may speak to us through the Qur'an, despite

---

27. Quoted in Saint-Albin, "Friendship in Tibhirine," 19n26.
28. Chergé, *Dieu*, 516.
29. Chergé, *Dieu*, 536.
30. Chergé, *Lettres*, 224.
31. Chergé, *Dieu*, 516.
32. Vrensen, "Formation," 359.
33. Chergé, *Dieu*, 529.

the potential for having our religious certitudes unsettled, or by trusting the call to remain in Algeria coming from Muslim neighbors and the local church, despite the evident dangers, it was precisely by stepping into the place of vulnerability that Christian de Chergé and the monks of Tibhirine found the freedom to hear and the availability to respond to the Gospel call to love.

MARTYRDOM OF LOVE

It is important to remember that the monks of Tibhirine were not looking to die. They took prudent steps in order to stay alive, hoping not only to survive the crisis but to be part of the rebuilding process after its conclusion. Christian de Chergé reminds us that Jesus' death was not suicide, and neither can a Christian martyr's death be suicide.[34] Willingness to die is not the same as desire to die. De Chergé is also very wary of the traditional definition of martyrdom as being killed out of hatred for the faith, *in odium fidei*. He recoiled at how certain some Catholic "martyrs" seem to have been about their own purity and about the wickedness of their enemy. He also observed how promiscuously both sides in the current conflict were referring to their own dead as martyrs.[35] There is a temptation to weaponize martyrdom. Instead, De Chergé frequently quotes Jesus in John's Gospel: "No one takes my life from me, but I lay it down on my own" (10:18). The martyr's life is given, not taken. He writes in his *Testament*: "I would like my community, my Church and my family to remember that my life was GIVEN to God and to this country."[36] It is the opposite of clinging to rivalrous victimhood as a way of condemning one's enemy. You cannot be a Christian martyr by turning your enemy into a murderer.

It is interesting that in 2019, Pope Francis beatified several Romanian Greek-Catholic martyr-bishops, and he remarked that they suffered "without showing hatred to their persecutors."[37] Understood properly, according to De Chergé, "the witness of Jesus, until his death, his 'martyrdom,' is a martyrdom of love."[38] De Chergé borrows the expression *martyrdom of love* from St. Jane de Chantal (1572–1641) who, with St. Francis de Sales (1567–1622), founded the Order of the Visitation in the early seventeenth century. To put it briefly, for St. Jane the martyrdom of love consists of all

---

34. Chergé, *Dieu*, 514.
35. Chergé, *L'Autre*, 419–21.
36. Salenson, *Theology of Hope*, 199.
37. Francis, "Divine Liturgy."
38. Chergé, *L'Autre*, 419.

the little, often hidden, ordinary ways in which one gives oneself in love to one's neighbor. She said that "martyrs of love suffer a thousand times more by staying alive to do God's will than if they had to give a thousand lives in witness of their faith."[39] Emblematic of Jesus' martyrdom of love, for De Chergé, is his washing of the disciples's feet on Holy Thursday. His witness, his martyrdom, is primarily service to his friends.

The theological key that unlocks the meaning of martyrdom therefore is not primarily the cross. It is the Incarnation, but only if we keep in mind that the various moments of Jesus' life cannot be separated from each other, nor any of them separated from the incarnation of the divine Word. The birth of Jesus is the incarnation of the Son, but so are the years at Nazareth during which Jesus was developing physically, psychologically, and spiritually, so are the years of Jesus's public ministry, and so are Jesus's last days when he suffered and was killed: "What happened during the hours of the Passion is the Incarnation continued," *Incarnation continuée*.[40] But then the reverse is also true. The earlier stages of Jesus' life, including the washing of his disciples's feet, his preaching and healing, and his early development, even his birth, already participate in his Passion, his witness, his martyrdom. The whole of his life is Incarnation. The whole of his life is a martyrdom of love. Most of Jesus's martyrdom therefore was neither dramatic nor noticed. It belonged, as St. Charles de Foucauld (1858–1916) would say, to the hidden life of Nazareth, with family and at work. That was the point St. Jane was making to her sisters, whose lives and deaths would remain hidden from most of the world, and that is the point De Chergé emphasizes in his chapter talks. Even in the face of a dramatic end, the monks are called to the daily, ordinary, constant martyrdom of love among each other and with their Muslim friends.

Not that doing so is easy, as De Chergé remarks: "Washing the feet of one's brothers on Holy Thursday, sure, but if it had to be done daily?" especially when "it is easier to . . . love this brother or sister rather than that one."[41] But that's precisely it. As De Chergé was fond of pointing out, Jesus washed the feet of both Peter and Judas. In fact, he washes the feet of both the Peter and the Judas "in me."[42] It is not for nothing, he notes, that St. Benedict associates suffering with the practice of "PATIENCE."[43] For De Chergé, the Cistercian vows of stability, obedience, and conversion of life,

---

39. Wright, *Bond of Perfection*, 154–55.
40. Chergé, *Dieu*, 542.
41. Chergé, *L'Autre*, 420–21.
42. Chergé, *L'Autre*, 455.
43. Chergé, *Dieu*, 544.

are anchors in living a martyrdom of love. Not in the sense of having one's life gloomily drained, but in the sense that one's very self is freely and joyfully given to others over the long term. So when the abbot general quips "that our order needs monks more than martyrs," De Chergé responds that "we are truly monks by continuing to live here the very mystery of Christmas, of GOD LIVING with men and women."[44] Of course, if that's true, he continues, then we must expect that we too may be exposed, from the cradle, to the massacre of the Innocents.

CONCLUSION

Let us return to the scene with which I opened the essay. After his Christmas Eve encounter at the monastery gate with Sayah Attiyah, Christian De Chergé found that, even though he knew of the bloodshed for which this man was responsible, he could not ask God to kill him. He found he could, however, pray that the emir be disarmed. Almost immediately, however, he realized that he had no right even to ask that, unless he and his community were willing to be disarmed themselves. Not from physical weapons, but from pre-judgments about the humanity, or lack thereof, of the rebels—whom they called the "brothers of the mountain"—or the Algerian soldiers—whom they called the "brothers of the plain"; about Islam, so quickly caricatured as inherently violent; about the meaning and value of safety; about vocation; and about what it means to be in the "school of the Lord's service," as the Constitutions call the Cistercian monastery.[45] From that point forward his regular prayer became, "Disarm me; disarm them."[46] Christian Salenson has pointed out that De Chergé was acutely aware of his own complicity in the French colonialist violence that continued to plague Algerian history.[47] When we are authentically disarmed—not just avoiding conflict—the ground is cleared, De Chergé observes, for the possibility of conversion, our own and that of others, as the good thief and the centurion can attest.[48]

St. Bernard of Clairvaux said: "Freedom of choice [is] something clearly divine."[49] Even if one is not faced with the deadly circumstances of Algeria in the 1990s, De Chergé may help us to recognize that in every situation *we*

---

44. Chergé, *Dieu*, 539.
45. Salenson, *Theology of Hope*, 171–72; OCSO, *Constitutions* c3.2.
46. Salenson, *Theology of Hope*, 31.
47. Salenson, "Un chrétien face," 200.
48. Chergé, *Dieu*, 514.
49. Bernard of Clairvaux, *Selected Works*, 266.

have a choice. We have a choice as to whether we emphasize death or life in our interpretation and communication of the Gospel; whether we interpret martyrdom in a defensive, competitive, triumphalist key that depends on the diminution of our rivals; or whether we interpret martyrdom as a witness of God's love for us, for others, for all, a key that depends on acknowledging the dignity of our rivals. Learning from De Chergé's experiments in freedom-through-vulnerability, substantial pastoral implications emerge. In Christian-Muslim dialogue, as *Nostra Aetate* says, we can focus on the moments of conflict in our history, or we can promote our shared devotions and virtues. We could therefore say the Church as a whole is called to what De Chergé names a martyrdom of love, a giving of herself in love to her Muslim friends and neighbors. It is a risk, but the Church must engage Muslims with a disarmed heart, while remaining ever-careful not to turn her love into a new weapon, a new way of feeling superior to Muslims.

As we saw, Christian discernment, according to De Chergé and the monks of Tibhirine, will involve listening to friends in concentric horizons of concern, always attentive to opportunities for being in solidarity with the most vulnerable among us. Even beyond the realm of interreligious dialogue, for example in dealing with the Catholic Church's history of sexual abuse and concealment, it is important to remember that we have a choice about how we engage with our victims, whether to meet them with compassion and understanding or with legalistic distance. We might imagine all sorts of other ways we as Church are tempted not to exercise solidarity with vulnerable peoples and wounded histories because some doctrine or some tradition makes it impossible. No. One lesson of Christian de Chergé and the monks of Tibhirine is that, while we must responsibly discern, and we must do so together, still *we have a choice.* It is risky, even dangerous, truly to listen, truly to give ourselves *hic et nunc*, in this place, at this time, with these people, not only bringing but also receiving Christ. Then again, who knows what might happen were we to be disarmed from all the things that keep us safe but not free?

REFERENCES

Beauvois, Xavier, dir. *Des hommes et des dieux*. Culver City, CA: Sony, 2010.

Bernard of Clairvaux. *Selected Works*. Translated by G. R. Evans. Mahwah, NJ: Paulist, 1987.

Chergé, Christian de. *L'Autre que nous attendons: Homélies de Père Christian de Chergé (1970–1996)*. Montjoyer, France: Bellefontaine, 2006.

———. *Dieu pour tout jour: chapitres de Père Christian de Chergé à la communauté de Tibhirine (1986–1996)*. Montjoyer, France: Bellefontaine, 2006.

———. "L'échelle mystique du dialogue." *Islamochristiana* 23 (1997) 1–26.

———. *Lettres à un ami fraternel*. Edited by Maurice Borrmans. Montrouge, France: Bayard, 2015.

Foulcher, Jane. *Reclaiming Humility: Four Studies in the Monastic Tradition*. Collegeville, MN: Liturgical, 2015.

Francis. "Divine Liturgy with the Beatification of Seven Greek-Catholic Martyr Bishops." Homily delivered in Blaj, Romania, June 2, 2019. https://www.vatican.va/content/francesco/en/homilies/2019/documents/papa-francesco_20190602_omelia-blaj-romania.html.

Leclercq, Jean. "Benedictine Freedom." *Cistercian Studies Quarterly* 16.4 (1981) 267–79.

Merton, Thomas. "The Ascetic Life, Experience of God and Freedom." *Cistercian Studies Quarterly* 9.1 (1974) 55–65.

Order of Cistercians of the Strict Observance (OCSO). *Constitutions and Statutes of the Monks*. https://ocso.org/wp-content/uploads/2023/11/01-CONSTITUTIONS-AND-STATUTES-OCSO-Monks_November-2023-EN.pdf.

Ray, Marie-Christine. *Christian de Chergé: Prieur de Tibhirine*. Montrouge, France: Bayard, 1998.

Saint-Albin, Godefroy Raguenet de. "Friendship in Tibhirine: Monastic/Muslim Dialogue in Algeria." In *Monks and Muslims II: Creating Communities of Friendship*, edited by M. Shomali and W. Skudlarek, 1–23. Collegeville, MN: Liturgical, 2014.

Salenson, Christian. *Christian de Chergé: A Theology of Hope*. Translated by Nada Conic. Collegeville, MN: Liturgical, 2012.

———. "Christian de Chergé: un chrétien face à la violence." *Islamochristiana* 43 (2017) 195–215.

Vrensen, Hedwig. "Formation." *Cistercian Studies Quarterly* 5.4 (1970) 354–62.

Wright, Wendy. *Bond of Perfection: Jeanne de Chantal & François de Sales*. Mahwah, NJ: Paulist, 1985.

2

The Freedom of the Contemplative
Thérèse of Lisieux in Dialogue with Louis Lavelle

MARY FROHLICH

In many regards, Thérèse Martin (known to us as Thérèse of Lisieux) lived a very small life. Born in 1873, she was only twenty-four years old when she died of tuberculosis in 1897. She spent her whole life—except for a few weeks of pilgrimage in Paris and Rome—in a small corner of Normandy in France. Her education was typical of her milieu, but quite poor by today's standards. At home she received instruction in faith, prayer, and piety, as well as in arts such as sewing and painting, then attended a convent school for a few years. The convent curriculum included "drawing, music, embroidery, sewing and dance," plus a little "grammar, arithmetic, geography and history."[1] The mentality of the time was that it was dangerous for young women to get involved in intellectual occupations.[2]

At fifteen, Thérèse received special permission to enter the Carmel of Lisieux—an enclosure comprising about six thousand square meters [85 x 85 yards] where she would reside for the rest of her life. Within that enclosure, the nuns' days were occupied with the mundane tasks of household and farm labor as well as fulfilling their vocational responsibility of liturgical and personal prayer. To earn their living, the Lisieux Carmelites also

---

1. Camille et Marie de la Rédemption, "Horizons de femmes," 27.
2. Camille et Marie de la Rédemption, "Horizons de femmes," 28–29.

made altar breads and did needlework and painting for hire.³ Enclosed Carmelites of that era generally knew relatively little about what was going on in the world beyond their walls, except what they could glean from letters received or from visitors in the parlor. Sometimes the prioress might deem it appropriate to inform them about certain local or national goings-on in order to solicit their prayers.

Another limiting factor in Thérèse's life was the cultural style of her milieu, which was a highly pious, defensive, and relatively rigid form of Catholicism. After the French Revolution dismantled the old alliance of Church and King, many Catholics who longed for the return of the old ways embraced an antirevolutionary politics of monarchism and ultramontanism. During the period of Thérèse's life, the Third Republic government which came into power in 1875 was enacting increasingly harsh anti-religious measures. Attempts at reconciliation, including Pope Leo XIII's 1892 *Ralliement*, were ineffective in stemming the tide of anticlerical legislation. It was common for devout middle-class Catholics to adopt a "citadel mentality" in which they withdrew into their own enclaves and perceived strong black-and-white lines between the "good" of their pious way of life and the "evil" of the broader society. Christopher O'Donnell writes that "For Thérèse's circle the Church was the secure refuge from an evil world."⁴

A woman whose life and activities were so limited would not seem to make a very promising icon of freedom. Yet this essay will make the case that Thérèse can be construed as just that. The trajectory of her life is a remarkable illustration of the contemplative process of growing in authentic inner freedom. The fruits of her inner freedom can be seen in her ability to see through and reframe aspects of her cultural and theological milieu that she recognized as incompatible with the freedom-in-God that she was discovering. This does not mean, of course, that she shucked off all the attitudes, habits, and customs in which her milieu had formed her. Unsympathetic readers of Thérèse are often put off by what they perceive as her childish, sentimental, overly pious language and practices. Up to the end, she expressed herself in the language of her surrounding culture—as do we all. Perhaps this makes it all the more remarkable that we can discover, shining through that unpromising veil, the light of a free soul.

The specific project of this essay is to place Thérèse's trajectory toward freedom in dialogue with the philosophy of Louis Lavelle (1883–1951). Lavelle was born ten years later than Thérèse, so his period of philosophical productivity occurred after her death—although, if she had lived a normal

---

3. Camille et Marie de la Rédemption, "Horizons de femmes," 45.
4. O'Donnell, *Love in the Heart of the Church*, 26.

lifespan of sixty or seventy years, the same years would likely have been her period of mature productivity as well. However, this essay is not attempting to make a claim that Thérèse was in any direct sense influenced by the philosophical thought of her time, nor that she necessarily would have recognized herself in the kind of language Lavelle uses in talking about the path to inner freedom. The value of placing her life in dialogue with Lavelle's philosophy is the potential to articulate her trajectory of contemplative growth in terms that can be recognized within broader discussions of authentic human freedom.

LAVELLE'S PHILOSOPHY OF FREEDOM

Louis Lavelle's philosophy is a late fruit of the nineteenth-century movement known as "French spiritualism."[5] This movement, which is usually identified as beginning with Maine de Biran (1766–1824), accepted from Descartes the analytic method of interior reflection but sought to avoid his body-soul dualism by finding the primordial metaphysical reality in "effort," "will," or "act" rather than in "thinking." Thus, French spiritualism claims not to be a version of idealism (which asserts that mind or spirit is the fundamental substance of reality), but rather a metaphysics of being as univocal, dynamic, conscious, and participative.

In Lavelle's articulation, the primitive act upon which both my being and that of the world depend is discovered in "my active presence to myself. This is my feeling of responsibility to myself and the world."[6] Reflection on this "act" that we discover as our most intimate reality, he asserts, awakens the intuition that our act of being is a finite participation in the pure Act that is eternally engendering myriad free beings with the vocation to participatively create themselves. In a short essay that he wrote shortly before he died, Lavelle testified that this grounding intuition arose in him even before he knew what philosophy was, and that his life's work consisted in faithfully unfolding its implications.[7] He summarized: "The secret of the world, the principle of all intelligibility and joy, consists in the admirable eternal circuit through which the pure Act is given for participation to all beings so that

---

5. Hardy, "French Spiritualism," 190–202; Sinclair and Antoine-Mahut, "Introduction to French Spiritualism," 857–65.

6. Lavelle, *Of the Act*, 3.

7. Lavelle, *De l'intimité spirituelle*, 281–85.

they may consent to make it living within them."[8] He called this a "psycho-metaphysics"[9] based in the concreteness of human life and experience.

This pure Act can also be called the "All," but it is emphatically not a substance; it is, rather, a "universal self" or "universal subjectivity," participation in which grounds our own capacity to be a self and to say "I."[10] Lavelle calls the Act the "hearth" and "heart" of all personal existence, indicating by these metaphors that not only is our personhood animated by this source but that it is also continually drawn to reach out toward coinciding more fully with it. Our own personhood, then, is primarily defined not by our individual characteristics or "personality," but by the vocation to surpass ourselves in the direction of the shared life of the All.[11] Indeed, Lavelle goes further, affirming that the pure Act is a person, for "The Act cannot found our personal life and at the same time fall short of it."[12] Although his sources and style of thinking are clearly philosophical rather than theological, Lavelle not infrequently employs God-language to describe the pure Act.

For Lavelle, participation and freedom are inseparable. As spiritual beings, we humans are not simply parts of a world that pre-exists us; rather, we are called to participate freely in "an act that is in the midst of being accomplished."[13] The self, writes Lavelle, "can be defined as the vehicle and the place of participation."[14] Our participation takes place on three levels, namely, nature, society, and spirit. We participate in nature through our necessary subjection to the laws of nature. In human society, we imbibe the norms of participation through relationships and traditions. The highest and most true participation is that of the spirit, for it is here that we truly exercise participative freedom. At the level of spirit we creatively invent ourselves, while also (potentially) promoting the good of nature, society, and other beings.[15] Our participative freedom is the very center or heart of our existence, constantly urging us toward the fullest degree of being of which we are capable.

Lavelle says that while our existence is received as a gift, it is our own choices that create our essence. Existence is only the possibility of essence, until liberty has actually been exercised. As Émérita Quito puts it, "The

---

8. Lavelle, *Of the Act*, 84.
9. Lavelle, *Leçon Inaugurale*, 24.
10. Lavelle, *Of the Act*, 96–99.
11. Lavelle, *Of the Act*, 105–8.
12. Lavelle, *Of the Act*, 107.
13. Louis Lavelle, *De l'acte*, 164, my translation.
14. Lavelle, *De l'acte*, 342, my translation.
15. Lavelle, *De l'acte*, 174–75.

formation of an essence, or of a self, is for Lavelle not only a property of the human being, but also a duty, a profound acceptation, a consent to recognize 'the role that I have to fill in the universe.'"[16] Robert Jones summarizes the meaning of "essence" in Lavelle's thought as "the precise shape an individual gives the soul through choices made from a range of possibilities, necessarily constrained by worldly limits."[17] The pure Act offers itself as an infinity of possibilities, leaving each of us free to recognize a more limited range as actual possibilities for ourselves—and then to choose which ones to actualize. This is a process that does not take place just once but occurs repeatedly in each moment of our lives.

Our freedom only remains pure, however, "if it holds fast to possessing nothing and never ceases to sacrifice everything it has."[18] Lavelle affirms that the nature of individual existence is that "it must be continually sacrificed precisely in order to acquire an essence."[19] Although existence demands that we constructively engage with nature and society, it is not in our historical achievements that our essence is to be revealed. As Philippe Perrot puts it: "it is ultimately neither in the world nor in History that human freedom takes possession of itself, but in the imitation of the pure Act to which the act of contemplation initiates it."[20] Ultimately, it is only by freely letting go of possession of worldly goods and success, indeed of one's very self, that one can be joined to the being of the All.[21]

Our choices, to be sure, are not strictly autonomous since they are a participation in the efficacity of the Act. Our particular location within nature and society also places constraints on us. Nonetheless, the participative act of the spirit "founds rather than destroys autonomy."[22] This highest act of participative freedom involves both dependence and initiative, for it is both a "pure consent to being" and a "personal and creative process by which we assume the responsibility to be that which we are and must be."[23] It is noteworthy that Lavelle's existentialism differs from the portrayal of "anguished freedom" in Sartre or Heidegger in that the (pure) "Act reaches

---

16. Quito, *La notion de la liberté participée*, 66, my translation.
17. Lavelle, "Act of Presence," xxix.
18. Lavelle, *Of the Act*, 130.
19. Lavelle, *Of the Act*, 70.
20. Perrot, "Action et Contemplation," 81, my translation.
21. Lavelle, *Of the Act*, 149.
22. Lavelle, *Of the Act*, 125–26.
23. Quito, *La notion de la liberté participée*, 56, my translation.

out a benevolent hand to humans, so that they can realize the possibilities that are in them."[24]

A DIALOGUE BETWEEN PHILOSOPHER AND SAINT

In a dialogue such as this between a philosopher and a saint, two different sets of terms are deployed in hopes that they can bring forth new insights. The challenge in this particular dialogue is that reflection on "freedom" is absolutely central in Lavelle's philosophy while it was not a significant, explicit theme for Thérèse. In fact, she only used the words *libre*, *librement*, or *liberté* thirty-one times in all her writings, and many of these refer either to "free time" or to God's freedom, not human freedom.[25] A very major theme for her, on the other hand, is grace. She employs the word *grâce* 265 times in her writings, nearly always to refer to grace as a gift or act of God on someone's behalf.[26] These two perspectives—Thérèse's that frequently focuses on what God does, Lavelle's that focuses much more on what humans can and must do—may seem to rub against each other at times. Yet they also can enlighten one another.

Some have even asked whether Lavelle edges into Pelagianism—e.g., the affirmation that humans do not need grace in order to make the choices necessary for salvation. Full exploration of that question would require a much more detailed analysis of his thought. However, when Lavelle writes that "The secret of the world, the principle of all intelligibility and joy, consists in the admirable eternal circuit through which the pure Act is given for participation to all beings so that they may consent to make it living within them,"[27] he clearly affirms that our very existence is a gift of the pure Act and that our fulfillment lies in "consent" to its ongoing gifts. This is his way of talking about grace. He frames the dynamic between giftedness and choice, or passivity and activity, not as fundamentally opposing forces but as a productive tension within acts of participation, with participation itself being the most fundamental gift. As we trace Thérèse's trajectory, our challenge will be to identify this productive tension without overbalancing to one side or the other.

---

24. Quito, *La notion de la liberté participée*, 57, my translation.
25. Geneviève et al., *Les Mots de Sainte*, 485.
26. Geneviève et al., *Les Mots de Sainte*, 397–400.
27. Lavelle, *Of the Act*, 84.

TRACING THÉRÈSE'S PATH OF FREEDOM

In a short essay such as this we can only review a few highlights of Thérèse's trajectory. I have selected nine key events (some short in duration, others more extended) in which Thérèse's freedom was challenged. Through her choices in these situations, she "co-created" herself as the saint we have come to know.

1. *Traumatic infancy.* Marie-Françoise-Thérèse, the ninth (and last) child of Louis and Zélie Martin, was born on January 2, 1873. In the six years prior to her birth her parents had buried four of their own children as well as a nephew. Three of the Martin children had died as infants, wasting away within a few months of birth. Even before these tragic events, Zélie's temperament tended toward pessimism and anxiety. Although her staunch Catholic faith required that she accept her babies' deaths as the will of God, deep sorrow and grief undoubtedly permeated her being. In addition, she had already been ill for some time with the breast cancer that would take her life only four years later.[28]

When Thérèse was just two weeks old, Zélie was already expressing concern that she might follow her siblings into death.[29] At two months, Thérèse was sick with enteritis and was no longer taking nourishment from her mother's breasts. The situation escalated until Thérèse, refusing completely to nurse, was extremely weak and agitated. In a panic, Zélie walked six miles "with death in her soul"[30] to bring home a peasant wetnurse, Rose Taillé. Instantly, Thérèse suckled "with all her heart" and fell into a deep, peaceful sleep.[31] She was then sent home to the countryside with Rose, where she lived happily until returning to the Martin household more than a year later.

It may seem odd to reflect on the events of infancy in terms of "freedom." Still, even an infant is not strictly passive. The path initiated in infancy profoundly shapes the whole future trajectory of freedom. The infant Thérèse did indeed make a choice here, even if it was an instinctive one: she refused the breast that was permeated by grief, anxiety, and illness. When offered the life-giving breast of Rose Taillé, she leaped toward life. Yet at the deepest level of her psyche, she was already marked by this primordial confrontation with death—and by her own response of choosing life.

---

28. Renda, *Call to Deeper Love*, 15–16.
29. Renda, *Call to Deeper Love*, 106.
30. Renda, *Call to Deeper Love*, 110.
31. Renda, *Call to Deeper Love*, 111.

2. *Her mother's death.* On August 28, 1877, Zélie Martin died of breast cancer. Thérèse was four and a half years old. Years later, she recalled standing all alone in a hallway looking up at the lid of her mother's coffin, which appeared "large and dismal." After the funeral, the five Martin sisters (who at that time ranged in age from seventeen to four) were together when Léonie, the middle sister, commented that the two youngest—Céline and Thérèse—were now "orphans." Eight-year-old Céline immediately ran to her oldest sister, Marie, saying "You will be my Mama!" Just as quickly, Thérèse turned to the next oldest and exclaimed, "As for me, it's Pauline who will be my Mama!" In *Story of a Soul*, Thérèse says explicitly that "I chose her freely."[32]

Once again, faced with the potentially fragmenting disaster that mother-loss can be for such a young child, Thérèse found a way to choose life. Then almost sixteen, Pauline took her mothering duties seriously and cared well for Thérèse. Thérèse notes, however, that "my happy disposition completely changed after Mama's death. I, once so full of life, became timid and retiring . . . I could not bear the company of strangers and found my joy only within the intimacy of the family."[33] In Lavelle's terms, Thérèse's existence—the human, historical ground on which she would stand as she faced the question of discovering her real essence—had once again been primordially wrenched by loss and death.

3. *A strange illness.* On October 2, 1882, Pauline Martin—Thérèse's chosen "Mama"—entered Lisieux Carmel. This was a terrible shock for nine-year-old Thérèse. She was not told directly of Pauline's impending departure, but instead overheard the news when her two oldest sisters were conversing. Of the heartbreaking effect of the news that Pauline was leaving her, Thérèse later wrote: "Ah! How can I express my anguish of heart! In one instant, I understood what life was . . . I saw it was nothing but a continual suffering and separation."[34]

About six months later, on Easter Sunday, Thérèse suddenly fell ill with a bizarre set of symptoms. She was weak and trembling, and during frequent crises she hallucinated frightening objects and was overtaken by violent bodily contortions. Sometimes she banged her head against the headboard or threw herself out of bed. She later testified that she never lost the use of reason, yet at times she could not speak and at other times she screamed nonsense. After two weeks she revived briefly to attend Pauline's reception

---

32. Thérèse de Lisieux, *Story of a Soul*, 34 [Manuscript A 12v].
33. Thérèse de Lisieux, *Story of a Soul*, 34–35 [A 13r].
34. Thérèse de Lisieux, *Story of a Soul*, 57–58 [A 25v].

of the habit, but by the next day the symptoms had redoubled.[35] The physicians who were consulted were powerless to provide any remedy or hope.

On Pentecost Sunday, Marie, Léonie, and Céline were all in Thérèse's room, praying on their knees in front of a statue of the Blessed Virgin. Thérèse too was praying. As she told the story later: "All of a sudden the Blessed Virgin appeared *beautiful* to me, so *beautiful* that never had I seen anything so attractive . . . what penetrated to the very depths of my soul was the *'ravishing smile of the Blessed Virgin.'*"[36] From then on, Thérèse began to get better.

Many explanations have been offered for Thérèse's strange illness, ranging from physical sickness to psychosomatic reaction to demonic possession. Stripped to its essentials, however, two elements stand out: the gift of grace in yet another "saving Mother," and the resilience of young Thérèse who "consents to being" (Lavelle's language for acceptance of grace) and once again bounces back from the brink of devastation.

4. *The "Christmas conversion."* It had always been a Martin family tradition to have little gifts for the children to discover in their shoes by the fireplace when they returned home from Midnight Mass. On Christmas Eve, 1886, Thérèse was almost fourteen years old and really past the age for such customs, but her sisters had prepared it for her anyway. Louis Martin was very fatigued due to the lateness of the hour, and, perhaps, his impending illness (which first manifested itself only four months later). As the family entered the house, he commented with annoyance that he was glad it was finally the last year for this. Thérèse's first reaction was the instinct to break into tears and cause an emotional scene. Instead, she forced back her tears and made sure to give her father joy as he observed her delight in receiving the gifts.

The incident could hardly be more mundane, yet it is marked in Thérèse's memory as a radical turning point in her spiritual journey. She wrote: "Thérèse was no longer the same; Jesus had changed her heart . . . I felt *charity* enter my soul, and the need to forget myself and please others."[37] On a psychological level, it seems that in this moment thirteen-year-old Thérèse made a leap that many never master: the realization that one does not have to be controlled by spontaneous emotional reactions but can make a choice about how to respond. Thérèse herself understood this leap, in which "work I had been unable to do in ten years was done by Jesus in one instant," as sheer grace. Understood in Lavellian terms, it was both a

---

35. Gaucher, *Sainte Thérèse de Lisieux*, 139–43.
36. Thérèse de Lisieux, *Story of a Soul*, 65–66 [A 30r–v].
37. Thérèse de Lisieux, *Story of a Soul*, 98–99 [A 45r–v].

"consent to being" (e.g., acceptance of grace) and a free act. The reason it is so significant in Thérèse's life trajectory is that it apparently was the first time that she made such a consensual and free act with full consciousness. She had certainly made many choices and efforts to conform to grace before this, but this one was deeper and more complete than any earlier ones, and she knew it. "Thérèse was no longer the same."

5. *Entering Carmel*. When Pauline left for Carmel, nine-year-old Thérèse had determined that she would follow her when she could. She felt deeply that this was a divine call, and that she wanted to go "not for Pauline's sake but for Jesus alone." When she confided this desire to Pauline and, later, to the Prioress at Lisieux Carmel, both confirmed it as authentic while reminding her that she would have to wait until she was sixteen before entering.[38] After her Christmas conversion, however, Thérèse became convinced that the time had come. She set out on a campaign to convince others that, at fourteen, she was ready to become a Carmelite. Not surprisingly, the first response of each authority figure was to oppose her plan. She was so determined that when her pilgrimage group participated in a group audience with the Pope, she disobeyed direct and explicit directions not to speak to him in order to make her request that he intervene on her behalf. When he responded "You will enter if God wills it!" she took his words as at least a partial affirmation. She was heartbroken afterwards, however, because the walls of opposition still stood.[39]

In the end, Thérèse was permitted to enter in April 1888, at the age of fifteen years and three months. Religious life in Carmel was clearly her choice, made firmly and decisively. But how "free" was this choice? She was an ambitious young woman who lived in a cultural milieu that held up religious life as intrinsically superior to any other way of life, and Carmel as the peak of the peak. Her family endorsed this hierarchy so firmly that all five daughters became religious, even though several of them (Marie, Léonie, Céline) struggled mightily with this choice.[40] Thérèse never seems to have even remotely considered marriage; men were a strange species to her. In entering Carmel, she rejoined her two older sisters and, a few years later, was passionately insistent that Céline join them there as well. It has been commented that there is something incestuous in this urgent need to reconstitute the family behind the walls of Carmel.[41]

---

38. Thérèse de Lisieux, *Story of a Soul*, 58–59 [A 26r–v].
39. Thérèse de Lisieux, *Story of a Soul*, 134–36 [A 63r–64v].
40. Bourreille, *De Thérèse Martin à Thérèse de Lisieux*, 55–61.
41. Bourreille, *De Thérèse Martin à Thérèse de Lisieux*, 50–51.

Thérèse's choice was certainly "free" in the sense that she was not coerced; on the contrary, she did her best to coerce others into cooperating with her chosen path! The freedom in question is on a more profound level. In Lavelle's language, it is the freedom consciously to recognize and actualize "the role that I have to fill in the universe."[42] Claude Bourreille makes the distinction between choosing a mode of life and discovering one's real vocation. When she entered Carmel, Thérèse decisively settled the question of her mode of life.[43] She still had a long journey to make, however, to discover the particular contours of her unique vocation—her "essence," in Lavelle's terms.

6. *Her Father's illness.* From childhood, Thérèse had a very tender relationship with her Father. He called her his "little Queen," and he was her "King." She loved accompanying him when he went fishing or on rambling walks in the countryside. In 1887, even before Thérèse entered Carmel, he had several strokes. Only ten weeks after Thérèse's entrance, however, an episode occurred that revealed that he was beginning to suffer from significant dementia. On June 23, 1888, Louis Martin disappeared for five days. He was finally located in Le Havre, claiming that he intended to go to Canada and live in solitude. He was brought home, but over the following months he endured more strokes. Finally, on February 12, 1889, Louis was found waving a pistol in the air while hallucinating battles and revolutions. Due to the fear that he might harm his daughters or someone else, he had to be hospitalized at the Bon-Sauveur asylum in Caen. He would remain there for three years, returning home only when his dementia was so advanced that he could be easily cared for by his daughters. He finally died on July 29, 1894, at the age of 71.

These long years of Louis's suffering were also a time of deep suffering for Thérèse. In her eyes her father was a saint, so the theodicy question—"Why do the just suffer?"—was heartrending for her. To make matters worse, there was gossip about whether his dementia was the result of syphilis, or whether it was the fault of his daughters for abandoning him when they departed for religious life. While the family's suffering itself was clearly not chosen by Thérèse, she had many choices to make about how to bear this reality and incorporate it within her spiritual life. From the beginning of the ordeal, in fidelity to the spirituality of her milieu, she made many comments similar to this one: "What a privilege Jesus grants in sending us

---

42. Lavelle, *Les puissances du moi*, 167, my translation.
43. Bourreille, *De Thérèse Martin à Thérèse de Lisieux*, 65.

such a great sorrow ... He is giving us his favors just as he gave them to the greatest saints."[44]

One hundred and thirty years later, such comments do not sit so easily with the spirituality of our times as they did with hers. For Thérèse, however, her father's suffering was truly an existential issue. Would she rage against God, numb herself so as not to feel the pain, put on a false cheerfulness, or fall into hopelessness? Her choice was to frame the suffering completely in terms of participation in the life and mission of Jesus. She wrote: "I found the secret of suffering in peace ... the canticle of suffering united to [Jesus's] suffering is what delights His Heart the most!"[45] Louis Martin's long agony formed his daughter's apprenticeship in the discovery that "suffering makes us like [Jesus]."[46] In Lavelle's terms, she was growing in the art of sacrifice for the sake of participating radically in the All.

7. *The Oblation to Merciful Love.* About one year after Louis's death, on June 8, 1895, the death notice of Sr. Anne-Marie of Jesus of Luçon Carmel was read in the refectory of Lisieux Carmel. Sr. Anne-Marie, like many devout Catholics of that era, had offered herself as a victim of divine justice. After a lifetime of extreme and debilitating penance, she died in agony crying out, "I do not have enough merits, I must acquire them!"[47] The next day, which was Trinity Sunday, Thérèse was inspired to make her own offering. Noting that she did not feel drawn to imitate those who offered themselves as victims of God's justice, she instead offered herself to God's Merciful Love.[48] Here is the climax of her prayer:

> In order to live in one single act of perfect Love, I OFFER MYSELF AS A VICTIM OF HOLOCAUST TO YOUR MERCIFUL LOVE, asking You to consume me incessantly, allowing the waves of *infinite tenderness* shut up within You to overflow into my soul, and thus I may become a *martyr* of Your *Love*, O my God! ... I want, O my *Beloved*, at each beat of my heart to renew this offering to You an infinite number of times, until the shadows having disappeared I may be able to tell You of my *Love* in an *Eternal Face to Face!*[49]

The Oblation constitutes a turning point in Thérèse's positive experiential awareness of her self-giving into Divine Love. It is clearly a conscious,

---

44. Thérèse de Lisieux, *Letters*, 1:541–42 [LT83].
45. Thérèse de Lisieux, *Letters*, 1:553 [LT87].
46. Thérèse de Lisieux, *Letters*, 2:897 [LT173].
47. Gaucher, *Sainte Thérèse de Lisieux*, 424–25, my translation.
48. Thérèse de Lisieux, *Story of a Soul*, 180–81 [A 84r-v].
49. Thérèse de Lisieux, *Story of a Soul*, 277.

whole-hearted act in which she freely reaches out to co-create herself as "oblation of merciful love." It is important to note that in framing her offering this way, she manifests the inner freedom to refuse the frame that was so strongly promoted by her culture, that of being a suffering "victim of divine justice." Insofar as it is within her ability to make an active choice of radical participation in God's love and mission, she has now done so.

8. *The night of faith.* In less than another year, on April 5, 1896—Easter Sunday—Thérèse was shockingly precipitated into an entirely different experience: that of the loss of all consoling awareness of God's presence. She wrote: "[God] permitted my soul to be invaded by the thickest darkness, and that the thought of heaven, up until then so sweet to me, be no longer anything but the cause of struggle and torment."[50] This occurred at the same time that she began coughing up blood from her lungs—the sign that her tubercular infection was entering a far more serious stage. The remaining eighteen months of her life were spent largely in spiritual darkness, at the same time that her health was rapidly declining.

During this period of her life, Thérèse faced the ultimate test. She was tormented as if by the voice of "sinners" mocking her and saying: "Advance, advance, rejoice in death which will give you not what you hope for but a night still more profound, the night of nothingness."[51] Having lived her whole life in a milieu deeply committed to imagining God, heaven, holiness, and virtue in very specific ways, she suddenly was faced with the collapse of this entire imaginative superstructure. This was particularly frightening and humiliating for Thérèse because she had devoted herself so fiercely to "advancing" within the spiritual path described by this superstructure. Her primordial confrontation with death and abandonment returned with a vengeance, now framed in the ultimate existential terms of despair and nihilism. As she peered into the abyss, Thérèse faced a choice more demanding than any she had made up to that time.

What she chose was to accept her place as that of being in active solidarity with sinners. She wrote that she did not "wish to rise up from this table filled with bitterness at which poor sinners are eating until the day set by You. Can she not say in her name and in the name of her brothers, '*Have pity on us, O Lord, for we are poor sinners!*'"[52] This was, in fact, the first time that Thérèse recognized, with her whole soul, that she was a sinner just as much as every other human being. Her core ambition of perfect virtue was stripped away from her; she could no longer rely either on her superlative

---

50. Thérèse de Lisieux, *Story of a Soul*, 211 [C 5r–v].
51. Thérèse de Lisieux, *Story of a Soul*, 213 [C 6v].
52. Thérèse de Lisieux, *Story of a Soul*, 212 [C 6r].

achievements or her fervent imagination. In the darkness, she had nowhere to go except to consent to being at one with the great mass of suffering sinners, humbly doing what little she could to lighten the burden of her sisters and brothers.

9. *Manuscript B*: Five months later—and just one year before her death—Thérèse wrote the remarkable text that is termed Manuscript B (and included as chapter 9 in *Story of a Soul*). Her sister and godmother Marie, also a nun of Lisieux, had requested that during Thérèse's retreat of September 7–18, 1896, she write something to explain her "little way." Thérèse responded in the form of a letter to Jesus. The text is far too rich to review in detail. The core of it is her description of her discovery of her true vocation. She begins by reviewing all the vocations that she desperately longs to fulfill. In addition to being Carmelite, Spouse, and Mother, she wants to be Warrior, Priest, Apostle, Doctor, Martyr, Crusader, Papal Guard, Prophet, and Missionary. These desires were causing her a "veritable martyrdom," she writes, until her eyes fell on 1 Corinthians 12–13. This was her discovery:

> I understood that the Church had a Heart and that this Heart was BURNING WITH LOVE. I understood it was Love alone that made the Church's members act, that if Love ever became extinct, apostles would not preach the Gospel and martyrs would not shed their blood. I understood that LOVE COMPRISED ALL VOCATIONS, THAT LOVE WAS EVERYTHING, THAT IT EMBRACED ALL TIMES AND PLACES . . . IN A WORD, THAT IT WAS ETERNAL!
>
> Then, in the excess of my delirious joy, I cried out: O Jesus, my Love . . . my vocation, at last I have found it . . . MY VOCATION IS LOVE!
>
> Yes, I have found my place in the Church and it is You, O my God, who have given me this place; in the heart of the Church, my Mother, I shall be Love. Thus I shall be everything, and thus my dream will be realized.[53]

This is Thérèse's culminating testament, both personally and theologically. On the theological level, it is a remarkably fresh ecclesiological statement that has yet to be plumbed for all its riches. On the personal level, it is an exuberant expression of the fullness of Thérèse's discovery and choice of radical participation in the divine mission of Love; or, in Lavellian language, in the pure Act of the All. Thérèse concludes her proclamation with a fresh reiteration of the principle of sacrifice: "Yes, in order that Love be fully satisfied, it is necessary that It lower Itself, and that It lower Itself to nothingness

---

53. Thérèse de Lisieux, *Story of a Soul*, 194 [B 3v].

and transform that nothingness into *fire*."[54] When Thérèse died on September 29, 1897, she was only twenty-four years old; yet there is ample evidence that she had lived as fully and radically as is possible for a human being.

THE FREEDOM OF THE CONTEMPLATIVE

A question that runs throughout this anthology is how spiritual practice fosters the freedom to resist evil. Unlike some of those featured in these essays, Thérèse was never faced with an outright, death-dealing social or political threat. Yet as we have seen, her life was marked from its origins by a primordial confrontation with the shattering effect of death and loss. Even as an infant and small child, she had to locate a way to choose relationships that would foster life and wholeness rather than acceding to the potential for psychological disaster. At age thirteen, in the "Christmas conversion," she awakened to her capacity to make such choices freely and consciously. The venue of this choice was small and mundane, yet cosmically life-changing for Thérèse. It became a template she could enlarge upon as she proceeded into making the choices that would constitute her heritage in the Church.

The five years of Louis Martin's suffering were an agony for his daughters as well. With the passion and death of Jesus as her constant model, Thérèse had to learn over and over again what Lavelle calls the principle of sacrifice. The true mettle of a person's life is not found in the sum of their worldly successes, but in the fruits of their fidelity of heart to the invitation to participate in the movement of the cosmos toward the fullness of life. In Thérèse's language, this is letting go of everything else for the sake of full participation in Jesus's mission of bringing into being the kingdom of God. How deeply Thérèse had made this principle of sacrifice her own was stunningly revealed when she made her "Oblation to Merciful Love." Explicitly rejecting the masochistic form of "victim spirituality" that was prominent in her milieu,[55] she prayed for the "martyrdom" of having God's "waves of infinite tenderness" overflowing within her and consuming her. The language is radically participatory, expressing the ecstasy of freely choosing to "consent to being" in the fullest possible way.

The shock of being cast from this ecstatic joy of overflowing experiential participation into the darkness and radical doubt of the "night of faith" was extreme. Suddenly the abandonment Jesus experienced on the cross was no longer something only to be imagined, admired, and imitated; it was

---

54. Thérèse de Lisieux, *Story of a Soul*, 195 [B 3v].

55. Manzoni, "Victimale (Spiritualité)," 531–45; Kane, "She Offered Herself Up," 80–119.

now her daily life, shorn even of any consolation of feeling his companionship. Here was the true test of the principle of sacrifice. Sacrifice is most radical when one is so completely stripped that there is no longer even the possibility of self-congratulation for the merit of one's sacrifice. Thérèse's response was to accept her meritlessness, recognizing her solidarity with her brother and sister sinners. Now she prayed for them not from a place of privilege, but from among them. She had learned that "consent to being" is not an act that lifts one to a special status above the rest of living beings, but rather reveals the profound truth of one's participation in the entire web of life.

The final fruit of this discovery of solidarity comes in Thérèse's Manuscript B proclamation that she has found her vocation, and that it is love—the burning love that constitutes the very Heart of the Church and that fuels every vocation and every movement toward God. While Thérèse had always been staunchly committed to the Church and its labors on behalf of humanity, it is only here at the end of her life that she has the inner freedom to identify herself as standing in the most literal sense at the very center of the Communion of Saints, participating with her whole being in the immense energy of its shared life. Christopher O'Donnell has suggested that Thérèse's most profound ecclesiological contribution is this recognition that it is only in the fullest level of participation in the Communion of Saints that the Church lives and advances.[56]

CONCLUSION

Even though many in her devout Catholic milieu framed their lifestyle choices in terms of resistance to the evil of secularism, this was not the primary venue in which Thérèse confronted destructive, life-denying forces. Her battle was at the deepest interior level where psychological fragmentation and spiritual meaninglessness repeatedly threatened her. Her explicit articulation of how she found her unique and extraordinary vocation in the very midst of this supremely debilitating challenge emphasizes the gracious acts of God. In the words of one of her signature images, "The elevator which must raise me to heaven is your arms, O Jesus!"[57] The value of placing her life trajectory in dialogue with Louis Lavelle's philosophy is by no means to downplay the power of her insight into the absolute necessity of grace. It is, rather, to lift up how grace operates in a dynamic rhythm with the free and creative choices necessary for the discovery and unfolding of human

---

56. O'Donnell, *Love in the Heart of the Church*, 215–18.
57. Thérèse de Lisieux, *Story of a Soul*, 208[C 3R].

vocation. If Thérèse's own life is the best exemplar of her "little way," it is far from simply being a way of submission and passive acceptance. Rather, this way calls for active participation in the co-creation of one's life with all the courage, creativity, and freedom of which a human being is capable.

REFERENCES

Bourreille, Claude. *De Thérèse Martin à Thérèse de Lisieux: devenir soi*. Paris: Consep, 2005.

Camille et Marie de la Rédemption. "Horizons de femmes à la fin du XIX seècle à Lisieux: la bourgeoisie et le Carmel, cadre de la vie de Thérèse." In *Thérèse carmélite*, edited by Dominique Poirot, 25–48. Paris: Cerf, 2004.

Gaucher, Guy. *Sainte Thérèse de Lisieux: 1873–1897: Biographie*. Paris: Cerf, 2010.

Geneviève, OP, et al., eds. *Les Mots de Sainte Thérèse de l'Enfant-Jésus et de La Sainte-Face: Concordance Générale*. Paris: Éditions du Cerf, 1996.

Hardy, Gilbert G. "French Spiritualism: Background and Basic Tenets." *Philosophy Today (Celina)* 12.3 (1968) 190–202.

Kane, Paula. "'She Offered Herself up': The Victim Soul and Victim Spirituality in Catholicism." *Church History* 71 (2002) 80–119.

Lavelle, Louis. *De l'acte*. Paris: Compagnons de Humanite, 2022.

———. *De l'intimité spirituelle. Philosophie de l'esprit*. Paris: Aubier, 1955.

———. *Leçon Inaugurale Faite Au Collège de France Le 2 Décembre 1941*. Paris: L'artisan du livre, 1942.

———. *Les puissances du moi. Bibliothèque de philosophie scientifique*. Paris: Flammarion, 1948.

———. *Of the Act*. Translated by Robert Jones. Queensland, Australia: Robert Jones, 2013. http://association-lavelle.chez-alice.fr/Traduction.htm.

———. "The Act of Presence: Works of Louis Lavelle." Translated by Robert Jones, 2012. http://association-lavelle.chez-alice.fr/Traduction.htm.

Manzoni, Giuseppe. "Victimale (Spiritualité)." In vol. 17 of *Dictionnaire de Spiritualité Ascétique et Mystique, Doctrine et Histoire*, 531–45. Paris: G. Beauchesne, 1932.

O'Donnell, Christopher. *Love in the Heart of the Church: The Mission of Thérèse of Lisieux*. Dublin: Veritas, 1997.

Perrot, Philippe. "Action et Contemplation Chez Louis Lavelle." *L'Enseignement Philosophique 63e Année* 1 (2013) 72–81.

Quito, Émérita S. *La notion de la liberté participée dans la philosophie de Louis Lavelle*. Vol. 49. Studia Friburgensia. Fribourg: Ed. Universitaires, 1969.

Renda, Frances, ed. *A Call to Deeper Love: The Family Correspondence of Saint Thérèse of the Child Jesus, 1863–1885: Blessed Zélie and Louis Martin*. Translated by Ann Connors Hess. Staten Island, NY: Society of St. Paul, 2011.

Sinclair, Mark, and Delphine Antoine-Mahut. "Introduction to French Spiritualism in the Nineteenth Century." *British Journal for the History of Philosophy* 28.5 (2020) 857–65.

Thérèse de Lisieux. *Letters of Saint Thérèse of Lisieux*. Translated by John Clarke. 2 vols. Washington, DC: Institute of Carmelite Studies, 1982, 1988.

———. *Story of a Soul: The Autobiography of Saint Thérèse of Lisieux*. Translated by John Clarke. 3rd ed. Washington, DC: Institute of Carmelite Studies, 1997.

3

Fire's Triptych

Rimbaud, Virgil, and Annie Dillard's Contemplative Transformation

KRISTEN DRAHOS

Annie Dillard, contemporary American writer turned naturalist, transcendentalist, scholar, and visionary, redirects the contemplative gaze. Instead of finding God through the soul's interiority, Scripture's revelation, or wisdom distilled in the crucible of asceticism, Dillard looks outward and into the teeming world around her. Nowhere is off limits—she seeks God in northern ice floes and Ecuadorian jungles as much as in her backyard. The method Dillard employs is one of openness and attention, witnessing both the abundance of life and the forms of pain that appear before her. Finding God begins with open eyes.

As she watches, the suffering she encounters increasingly clamors for more than observation alone. Dillard is yanked from the sidelines as her contemplative surveillance takes an abrupt turn to a new form of practical participation. Fire bursts forth in *Holy the Firm* as a radical spiritual practice of contemplation. A collision of opposites provides the landscape for Dillard's fertile mind, where she advances a vision that risks personal safety and comfort for the sake of one's neighbor, demands justice for wounds that gush with pain, and drags Dillard into the very shape of a God whose transformational love emerges through crucified death. Knowing God issues new requirements as contemplation's witness enmeshes itself with the work of responding to suffering. Dillard presses her readers to take seriously the task presented by one of the most brutal yet fascinating images in her corpus—the blazing moth-nun whose head is permanently alight with fire's transfiguring flame—as a path to addressing the suffering of one's neighbor.

Dillard's conclusion shocks and alarms, since the risk presented is consuming and defies boundaries. Perhaps, however, this kind of contemplation is necessary in a world awash with the brutal legacies of discrimination, racism, poverty, and other forms of inequality that linger and continue to create suffering today. As Dillard herself models, there may be a form of Christian love that makes transformative fire immanent, burning through prejudicial barriers, conveying suffering to God as a sacred offering, and generating a form of love that fuels works of justice to bring about a new world through the transformation of the old.

This chapter proposes that Annie Dillard calls Christians to embrace a united vision of the contemplative's watchful waiting with an active response to suffering neighbors. First, I differentiate Dillard's contemplative blaze from the poetic fire of Rimbaud, and particularly the poetic seer in his letter to Paul Demeny (1871).[1] I claim that Dillard's engagement with the French poet provides the initial outlines for contemplation that promotes a new kind of agency, where the fire burns through the distance between seer and the world and challenges injustice's ubiquitous presence afresh. Dillard binds poetic creativity to the needs of those who suffer. Fire is that which helps Dillard ensure thinking leads to action and creativity's generation never wipes away the meaning found in wounded experience. Next, I propose that Dillard presents a dramatic model of contemplative fire, which challenges the religious temptation to theory and abstraction. Using a contrasting poetic example drawn from fire in book 7 of Virgil's *Aeneid*, I argue that Dillard's fire promotes practices of inclusion, solidarity, and sacramental transformation. Finally, I conclude that Dillard's reaffirms that a contemplative vocation must be an active one, breaking the perceived binary separating the two, and calls upon Christians to take up practices that set alight the holy and searing fire of love's transformation.

---

1. Rimbaud's vision of a seer appears in letters to Izambard and Demeny from May 13 and 15, 1871, which were written prior to and after his younger sibling Isabelle's first communion on May 14 (Robb, *Rimbaud*, 84). The first letter's most famous line poses a response to Descartes's thinking self. For purposes of scope, I have focused on the second letter, more commonly referred to as "Letter of the Seer."

A SEER'S FIRE

In *Holy the Firm*, readers meet Dillard tangled in the world's raw materials in northern Puget Sound, surrounded by both mountains and sea. Divinity saturates the world and covers Dillard: "the day is real" as "today's god rises . . . holding all and spread on me like skin."[2] At first, she appears as the contemplative writer who explores this abundance.[3] Reminiscent of *Pilgrim at Tinker Creek*, Dillard's text opens with the simplicity of life with her cat and observations about the sow bugs, spiders, and moth husks that litter her bathroom.[4] Yet Dillard does not linger in joy, and her observations shift as she creates a disturbing hypothesis in the first pages of her text. She notes that on the floor, the "empty moths, stagger against each other, headless . . . like a jumble of buttresses for cathedral domes, like nothing resembling moths." Death offers a spectacular transformation for the insects as Dillard weds their vacant exoskeletons to a church's sacred ground, all of which she finds in the immediacy and immanence of her bathroom. Death that hollows can hallow, and she describes a moment when she witnessed this transformation firsthand.

Dillard recalls an evening as a teenager spent reading a book about Rimbaud by candlelight in the Blue Ridge Mountains, where moths continuously flew into her candle's flame. Their singed wings acted as glue that adhered their melting bodies to various pans nearby. One, though, stuck in the candle's wax. "Her moving wings ignited like tissue paper . . . vanished in a fine, foul smoke . . . her six legs clawed, curled, blackened, and ceased, disappearing utterly . . . her antennae crisped and burned away . . . her head was . . . gone, gone the long way of her wings and legs."[5] What begins with devastation, however, transforms as the moth's body begins to act as a second wick for the candle. She writes that the moth became a "saffron yellow flame . . . robed . . . to the ground like any immolating monk . . . her head was fire."[6] Dillard concludes by juxtaposing this "hollow saint" and "flame-faced virgin" to Rimbaud, who "burnt out his brains in a thousand poems."[7] The all-consuming vocation that these two figures convey—moth and poet—seems as dangerous as it is powerful, yet it is precisely the idea

---

2. Dillard, *Holy the Firm*, 12.
3. Dillard, *Holy the Firm*, 22.
4. Dillard, *Holy the Firm*, 13–14.
5. Dillard, *Holy the Firm*, 16.
6. Dillard, *Holy the Firm*, 17.
7. Dillard, *Holy the Firm*, 17.

that Dillard finds she needs in answer to the acute suffering she faces in the following pages.

The poetic image she invokes emerges most clearly in Rimbaud's 1871 letter to Paul Demeny. Rimbaud, once described as a "furious angel," inverts the promethean promise of fire to spark civilization, technology, and progress.[8] While Rimbaud's poet is "truly the thief of fire," he conveys "all forms of love, suffering, and madness" and rejects what conforms to agreeability, intelligibility, and pleasure.[9] The three poems Rimbaud includes in his letter amplify a world that upends traditional ideas and brims with celebrations of the grotesque and its fruits. Paris will receive its spring-like renewal only when watered by revolutionary "showers" of gasoline; the lovers that Rimbaud extols are the "ugly ones," infected with sores and blisters, able to destroy erotic sentimentality to discover embodied creativity; the institution of religion turns into a farce as the ordained brother strains and trembles not over ecclesial matters, but rather on account of an upset stomach upon his chamber pot.[10] By putting the scandalous on display, Rimbaud strips away the veneers that political order, love, and religion use to cover the world's ugliness and enervate its creativity through the imposed artificiality of form and order.[11] He rejects the world's presentation as a "great dream" of fictitious ideals, where life is exchanged for what is "deader than a fossil."[12]

Rimbaud not only challenges these positions, but by intentionally embracing "rational derangement of all the senses" and "unspeakable torture," the poet-seer can draw forth the "unknown" and the "unheard of and unnamable things" that remain inaccessible to others.[13] He claims that real creativity and true transformation depend on this poetic work.[14] The poet

8. As quoted from Bays, *Orphic Vision*, 132.

9. Rimbaud, *Complete Works*, 376.

10. Rimbaud, *Complete Works*, 73–81. Debates about Rimbaud's relation to religion and Catholicism abound, beginning with his sister, who insisted that her brother died a good Catholic, through various debates among later scholars in their interpretations of his life and work's relation to religion, Romanticism, philosophy, and politics. See Bays, *Oprhic Vision*, 131–39.

11. Ross Chambers points out that these poems combine the cliché and sublime of religious language to create a space for the unmeasurable and unattainable of poetic newness. Chambers, "On Inventing Unknownness," 32.

12. Rimbaud, *Complete Works*, 375, 379.

13. Rimbaud, *Complete Works*, 377.

14. As Chambers notes, such creativity "is not something pre-existing . . . but an outcome, something that *can* exist *only* as a consequence of its having been poetically 'invented' . . . or found" (Chambers, "On Inventing Unknownness," 15). Such an act relates to, but differs from, a thinker like Pascal, whose contemplation is a "response to

breaks "endless servitude" and creates new forms for living that will not be "strangled by the old form."[15] To give birth to a new world requires embracing the strange, horrific, irrational, and absurd, since these spaces brim with unseen resources for the poet's work. In such work the known of the world "cannot be fully and incontrovertibly left behind, let alone transformed," yet poetry does work on it nevertheless.[16] Such efforts differ from a recovery project, which can only lead to stillborn creations with nothing vital to offer.[17] In contrast with academic intellectuality and religious piety, the poet demands that new voices enter a world and create, rather than regurgitate.[18] Poets are those who can bestow "form" and "formlessness," going beyond papering over the recherché to scaffold and inaugurate transformation for what festers and rots.[19] They are the ones whose words "give rhythm to action" to incite change and apocalyptically create the future in the present.[20] Although the poems in Rimbaud's letter unveil more than create, he promises a new future for poetic utterance.

At first blush, Dillard aligns with Rimbaud's impulse to peel and peer beneath exterior dressings. Dillard too denounces the ubiquitous temptation to paint over suffering rather than admit that it cannot merely be counted as one of the "deep-blue speckles" of an otherwise ordered and beautiful world.[21] Suffering seers, blisters, and scars, and to say otherwise perpetuates disfiguration. Initially, she is an artist like Rimbaud, one who "lives jammed in the pool of materials."[22] Dillard declares that she has come "to study hard things—rock mountain and salt sea—to temper my spirit on their edges."[23] Three years after his letter to Demeny, Rimbaud declared "Saints are the strong ones!" while simultaneously bemoaning that "anchorites are artists

---

the unknown itself—not to any inventing of unknownness" (Chambers, "On Inventing Unknownness," 24). Chambers traces Rimbaud's turn to invention of the unknown to a more proximate source in the 1819 poetry of Giacomo Leopardi. See Chambers, "On Inventing Unknownness," 22–25.

15. Rimbaud, *Complete Works*, 379.
16. Chambers, "On Inventing Unknownness," 30.
17. Rimbaud, *Complete Works*, 381.
18. Rimbaud, *Complete Works*, 381.
19. Rimbaud, *Complete Works*, 379.
20. Rimbaud, *Complete Works*, 375. Later Rimbaud claims that the poet goes further—acting "in advance" of action. Here Rimbaud changes his mind and pulls back from the idea that the poet creates the dynamic movement that prompts change, but rather accelerates the timeline—the poet acts before all. Rimbaud, *Complete Works*, 379.
21. Dillard, *Tinker Creek*, 232.
22. Dillard, *Holy the Firm*, 22.
23. Dillard, *Holy the Firm*, 19.

not wanted any more!"[24] Dillard, however, reclaims and adjusts the meaning of both the saint and the idea of the one barnacled to sacred ground and nourished by transfigured elements. Dillard realizes that her words will not make sense to many. As with Rimbaud, they will merely think she is "raving again" when she offers wisdom that emerges from "the edge of the known and comprehended world."[25]

Like the moth trapped in the pool of wax, Dillard's contemplation transforms by taking up the world's molten swirl. Where Rimbaud took from the rejected of the world and attempted to create new forms within it, Dillard begins to absorb the world she witnesses. She describes a threefold triptych for her mission, where artist, thinker, and nun fuse and inform one another.[26] Distance remains in Rimbaud between the poet and the grotesque—his power comes from touching but not sickening from the ooze of the sores on his lover's breast. Dillard, however, wades into suffering and molds a new form of solidarity by removing the distance between herself and the world's mess. The artist becomes an anchorite by welding herself to the holiness of the world around her: she wakes and rests "in a god," the dead bodies of those around her make her cathedral's buttresses, and she is immersed into wax that becomes liquid with pain in the suffering of the book's second half.

Next, Dillard adapts the thinker who "lives in the bright wick of the mind."[27] Observation merges with encounter, and Dillard's thinking presents a new form of participation with what she finds through contemplation and writing. Dillard recognizes that idealized forms will not suffice, but that does not mean the mind has nothing to contribute. Contemplation and writing grant changed vision—the forms of "the Middle Ages" become "my Middle Ages," making a new "illuminated manuscript" that participates in the artist's work of conveying beauty's invitation to participation.[28] As the thinker, Dillard offers a new vision to the one who suffers. The mind must seek out new patterns that never erase the meaning of the sufferer's experience yet simultaneously find ways to address the pain endured. In a

---

24. Rimbaud, *Complete Works*, 273.

25. Dillard, *Holy the Firm*, 18, 20.

26. Rachel Matheson invites readers to see each vocation aligning with one of the book's three parts, which she describes through the arc of creation, fall, and redemption. "Dillard presents a configuration in which spirit, mind, and matter, as well as nun, thinker and artist, are distinct yet integrated" (Matheson, "Sacramental Vision," 67). The contemplative's final ecstatic vision at the work's end shows the unity and differentiation of all three and within the fullness of time's arc.

27. Dillard, *Holy the Firm*, 23–24.

28. Dillard, *Holy the Firm*, 23–24.

final moment of transformation, though, Dillard takes the shape of a mystic as a nun who "lives in the fires of the spirit." She writes, "I am hollow," like the moth's vacated body.[29] Yet instead of removal from the world, the world's proximity channels up her body. She becomes part of the change she envisions as she moves from observation to participation and service. By fusing her fate to suffering and taking it on as her own, her vision as a thinker never loses itself in abstract reflection, and her practical creativity in addressing pain takes on utmost urgency. The agency she develops demands an active agenda of seeking out suffering, of embracing extreme personal risk that refuses distance's safety, and of offering all of one's creativity and talents to usher forth the distinctive and holy gifts embedded in suffering's depths. Unlike the moth who unwittingly flew into her flame in the mountains, Dillard freely embraces her mission turned vocation. Rather than Rimbaud's poet-seer, Dillard casts the moth-nun with her head set on fire as the one who will inaugurate change within the world, and wills us to desire a similar fiery fate.

DRAMA AND FIRE'S VOCATION

In the second part of *Holy the Firm,* Dillard puts her dynamic image to the test as she considers its relation to the horrific suffering of a child, Julie Norwich. Burning in this section blazes into horror as "into the world fell a plane . . . one wing snagged on a fir top . . . and smashed . . . the fuel exploded; and Julie Norwich seven years old burnt off her face."[30] The child forces readers to look suffering in the face—"her eyes naked and spherical, baffled"—where no abstract consideration will suffice.[31] Her name evokes the English anchoress, Julian of Norwich, who contemplates the goodness and providence of God in the midst of the plague's ravages. Dillard's placement of it upon the child's suffering raises questions of theodicy afresh. Here innocence and helplessness come to a point, and Dillard exclaims, "what . . . is going on here? The works of God made manifest? Do we really need more victims to remind us that we're all victims?"[32] She points out that for all that the world has changed since the fourteenth century, technology fails to fully transform suffering.[33] Julie lacks lips to scream after her accident,

29. Dillard, *Holy the Firm,* 24.
30. Dillard, *Holy the Firm,* 35–36.
31. Dillard, *Holy the Firm,* 36.
32. Dillard, *Holy the Firm,* 60.
33. In Julie's case, "because burns destroy skin: the drugs simply leak into the sheets" (Dillard, *Holy the Firm,* 60).

but her agony resounds in Dillard's text. At the outset, divine mercy also has seemingly burnt away with her skin. There is "no wind, and no hope of heaven" on such a day.[34] Julie's name seems to render its medieval origin mawkish. It forces Dillard into a confrontation not only with God, but with the transformative and liberational efficacy of her threefold vision.

Julie in Dillard's text particularizes suffering and places it on the reader's doorstep, much as it is set before Dillard. Suffering becomes drama—it cannot be regulated to theoretical opining about the nature of mercy and grace, it resists segregation, and it integrates itself into the fabric of human existence writ large. While readers will never meet the child Julie, we need only to open our eyes and realize that there are a hundred individuals with their own seared skin, gasping mouths, and unblinking eyes living next door. "This is evidence of things seen: one Julie, one sorrow, one sensation bewildering the heart, and enraging the mind, and causing me to look at the world stuff appalled. . . . Have I once turned my hand in this circus, have I ever called it home?"[35] In a deluge of questions, she grows frustrated with theological theory that lacks a dramatic domain. The God whose transcendence creates the total distance of incomprehensible otherness, where "he knows himself blissfully as flame consuming, as all brilliance and beauty and power," yet leaves "the rest of us . . . [to] go hang."[36] The God who sends Christ for a singular moment of divine intervention can only give "a kind of divine and kenotic suicide" that offers a singular instance of meaningful suffering, "pulling his cross up after him like a rope ladder home."[37] Each answer dissatisfies Dillard—she is left "chewing the bones in [her] wrist" as she ponders what it means to "pray for them"—for the world of sufferers including Julie, her father, and her mother. Prayer, she senses, must do much more than merely act as a theological reminder and placeholder for action. Something must be done, and God must get involved. But "who will teach us to pray?"[38]

Much as Dante depended upon Virgil for guidance through hell and purgatory, the Roman poet can assist Dillard's intuition that she and Rimbaud share about the significance of fire, particularly as it applies to the problem of suffering via the dramatic. Virgil extends Dillard's sightlines for understanding the effects of fire in the drama of human existence. Although Dillard does not draw upon him herself, Virgil likewise recognized that

---

34. Dillard, *Holy the Firm*, 36.
35. Dillard, *Holy the Firm*, 46.
36. Dillard, *Holy the Firm*, 48.
37. Dillard, *Holy the Firm*, 47–48.
38. Dillard, *Holy the Firm*, 49.

transformation was as inherently dangerous as it was potentially valuable. Like Dillard, he embraces the symbol of fire to offer warnings and sightlines for transforming the pain of destruction into the glory of a new nation. Exploring Dillard through references to the *Aeneid* makes visible and explicit specific dangers that Dillard's project avoids, while also amplifying strategies that make her ideas potent and effective in changing the world around her.

Throughout book 7 of the *Aeneid*, fire dominates and shapes what will unfold in the rest of the text, offering insights and warnings about its power and presence. In this book, Aeneas and the Trojans have recently arrived in Italy, and it opens with the hope of a peaceful union of people, Latins and Trojans, through marriage between King Latinus's daughter, Lavinia, and Aeneas. Fire in this drama, however, threatens the entire affair—first burning an ambition in the queen mother's heart to wed her daughter to a local suitor rather than Aeneas, and moments later engulfing Lavinia at the altar, where "her flowing hair caught fire, her lovely regalia crackled in the flames, her regal tresses blazed, her crown blazing . . . the next moment the girl was engulfed in a smoky yellow haze."[39] The fire that overwhelms Lavinia, however, takes a twofold form. It is a sign of both "wonder" and "terror."[40] Prophets simultaneously declare that it portends the burnish of brilliant fame as much as the horror of a grueling war between the Latins and Trojans. Fire's immanence is both threat and political glory.

On one level, the gods control the dramatic action of this story, where Jove and the fates decree that Aeneas will found Rome in Italy, and the goddess Juno can only delay the day's coming, rather than avert what is already destined. Like Julie, whose accident is framed in passive voice, the macro-drama that occasioned Lavinia's suffering is out of human control.[41] However, human volition plays a significant role in the way the drama unfolds in both the *Aeneid* and Julie's story. What was a fire already burning in the queen mother's heart is stoked into a fully venomous viper that "breathes its fire through the frenzied queen" and "becomes the gold choker around her throat . . . braiding through her hair [and] writhing over her body."[42] Fire takes over the queen, seizing her mind and robbing her of rational thought

---

39. Virgil, *Aeneid* 7.80–84.

40. Virgil, *Aeneid* 7.87.

41. Matheson points out that Dillard's rare passive construction frames suffering as interruptive and non-volitional, which she uses to explore the structure of Dillard's work as aesthetic appreciation of creation, intellectual contemplation of the Fall, and mystical vision of Christic and sacramental redemption. See Matheson, "Sacramental Vision," 79n26.

42. Virgil, *Aeneid* 7.410–12.

and speech.[43] Unlike Lavinia's blaze, the queen's fire lacks double directionality. The queen's determination to reject the newly arrived Trojans, despite divine prophecy and omens, establishes a single and deadly trajectory for the flames she conveys. Recalling Queen Dido's unhappy self-immolation in book 4 after Aeneas's decision to prioritize Rome's foundation over his personal erotic affection, the Latin queen expands the symbol of a self-chosen horrific funeral pyre as she burns through the city and incites violence in others.[44] Her unwillingness to risk offering up what she willed for her daughter by clinging to the past as a vision of continuity, safety, and prosperity turns deadly for herself and others. Yet she is not alone in stoking flames that will create great suffering and consume many in war. Like the queen, the will of the gods frustrates Turnus, a forerunner of Lavinia's suitors, and his desire to wed Lavinia, but ironically it is his passivity and derision that stoke the incendiary flames that consume him. In his case, Juno's emissary finds herself having to goad Turnus into taking up arms.[45] It is not until Turnus laughs and derides her message that Alecto "ignite[s] in rage" and lodges a violent flame of war in his chest.[46] His initial unresponsiveness turned to mockery leads to his donning of a helmet that "raises up a Chimaera with all the fires of Etna blasting from its throat and roaring all the more, its searing flames more deadly the more blood flows and the battle grows more fierce."[47]

Within the macro-drama, the mortals' decisions significantly configure their trajectories and ends. The queen's refusal to entertain an alternative to the stranger at her doorstep contrasts both with Lavinia's and the king's openness to conceiving what other possibilities the future might hold. This is not to say that accepting the Trojans and Aeneas is not without risk—the doubled meaning of Lavinia's flaming hair makes the danger visible and present to all who see it. Yet it is precisely their ability to open themselves to what is unsafe, new, and strange on their shores that gives these characters a new role to play in transforming the old empire to a new one—one that will eventually lead to a mixture of custom, language, and blood, rather than Trojan hegemony. In addition, Turnus's initial indifference and scornful

---

43. Virgil, *Aeneid* 7.14–17.

44. Dido's death is "not fated or deserved," but rather self-chosen (Virgil, *Aeneid*, 4.866). Where Lavinia and Dido have parallels with respect to Aeneas as an erotic partner, the violent agency Dido displays in her death connects her to Queen Amata. The violence incited spreads quickly, most notably in the Latin mothers. See Virgil, *Aeneid*, 7.455–74.

45. Virgil, *Aeneid* 7.490–508.

46. Virgil, *Aeneid* 7.509–10, 523.

47. Virgil, *Aeneid* 7.911–13.

laughter point to the importance of human reactions to the drama's unfolding. Turnus's disdain launches him into a trajectory where the flames of war are placed upon his head, symbolized by his helmet, which will ultimately destroy him. Where Lavinia's crowning fire turns to glory, Turnus's bellicose flames lead to his glory-seeking grasp of slain Pallas's sword belt. Turnus's flaming head cannot transpose war's weaponry, which he dons head to hilt, and Aeneas's rage at the sight overwhelms the victor's impulse to mercy.

By contrast, Dillard's project reveals specific approaches to openness to what is foreign, solidarity with risky, and the potential for abundance that emerges from the service of sacrifice. Unlike the queen, Dillard's heart is moved by the entrance of another person within her world. While Julie has no claim upon her affection—she is not Dillard's child nor is Dillard indebted to her—Dillard embraces the changes Julie brings to her world, and in particular a change that involves entering into suffering's drama. Both the queen and Dillard recognize that those who come will refashion their worlds if allowed in. Dillard, unlike the queen, walks boldly into a changed world. In consequence, she seeks new trajectories from God for the suffering at hand. The queen remains singly focused, wed to the course she desired for her daughter's life, which ultimately leads to diseased madness on account of the permanent discontinuity between what was outside her control and her unquenched desires. Dillard's open embrace of difference, though, challenges the status quo. She voices dissent about the suffering she encounters, and through it she finds "the heart's slow learning where to love and whom."[48]

Unlike Turnus, Dillard does not sit unaffected. What begins Julie's tale by accident with "into this world falls a plane" mirrors the draw of insects, where "moths kept flying into the candle." Like the moths, Dillard feels a pull toward Julie in her suffering. Unlike the moths, Dillard must willingly choose to enter the fray, which brings two seemingly distant moments in time and drama together. Earlier she notes that she and Julie resemble one another, but it is not physicality that holds the two together. Instead, Dillard's work transposes Julie's suffering into herself by lighting "the short string of [her] gut." Drama creates the conditions for a new form of solidarity between Dillard and Julie that is transformative in and through its being offered to God.

In the *Aeneid*, the immanent domain traps fire within the realm of petty gods and rulers. Even the glory of Rome presages a future fueled by violence, conquest, colonialism, and war as fire remains bound to the desires and frailties of mortal leaders and the whims and quarrels of the gods.

---

48. Dillard, *Holy the Firm*, 62.

Yet in Dillard, what was seemingly Julie's fate to wear "that skinlessness, that black shroud of flesh in strips on your skull" becomes Dillard's and transforms her work as an artist and thinker to that of the sacrificial nun who welds horizontal care to vertical offering.[49] She puts on the habit of one bold enough to wade into the fray of suffering and risk setting her own head on fire with love rather than rage. It will be Dillard who is "held, held fast by love in the world like the moth in wax, your life a wick, your head on fire with prayer."[50] She becomes an embodiment of the form of Christ with "face [that] is flame like a seraph's, lighting the kingdom of God for the people to see; his life goes up in the works . . . spanning all the long gap with the length of his love, in flawed imitation of Christ on the cross stretched both ways unbroken and throned."[51] The fiery nun transposes the candle-flame of the artist to a votive that binds her fate to the suffering one's and raises earth to heaven.

Like Francis after his vision on Mount Alverna, this revelation changes Dillard's life and work.[52] Although she recognizes that Julie's scars and experience will alter, the permanence of what Dillard becomes does not fade. Dillard's enduring transformation testifies to the lasting impact that the world's suffering and pain create. They mark history, even as their acuity passes. With her new vocation, Dillard becomes the living candle who participates in making an ongoing offering of Julie's pain, unforgotten but transformed. In a moment of solidarity born out of her witness of the child's pain, she declares, "Live. I'll be the nun for you now. I am now."[53] Unlike one locked away, Dillard's new contemplative role further enmeshes her in the world. "There are two kinds of nun," she writes—"out of the cloister or in."[54] Dillard is the one whose cloister widens. There is nowhere she will not convey the work to which she is called.

At the book's end, Dillard shifts the domain of the common and its intersection with the holy from her bathroom floor to the grocery shelf, where she buys wine for her Church's communion. Eucharist and sacrament dominate the book's conclusion. Like the wine that begins in the mundane,

---

49. Dillard, *Holy the Firm*, 74.

50. Dillard, *Holy the Firm*, 76.

51. Dillard, *Holy the Firm*, 72.

52. See also Drahos, "Nailed and Aflame." This image also invites a conversation with Walter Benjamin and his focus on Klee's angel of history, who gazes in horror at the world's ruination. Dillard's flaming seraph offers a vision of one who can accomplish the work that Klee's angel could not by creating a living conduit from one moment to another and conveying the world's wounds into the power of God.

53. Dillard, *Holy the Firm*, 76.

54. Dillard, *Holy the Firm*, 74.

the everyday has the potential to change and become something infused with power. That which starts out as "Christ with a cork" becomes salvific as God's transformative power traverses boundaries of heaven and earth, the sacred and the secular, and the wounded and the whole.[55] "The world is changing. The landscape begins to respond as a current upwells" as Dillard sets off on a walk with wine on her back.[56] "Through all my clothing, through the pack on my back and through the bottle's glass I feel the wine. Walking faster and faster, weightless, I feel the wine. It sheds light in slats through my rib cage, and fills the buttressed vaults of my ribs with light pooled and buoyant. I am moth; I am light. I am prayer and I can hardly see."[57] This epiphanic, eucharistic transformation happens precisely as Dillard goes on a journey into suffering, engulfing her in the mysterious transfiguration of the common to the rare. Dillard becomes a living sacrament. Her body becomes a new cathedral for hosting the holy and its transfiguring power, even where what is common appears beyond redemption.

Where Turnus's fiery helmet of war fixed his trajectory, Dillard's embrace of the moth-nun breaks her vocation wide open and thrusts her from mystical contemplation to active service. "Here am I; send me," she writes, echoing the prophet Isaiah.[58] The form of Dillard's task shines brightly: solidarity unites her with the personal shape of suffering and charges her with carrying it, conveying it up the hill such that it might be charged with the glory of God and part of a divine economy. As Matheson notes, "she no longer demands an explanation for the existence of suffering, but rather seeks a proper response to its presence."[59] Her constancy, and the sacrifice put upon her and symbolized by the moth's lost wings and burned away legs and antennae, transform her into something entirely new and dramatic—the nun become servant and continual martyr.[60] She is a flaming wick for

---

55. Dillard, *Holy the Firm*, 64. While she notes the significance of encountering God in churches high and low earlier, she points out that God's transformative presence is not contained by the walls of buildings or the consecration of particular space. See Dillard, *Holy the Firm*, 59.

56. Dillard, *Holy the Firm*, 64.

57. Dillard, *Holy the Firm*, 65.

58. Dillard, *Holy the Firm*, 73.

59. Matheson, "Sacramental Vision," 77.

60. Matheson amplifies the first aspect, where "the sacramental opens the ability to see the world anew, but it also invites a response to that vision, which Dillard discerns as an act of compassion, of sharing in another's suffering" (Matheson, "Sacramental Vision," 90). Yet I add the second condition to unite the moth-nun to the vocation of a martyred writer, which gives practical dimensions to the point of reference that the moth-nun points to—a crucified Christ in the form of the stigmatic Seraph who changes the trajectory of St. Francis's earthly vocation. Dillard's martyrdom follows the

the wax, yet still selfsame—it is her body and her head that blaze with fire as she joins the sacramental work of Christ by "emulat[ing] the self-abasing love of Christ who took on the form of a servant."[61] It is the integration of artist-poet, thinker, and nun that makes this work possible.[62]

Dillard is ready to be sent wherever suffering requires transformation and to call the world to account. The entire world is her pool of wax. She charges those who read her book with a similar mission. The illumination of the moth-nun broke into Dillard's consciousness and ignited her mind and heart. In similar fashion, Dillard's writing breaks into her reader's consciousness. She is now the flame to which other moths are irresistibly drawn, and she keeps the wax that will become pools for their bodies flowing. "Which of you want to give your lives to be writers?"—she asks.[63] Writing is the specific form that her vocation has taken, but the call is universal. To love those who suffer also entails confronting the world with a light that cannot be ignored or sidestepped, giving one's life for the suffering and drawing others into the same light. Although such love will create the conditions of a form of martyrdom for those drawn to it, that same love will ignite the work of compassion, solidarity and transformation.

PRACTICES OF FIERY CONTEMPLATION

The fires conjured by Rimbaud and Virgil challenge readers to look beyond the comfort of the world's facades and the ease of the status quo. Both poets grasp the power of fire as a symbol that has the power to recreate the world and offer the foundation for what has yet to be imagined. Like these poets, Dillard recognizes the power of fire to address the needs she sees before her in the world's manifold suffering. Dillard harnesses the power of fire to

---

path of "white" rather than "red" martyrs, or those whose martyrial offering occurs without resulting in physical death.

61. Matheson, "Sacramental Vision," 77.

62. Matheson concludes her piece by drawing the service that Dillard describes into a final liturgical frame that reassumes a traditional contemplative posture, where she offers "a response of thanksgiving and wonder" in answer to the "drama of divine love to which we are invited to participate through communion with the other." She concludes by situating Dillard's "selfless sacrifice" within the context of "loving worship of the divine" (Matheson, "Sacramental Vision," 77). Matheson's liturgical framing is astute and compelling, but I argue it lacks attention to Dillard's active charge to embrace the life of a nun living beyond convent walls—whose final vocation is not cloistered contemplative adoration, but a prophetic and martyrial witness of service to and for others. Dillard's nun is sent forth from worship to break into and reform the world still groaning and journeying to its final end in God.

63. Dillard, *Holy the Firm*, 18.

reimagine Christian contemplation. Rather than passively observing, she jumps into the suffering quagmire before her. By embracing the freedom of the transformed poet, Dillard not only embraces a new life for herself, but she charts a bold trajectory for the faithful. Pain is personal, builds bonds between sufferers and those who encounter them, and can become a catalyst of transformation for individuals and of history's drama writ large. Dillard reworks the parameters of Rimbaud's seer to sketch a new form for contemplative witness—the vocation of a martyr brave enough to open her head to the fire of love and embrace the world through its animating draw. In so doing, she promotes important concrete practices: paying attention to the proximate, reaching out to those who suffer with courage, challenging theoretical answers that erase the personal and profound dimensions of pain, resisting collapsed trajectories for addressing pain's wounds, and opening oneself to joining the work of transforming pain into something radically new. Dillard holds up herself as the moth nun in her writing, but she also challenges all who call themselves Christians to embrace a form of this vocation as well.

REFERENCES

Bays, Gwendolyn. *The Orphic Vision: Seer Poets from Novalis to Rimbaud*. Lincoln: University of Nebraska Press, 1964.

Chambers, Ross. "On Inventing Unknownness: The Poetry of Disenchanted Reenchantment." *French Forum* 33 (2008) 15–36.

Dillard, Annie. *Holy the Firm*. New York: Harper and Row, 1977.

———. *Three by Annie Dillard: The Writing Life, An American Childhood, Pilgrim at Tinker Creek*. New York: Harper Perennial, 1990.

Drahos, Kristen. "Nailed and Aflame: Annie Dillard's Bonaventurian Mysticism." *Religion & Literature* 51.2 (2019) 91–112.

Matheson, Rachel. "Sacramental Vision in Annie Dillard's Holy the Firm." *Literature & Theology* 34.1 (2020) 64–82.

Rimbaud, Artur. *Rimbaud: Complete Works, Selected Letters*. Translated by Wallace Fowlie. Chicago: University Of Chicago Press, 2005.

Robb, Graham. *Rimbaud*. New York: Norton, 2000.

Virgil. *The Aeneid*. Translated by Robert Fagles. New York: Penguin, 2006.

THEORY

4

Kenosis and Freedom

JACOB W. TORBECK

Classical Christian theological notions of freedom do not entail a living-out of one's own personal will, but obedience to the will of God, insofar as possible uniting one's own will to the divine will. This necessarily entails a form of self-emptying, a *kenosis*, in the form of an *imitatio Christi*, after the apostle Paul's Christological hymn in Philippians, which highlights Jesus's humility and obedience manifest especially in the Incarnation and the Crucifixion. On one hand, this model of "Christian obedience as freedom" enables a freedom of the will that is not contingent upon social or political freedom. On the other hand, in the wake of the suppression or denial of social and political freedoms—freedoms that contribute to human flourishing—to vulnerable or marginalized persons, we may wonder if the vulnerability engendered by a spirituality of self-sacrifice might work *against* the promotion of these same social and political freedoms.

It takes very little research or imagination to determine how admonitions to imitate Christ's obedience and self-sacrifice can go (and have gone) wrong. Many of us have likely heard of battered spouses counselled by a spiritual director to remain married to their abusive partner, even being advised to "offer up" their suffering. As Jennifer Manlowe points out in her article "Seduced by Faith: Sexual Traumas and Their Embodied Effects," notions of empowerment or healing through prayer have historically perpetuated cycles of shame or self-blaming, and convinced abuse victims that their real problems are not their abusers, but rather their addictions, their "stubborn wills," or some other fault.[64] These admonitions to emulate Mary's or Christ's meekness and vulnerability open victims to further harm. Thus, to many, a kenotic understanding of freedom has uncomfortable connotations.

Even on a more mundane level, the thought of self-divestment strikes against the commonplace American understanding of freedom as including the exercise of the autonomous subject's unalienable right to pursue happiness through one's free choices. From the opposite perspective, there is a perception of the mystical spirituality which fosters and grows from kenosis as being at odds with any project of *communal* salvation. In this view, the mystic is engaged in a personal, individual project of *self-actualization* that places them *beyond* vulnerability. To elevate this model of spirituality might imply that the material concerns, sometimes forms of material oppression, from which these so-called mystics have detached themselves, are really of little importance for Christian holiness.

Each of these perceptions alerts us to real dangers inherent in the concept of self-emptying, as it has been experienced in history. In this essay, I put forward an articulation of kenotic freedom that conceives of (what is variously called) self-emptying, kenosis, or decreation as neither solipsistic nor oppressive. I do this first by briefly summarizing the historical values and broad debates that have led to the above critiques. Second, I draw definitions of kenosis and the freedom it engages and enables from the work of spiritual theologians and philosophers, especially Hans Urs von Balthasar and Simone Weil, for whom the "pouring out of oneself" forms the shape of Christian action, or the basis for Christian ethical life. Finally, I place these definitions in conversation with the work of Howard Thurman, whose own response to the question of the social role of the mystic broadens and clarifies the implications of kenotic freedom. Broadly speaking, conceiving of freedom in light of Christian kenosis reorients our understanding of social and political freedom away from common liberal notions of freedom, offering instead a renewed sense of autonomy as that state in which the Christian receives the gift of their own being for the sake of offering themselves back.

CONTEXT AND CRITIQUES OF KENOTIC FREEDOM

Liberal valuations of personal liberty and autonomy have played a role in diminishing the role that kenosis plays in contemporary understandings of freedom. The liberal view of freedom, typified in the thought of Hobbes and

---

64. Manlowe, "Seduced by Faith," 336. Aristotle Papanikolaou provides a number of other examples in "Kenosis and Abuse."

Locke, often understands liberty as "the absence of external impediments,"[65] a state through which individuals, endowed with equal individual rights, are free to pursue their own vision of the good life.[66] Charles Taylor, in *The Ethics of Authenticity*, summarizes this position by saying that "Self-determining freedom demands that I break the hold of all . . . external impositions, and decide for myself alone."[67] Because the elevation of individuals over the community is bound to produce conflict, where self-interests conflict, the state has the role of regulating social relations, putting limited constraints upon individual rights to minimize obstacles to the pursuit of individual desires.

As Ryan LaMothe notes, under the liberal view of freedom, "it was only the Leviathan that demanded some degree of self-limitation, broadly seen as refraining from impinging another individual's pursuits of the good life."[68] This was a paradigm shift from classical and Christian notions of freedom, which had entailed a broader expectation of social responsibility. In Greek thought, my welfare, your welfare, and so on, as well as our freedom, were linked to the welfare of the polis. In the work of Augustine and Thomas Aquinas, political freedom is obtained (always imperfectly) to the degree in which societies enable and participate in the "presence of the beauty of order," the order of the common good, or justice.[69] The freedom to live in and from this common good, however, is not the maximally unrestrained pursuit of individuals' notions of the good, but the individual and communal obedience to a common vision of God's goodness and justice. The adoption of liberal notions of freedom was also, then, a move into a new relationship to the sociality of freedom and the common good toward which it was ordered. Instead of sociality being constitutive of freedom, sociality became its obstacle. Or, as LaMothe puts it, "the idea of freedom loses its relational or social foundations and is increasingly seen as an individual possession."[70]

As one might have expected, this change in our understanding of freedom accompanied a concomitant escalation of critiques of kenotic and

---

65. Hobbes, *Leviathan* 14, quoted in Honneth, *Freedom's Right*, 21. The Leviathan is the potent political entity exercising governing power over the people, akin to the phrase "the State" or "the Crown."

66. LaMothe, "Social and Political Freedom," 262–63.

67. Taylor, *Ethics of Authenticity*, 27, quoted in LaMothe, "Social and Political Freedom," 263.

68. LaMothe, "Social and Political Freedom," 265.

69. Bauerschmidt, "Aquinas," 56, cited in LaMothe, "Social and Political Freedom," 262.

70. LaMothe, "Social and Political Freedom," 263.

mystical spirituality. The twentieth century especially bore witness to the perception of a worrisome relationship between mysticism and ethics. On the one hand, the notion of mysticism as private, incommunicable spiritual endeavor would seem to fit within the milieu of liberal notions of freedom. This, for some notable critics, was precisely the problem. Grace M. Jantzen notes in her 1994 article, "Feminists, Philosophers and Mystics," that with few exceptions, "books of popular Christian spirituality treat prayer and spiritual exercises as strictly private," sharing with philosophical studies of mysticism the assumption that mystical experience and mystical spiritual practice are private and subjective in such a way that the relationship between the mystic and social justice is rendered nebulous and obscure.[71] Indeed, in 1910, Bertrand Russell identifies the mystical mind as possessing "the absence of indignation or protest,"[72] which are states incompatible with the kinds of unity and peace that mystical consciousness is thought to produce. Reinhold Niebuhr seems content, in *An Interpretation of Christian Ethics,* to define mysticism as "really a self-devouring rationalism which begins by abstracting rational forms from concrete reality and ends by positing an ultimate reality beyond all rational forms."[73] Though making clear that not all rationalism must end in mysticism, no such caveats are given for the "mystical," which remains, in Niebuhr's view, the realm of a pessimistic dualism necessarily enacted through a "contemplative withdrawal from the world" that is reserved for the aristocratic class, as the "burden-bearers of the world" are not permitted "to harbour the illusions of either pure pessimism or pure optimism."[74] Karl Barth's well-known allergy to mysticism targets his perception of mystical spirituality as an endeavor of solipsistic self-actualization, divorced from participation in the Christian community.[75]

In saying this, these writers are not merely echoing the earlier philosophical critiques of the liberal capitalist milieu found, for example, in Marx and Hegel, nor are they are simply arguing for a nostalgic return to a pre-liberal Christian order. They are also adding voice to a resentment which had already been seen long ago in the *Cloud of Unknowing,* which refers to complaints levied "to this day" by "all actives" against contemplatives who "set themselves apart from worldly concerns."[76] We can hear such critiques

71. Jantzen, "Feminists, Philosophers, and Mystics," 202.
72. Russell, *Mysticism and Logic,* 11.
73. Niebuhr, *Interpretation of Christian Ethics,* 15.
74. Niebuhr, *Interpretation of Christian Ethics,* 15.
75. McIntosh, "Humanity in God," 24–25.
76. *Cloud of Unknowing,* 158–60.

sung more recently in Joe Hill's 1910 parody of the hymn "In the Sweet-By-and-By," which crows:

> Long-haired preachers come out every night
> Try to tell you what's wrong and what's right
> But when asked 'bout something to eat
> They will answer in voices so sweet
> You will eat (*You will eat*), by and by (*By and by . . .*)
> In that glorious land above the sky (*Way up high!*)
> Work and pray (*Work and pray*), live on hay (*Live on hay?!*)
> You'll get pie in the sky when you die (*That's a lie!*)

"The Preacher and the Slave," as Hill called his song, is evidence that concern about "pie-in-the-sky" spirituality was not simply an academic misperception by the likes of Barth, Niebuhr, and Russell. The perceived disconnect between receiving spiritual doctrines and practicing Christian life (often identified with the biblical figures of Mary and Martha) was well known and deeply felt, especially by those who were "living on hay." Thus, despite whatever errors we might see in certain evaluations of mystical experience and thought, the critiques resonate with a large portion of humanity.

It might nevertheless be tempting to say that critics like Barth misname the mystical disposition in a way that utterly misses "authentic" kenotic mysticism and the social freedom it offers. After all, would not a self-emptying, or kenotic, mysticism be antithetical to the solipsism that Barth and Russell decry? I believe this is possible, but there are still caveats to which we must attend. One strong warning comes from Jean-Luc Marion, who points to a misunderstanding of sacrifice as a method of autarchy, or self-appropriation. Rather than a kind of kenosis, sacrifice becomes a way for those who are already powerful and privileged to celebrate their self-sufficiency. He writes:

> Indeed, the wise and the strong want to rid themselves of a possession by destroying it and thereby becoming free of it; they alone can do this, and they prove it to themselves by surviving what they destroy in themselves: in making a sacrifice of other goods (by ascesis, renunciation, mutilation, and so forth), they demonstrate their autarchy to others; or rather they prove at least to themselves their autonomy and ataraxy. Sacrifice thus becomes the auto-celebration of the ascetic ideal, in which the ego attains a kind of causa sui by no longer owing anything to anyone, not even its own person to the world.[77]

---

77. Marion, "Sketch of a Phenomenological Concept," 437–38.

We are warned, in this passage, of a spiritual temptation—an attractive simulacrum of kenosis. Instead of an unselfing, the self is aggrandized. Rather than rendering oneself vulnerable, the act of renunciation becomes a performative gesture to demonstrate one's own invulnerability. The freedom that one takes here is not the freedom of Christ.

On the other extreme, insofar as *kenosis* is concerned, the vulnerability engendered by the practice of a kenotic mysticism can be exploited from the outside. As a number of feminist and womanist authors have noted since Valerie Saiving's classic article "The Human Situation: A Feminine View," the doctrine of kenosis has been employed to glorify gratuitous suffering, justify keeping women in subordinate positions in male-dominated hierarchies, and, as Jennifer Newsome Martin summarizes, "sanction self-evacuation particularly among those whose sense of self may already be compromised."[78]

Importantly, Saiving's critique of Niebuhr's own admonitions against the selfish will points out that for marginalized persons, in this case women, freedom as social self-determination has not yet been fully won. In their respective summaries of this and the subsequent feminist critique of kenosis, Aristotle Papanikolaou and Jennifer Newsome Martin each point to the debate between Daphne Hampson and Sarah Coakley as paradigmatic for the way it highlights the important issues. For Hampson's part, it is autonomy, understood as a practice of self-determination, that is the goal of feminism.[79] Thus, if we understand kenosis as an act or disposition of self-sacrifice in imitation of Christ, inasmuch as it is a *surrender* of self-determination, it would seem to be wholly incompatible with Hampson's articulation of the feminist obligation to promote women's autonomy.[80]

Coakley's rejoinder attempts to rehabilitate kenosis as a "contemplative 'power-in-vulnerability.'"[81] While admitting that earlier British kenoticists expressed their notions of kenosis in terms marred by sexism and classism, Coakley argues that scripture gives us reason to believe that "true divine 'empowerment' [could] occur most unimpededly in the context of a *special* form of human 'vulnerability.'"[82] She describes this vulnerability as "not an invitation to be battered," but instead as a practice of making space for God to

---

78. Martin, "Balthasar's Gendered Theology," 214.

79. Martin, "Balthasar's Gendered Theology," 216, referencing Daphne Hampson, "On Autonomy and Heteronomy."

80. Martin, "Balthasar's Gendered Theology," 216.

81. Martin, "Balthasar's Gendered Theology," 217.

82. Coakley, *Powers and Submissions*, 32, quoted in Martin, "Balthasar's Gendered Theology," 217.

dwell in a love that empowers.[83] Despite hoping to amplify the good he sees in Coakley's argument, Aristotle Papanikolaou notes that it is nevertheless difficult to see how the "gentle space-making" in Coakley's model, understood as happening in the personal prayer life of an individual, can be made manifest in human communities and relationships.[84] Martin herself draws upon Balthasar's reception of Bulgakov's sophiological *Urkenosis* to extend Coakley's argument and offer implications, including recontextualizing the cross as a model of divine love, and accenting the goodness of bodies and difference, that may make a feminist reconstruction of kenosis possible.[85] In short, because the event of Trinitarian and Christic kenosis are the pouring out of divinity not only into the event of the Cross but also into Creation and Incarnation as well, creaturely understandings and imitations of divine kenosis at once necessitate and facilitate the perception of divine goodness and love precisely in materiality and its diversity. According to Balthasar, materiality and difference are loci where freedom can be discovered—"If I bump up against a fellow human being, I discover two things especially: the border of my freedom and the reality of his freedom, for his freedom only becomes real to me when two bodies encounter each other."[86] It is only in this recognition of the other's alterity—that is, in the realization of separation—that a community can arise, and it is in the possibility of community that the reality and boundaries of freedom are revealed.

KENOSIS AS ORIENTATION TOWARD OTHERS

Indeed, the challenge of application is how to make kenosis and the kind of freedom it would manifest plausible and possible in earthly, human communities. One of the facets of kenosis that Balthasar and his interpreters helpfully underscore here is the priority and centrality of divine action and *historical* precedent in the kenotic freedom of Christ. Balthasar's understanding of kenosis and citations of it, like Martin's, tend to focus on the drama of redemption that the kenosis of Jesus Christ has enacted and fulfilled, and in which we are invited to participate. Anne M. Carpenter summarizes Hans Urs von Balthasar's understanding thus: "Kenosis is a version of the dispossessive, loving attitude that characterizes, among other things, the open attention of the knowing subject toward truth . . . the connotation

---

83. Martin, "Balthasar's Gendered Theology," 217. See Coakley, *Powers and Submissions*, 35.

84. Papanikolaou, "Person, *Kenosis*, and Abuse," 45–46.

85. Martin, "Balthasar's Gendered Theology," 231–32.

86. Balthasar, *Epilogue*, 104, quoted in Martin, "Balthasar's Gendered Theology," 232.

for kenosis is of a making room, or in Balthasar's parlance, a 'letting-be.'"[87] Importantly, Carpenter says, even in Christ this kenosis is a free act of human obedience that is a "willing of the other." In Jesus's obedience to the Father, she continues, his free kenotic act of obedience reveals his "I" in a manner that simultaneously "makes room in itself for every other human 'I' that ever will be—a breadth possible to him as God-man."[88] Carpenter reminds us that for Balthasar, this finite and human act of kenotic obedience is patterned after the infinite kenotic freedom of the Trinity, whose processions are themselves God poured out in love.[89]

Though she does not herself use the terminology of "kenosis," Simone Weil often writes of the importance of attention as an act of self-emptying that is oriented toward others. In her essay, "Reflections on the Right Use of School Studies with a View to the Love of God," Weil begins by saying that "prayer consists of attention."[90] To develop this faculty, she goes on to say, we must become aware of our own finitude, grow in humility, and understand that we do not come to practice attention through the force of our will, but through desire and surrender.[91] In other words, learning to attend is as much characterized by kenosis as the open attention, or "letting be," that Carpenter names above.

Much like in the Balthasarian definition, which names kenosis as a loving attitude that characterizes attention, Weil says that our love of God has attention for its substance, as does the love of our neighbor. With this assertion fresh in our minds, she then asserts that "Those who are unhappy have no need for anything in this world but people giving them their attention," with the caveat: "The capacity to give one's attention to a sufferer is a very rare and difficult thing; it is almost a miracle; it *is* a miracle. Nearly all those who think they have this capacity do not possess it."[92] To attend to the afflicted, she says, is to recognize that the sufferer *exists* outside of whatever categories I may be tempted to put them into. This recognition, Weil continues, happens when "the soul empties itself of all its own contents in order to receive into itself the being it is looking at, just as he is, in all his truth."[93] In other words, the recognition that accompanies the act or disposition of attention is a kind of "space-making," or "letting-be."

---

87. Carpenter, *Nothing Gained is Eternal*, 136.
88. Carpenter, *Nothing Gained is Eternal*, 136.
89. Carpenter, *Nothing Gained is Eternal*, 137.
90. Weil, *Waiting for God*, 59.
91. Weil, *Waiting for God*, 60–61.
92. Weil, *Waiting for God*, 64.
93. Weil, *Waiting for God*, 65.

KENOSIS AND FREEDOM

Weil presents the rare and miraculous capacity to attend to the afflicted as something like a virtue in Thomas Aquinas: attention can be fostered, practiced, and habituated (through school studies, for example), but is only found in its truest expression through the grace of God. However, because love of God and neighbor are the aim of a good life, Weil subordinates all academic excellences to the goal of attention. Furthermore, in undertaking the twin command of loving God and loving one's neighbor, we are obliged at the start to behold them, to recognize them, and this beholding requires already a form of kenosis. Christian life, then, if it involves following these commandments, must always be a kind of self-emptying. This self-emptying is what she elsewhere calls "decreation."[94]

What happens, then, in this self-emptying? What does decreation entail? As a form of self-dispossession, decreation sometimes raises questions about the well-being of the self in the self-other relationship. Weil anticipates these questions, and immediately cautions that decreation is not destruction, but the passing into the uncreated.[95] To more fully describe this process, we may look to a nearly synonymous concept in the work of Emmanuel Levinas, which he calls "substitution." Substitution is a disposition wherein one is oriented by the priority of the Other that, rather than any negation of the I, is instead the fundamental orientation of being; it is the transcendence of the I reaching toward goodness beyond being. He calls this non-acquisitive yearning for the transcendent "Desire." As Levinas puts it:

> To posit being as Desire and as goodness is not to first isolate an I which would then turn toward a beyond. It is to affirm that to apprehend oneself from within—to produce oneself as I—is to apprehend oneself with the same gesture that already turns toward the exterior to extra-vert and to manifest—to respond for what it apprehends—to express; it is to affirm that the becoming-conscious is already language, that the essence of language is goodness, or again, that the essence of language is friendship and hospitality.[96]

For Levinas, the I comes into apprehension of itself as *already* called by some Other. The I is not in the first place some active force which exercises the power of its attention as a subject acting upon the world. Accepting and acting—responding—from our being-as-being-addressed is the posture of the emergent I that experiences Desire (the yearning for the transcendent by which I am always already called) as a constitutive and authentic part

---

94. See esp. Weil, *Gravity and Grace*, 78–86.
95. See Cha, *Decreation and the Ethical Bind*, esp. 37–38.
96. Levinas, *Totality and Infinity*, 305.

of its own existence. To "have oneself in hand," to apprehend oneself, to become a free ethical subject, is already to come to understand oneself as called to abdication, to a non-violent self-renunciation. Levinas contends that this substitution is neither self-harm nor resignation, but love.[97]

He summarizes this often in his works through the invocation of Dostoevsky's famous quote from *The Brothers Karamazov*: "We are all guilty of all and for all men before all, and I more than others."[98] The asymmetry in this statement seems even more radical when one considers that Levinas explains that this means that "one is responsible even for the other's responsibility."[99] Dostoevsky's words take on new meaning in Levinas, for whom our "responsibility" is not merely a liability (which can generate culpability), but also our ability to respond to the call of the other. It is both ability and liability because our response of attention to the call of the Other is already the condition of possibility for their response as well. The Other is, on the one hand, prior, but we are also the Other's Other. For Levinas, substitution means that ethically the boundary between myself and the other seems almost to dissolve; it is suspended, such that no matter the distinction in our perspectives or power, in the end I take their well-being as indistinguishable from mine.[100]

If this realization becomes something consciously taken up, then, according to Weil, it becomes decreation. In "The Love of God and Affliction," Weil likens our own decreation to a contracted form of divine kenosis: "God denied himself for our sakes in order to give us the possibility of denying ourselves for him."[101] That is, in pouring ourselves out, we make space for the Other who is Christ, who pours himself into us like living water, so that our decreation becomes not an annihilation, but a passing into grace. Here we can see how the event of Creation is bound to the event of the Christ's incarnation, life, death, resurrection, and ascension; the initial kenosis of God's speaking, seeing, loving Creation into being is recapitulated, and we are invited to an imitation, or reflection of this, in a contracted fashion.

Creation and decreation, so characterized by divine and human kenosis, are likewise what enable our freedom. Creation of the world, for Weil, is a divine pouring out that brings creatures into being that are distinct from

---

97. Levinas, *Totality and Infinity*, 253.

98. Dostoevsky, *Brothers Karamazov*, 264. See Levinas, *Ethics and Infinity*, 98.

99. Reed, "Decreation as Substitution," 30. See Levinas, *Ethics and Infinity*, 99.

100. This indistinguishability has some resonance with the Ignatian *indifferentia* of Balthasarian kenosis (Carpenter, *Nothing Gained is Eternal*, 13), and Weil's concept of detachment (*Gravity and Grace*, 57–61), though investigating the nuances is not something that can be undertaken here.

101. Weil, *Waiting for God*, 89.

divinity and thus able to exercise freedom. Now in the world, the only truly ethical activity comes about via a true understanding of the world, perceiving (through attention) the true and necessary relationships between the creatures.[102] Consent and obedience to this order, Weil says, is the only true freedom, and this comes about through decreation.

In summary, the kenotic self-dispossession Weil terms decreation finds harmonies in Balthasar and Levinas, as each writer highlights the attentive disposition of love that endeavors to accept the Other (whether this is a divine or human or some other Other) as they are revealed, not as a fitting into a limited role in a system of relations with myself at the center. By abdicating my efforts to fit the world into a totality of my own imagination and consenting instead to perceive the world's relations as they are, I participate in the creation of communal freedom, making room for others to act in kind.

There are obvious potential costs to this notion of freedom. In *Knowing Jesus*, James Alison underscores some of these when he notes that Jesus offers his followers liberation from the economy of violence.[103] In stepping outside of the relations of non-recognition that reduce persons to their role in a totality, and that make obligations into a *condition* for love, rather than the result of loving recognition, the followers of Christ make themselves vulnerable to all of the violence that Christ suffered. For Alison (as for Weil and Levinas), this is not *seeking* to be "lynched," as he puts it, even if such an ending is foreseen. Rather, it is the clear-eyed acceptance of the cost of freedom in a system where capitulation to the system of force is required for its perpetuation. He calls this, "the intelligence of the victim," the criterion for the moral life of the Christian, which is accompanied by and accompanies "moving into freedom."[104] What is absolutely essential to note here, is that the victimization that arises from this freedom is not itself the kenosis. Christ's self-gift, according to Alison, is *prior to* the passion.

SOCIAL AND POLITICAL FREEDOM AND KENOSIS

The above articulation of kenosis, decreation, or unselfing describes something other than a capitulation to the logic of self-sufficiency and independence as it is generally used in modern liberal societies. Even though, as I acknowledge above, calls for material liberation are just, this approach cannot mean that mystical unselfing is a direct path to ending the economic

102. McCullough, *Religious Philosophy of Simone Weil*, 148–49.
103. Alison, *Knowing Jesus*, 44–45.
104. Alison, *Knowing Jesus*, 48.

and social evils that have always plagued our societies *if by this* we mean something like raising everyone to be independent, autonomous subjects. As Howard Thurman notes, the mystic understands that the human needs that surround them are the sacred space for pursuing the desire of their heart, for the giving over of their selves in attention. According to Thurman, the mystic—the one who gives themselves over to the consciousness that accompanies and allows kenosis—"is not interested in social action because of any particular political or economic theory . . . but he is interested in social action because society as he knows it to be ensnares the human spirit in a maze of particulars so that the One cannot be sensed nor the good realized."[105] Thus, the task of the mystic, as true for Weil as it is for Thurman, is to relieve these situations so that it becomes *possible* for them to "ascend the mount of vision with freedom and abandonment."[106]

Thurman sounds very much like Weil when he writes, in his 1939 address to Eden Seminary in St. Louis, that this can only be done when individuals become persons; that is to say, when they are able to take themselves in hand. In Weilienne terms, those who are the afflicted, those ground down by the gravity of industrial life, for example, with little resources to even lift their eyes, the space-making that occurs in unselfing, which says to them "What are you going through?" can be part of their healing.[107] Thurman believed that those who have social power without a concomitant sense of social responsibility have very little hope of turning around, unfortunately.[108] Thus, the task of material liberation is one of radically altering the structure of social relationships such that what Thurman calls the "imperialistic will"[109] of persons can subside, replaced by the kind of freedom Alison spoke about. The mystic cannot leave this task aside. Just as Maximus the Confessor argues that what is seen in contemplation must become incarnate in the practice of the virtues,[110] Thurman affirms that "what [the mystic] experiences, [they are] under obligation to achieve in experience."[111]

This is why, for Simone Weil, decreative attention, the attention through which one is poured out for the sufferer, is a way of life, and often a shocking one. In Weil's letters, we see her efforts to come into radical solidarity and achieve an adequacy of perception of laborers by taking on factory and farm

---

105. Thurman, *Strange Freedom*, 120.
106. Thurman, *Strange Freedom*, 120.
107. This gloss of Weil's thought pulls from a variety of sources.
108. Thurman, *Strange Freedom*, 121.
109. Thurman, *Strange Freedom*, 121.
110. Maximus, *Ambigua* 10 (150–53).
111. Thurman, *Strange Freedom*, 121.

labor, and subsequently by advocating and helping other laborers advocate for better working conditions—conditions that would enable greater space for the contemplative life of the spirit and prevent the dehumanization of mechanistic toil. Her efforts and ideas also moved into extremes that seem to match the absurdity of the affliction she encounters: in one letter, she details a prospective plan to parachute nurses to the front lines of the war as a stark counter display to the force of arms. While we may disagree with the specific kinds of action that Weil imagined and even practiced, the shocking nature of these acts of solidarity is necessary, according to Thurman, to "shock the oppressor into a state of upheaval and insecurity."[112]

CONCLUSION

The freedom kenosis relies upon and makes possible is first of all a spiritual freedom. As Howard Thurman concedes in "Mysticism and Social Change," the proposition that the "basic ethical significance of mysticism" is personal, or individualistic, is difficult, if not impossible, to refute.[113] Nevertheless, he continues, the clarity of perception that accompanies the mystical moment carries with it the consciousness of communion not only with the divine but also with all creation, the order of the world. In other words, what begins as personal and spiritual becomes secondarily social and political.

> The ascetic impulse having as its purpose individual purification and living brings the realistic mystic face to face with the society in which he functions as a person. He discovers that he is a person and a personality in a profound sense can only be achieved in a milieu of human relations. Personality is something more than mere individuality—it is a fulfillment of the logic of individuality in community.[114]

The priority of this community means that for the mystic, the distinction between the personal and the social are ultimately illusory, at least where spirituality and sin are concerned. As in Weil, where the existence of affliction and injustice challenge our ability to authentically express our freedom,[115] for Thurman, the "affirmation mystic" must say, alongside the socialist, after Eugene Debs, "While there is a lower class, I am in it. While there is a criminal element, I am of it. While there is a man in jail, I am not

---

112. Thurman, *Strange Freedom*, 122.
113. Thurman, *Strange Freedom*, 116.
114. Thurman, *Strange Freedom*, 116.
115. Holsberg, "Decreation and the Creative Act," 65.

free."[116] Put differently, the mystic, in their kenosis, lives in the consciousness that "injustice anywhere is a threat to justice everywhere,"[117] and pours themselves out in the service of seeking justice, the beauty of the order of the world.

The freedom that arises from this form of kenosis is distinct from that of any project which has as its ultimate end the goal of creating self-sufficient individuals. Indeed, the achievement and exercise of kenotic freedom ultimately transcends and subverts this goal. Kenotic freedom is the free act of God and the free response of the mystic, who in their own decreative act of unselfing, breaks away from the logic of autarchy and social power. In the unselfing of kenosis, the mystic apprehends their own place not at the center of reality but amidst a community of others to whom they are called to attend. Through this attention, the attended stranger, their neighbor, is afforded freedom as they are given space to reveal themselves and be who they are in their own free response.

What this looks like varies. In Weil, we see advocacy for better material conditions for laborers; in Thurman, we read of moral appeal, mystical accompaniment, and nonviolent resistance to the violence of the oppressive and depersonalizing social forces. As understood by Balthasar and Weil and many others, this process mirrors and participates in the loving, creative, and sustaining vision of God, and imitates the saving self-gift of the Word in the Incarnation and life of Christ. This imitation, in the words of Howard Thurman, understands that "working and waiting," acting and contemplating, are distinct, but achieved together, as in working for the new day, the mystic awaits its coming which is "achieved by God and alone."[118] Until then, in this already but not yet, the kenosis advocated by Thurman, Weil, Balthasar, and others is aimed at engendering personal and social and political freedom by creating a community of persons in which holistic human flourishing can be pursued.

REFERENCES

Alison, James. *Knowing Jesus*. Springfield, IL: Templegate, 1994.
Balthasar, Hans Urs von. *Epilogue*. Translated by Edward T. Oakes, SJ. San Francisco: Ignatius, 1991.
Bauerschmidt, Frederick Christian. "Aquinas." In *The Blackwell Companion to Political Theology*, edited by P. Scott and W. Cavanaugh, 48–61. Oxford: Blackwell, 2007.

---

116. Thurman, *Strange Freedom*, 117, quoting Debs, "Social Reform," 89.
117. King, *Letter from a Birmingham Jail*.
118. Thurman, *Strange Freedom*, 123.

Carpenter, Anne M. *Nothing Gained is Eternal: A Theology of Tradition*. Minneapolis: Fortress, 2022.

Cha, Yoon Sook. *Decreation and the Ethical Bind*. New York: Fordham University Press, 2017.

The Cloud of Unknowing. Edited by James Walsh. Classics of Western Spirituality. Mahwah, NJ: Paulist, 1981.

Coakley, Sarah. *Powers and Submissions: Spirituality, Philosophy and Gender*. Oxford: Blackwell, 2002.

Debs, Eugene. "Social Reform." In *Labor and Freedom: The Voice and Pen of Eugene V. Debs*, edited by Phil Wagner, 89. St. Louis: Phil Wagner, 1916.

Hampson, Daphne. "On Autonomy and Heteronomy." In *Swallowing a Fishbone?: Feminist Theologians Debate Christianity*, edited by Daphne Hampson, 1–12. London: Society for Promoting Christian Knowledge, 1996.

Hobbes, Thomas. *Leviathan*. Edited by J. C. A. Gaskin. Oxford: Oxford University Press, 2008.

Holsberg, Lisa Radakovich. "Decreation and the Creative Act: Simone Weil and Nikolai Berdyaev." In *Simone Weil and Continental Philosophy*, edited by Rebecca Rozelle-Stone, 51–68. Lanham, MD: Rowman & Littlefield, 2017.

Honneth, Axel. *Freedom's Right: The Social Foundations of Democratic Life*. New York: Columbia University Press, 2014.

Jantzen, Grace M. "Feminists, Philosophers, and Mystics." *Hypatia* 9.4 (1994) 186–206.

LaMothe, Ryan. "Social and Political Freedom: A Pastoral Theological Perspective—Part I." *Pastoral Psychology* 70.3 (2021) 255–71.

Levinas, Emmanuel. *Ethics and Infinity: An Essay on Exteriority*. Translated by Richard A. Cohen. Pittsburgh: Duquesne University Press, 1985.

———. *Totality and Infinity: An Essay on Exteriority*. Translated by Alphonso Lingis. Pittsburgh: Duquesne University Press, 1969.

Manlowe, Jennifer. "Seduced by Faith: Sexual Traumas and Their Embodied Effects." In *Violence Against Women and Children: A Christian Theological Sourcebook*, edited by Carol J. Adams and Marie M. Fortune, 328–38. New York: Continuum, 1995.

Marion, Jean-Luc. "Sketch of a Phenomenological Concept of Sacrifice." In *Jean-Luc Marion: Essential Writings*, edited by Kevin Hart, 436–50. New York: Fordham University Press, 2013.

Martin, Jennifer Newsome. "The 'Whence' and the 'Whither' of Balthasar's Gendered Theology: Rehabilitating Kenosis for Feminist Theology." *Modern Theology* 31.2 (2015) 211–34.

Maximus the Confessor. *On Difficulties in the Church Fathers: The Ambigua*. Vol. 1. Translated by Nicholas Constas. Cambridge, MA: Harvard University Press, 2014.

McCullough, Lissa. *The Religious Philosophy of Simone Weil: An Introduction*. London: IB Taurus, 2014.

McIntosh, Mark. "Humanity in God: On Reading Karl Barth in Relation to Mystical Theology." *Heythrop Journal* 34.1 (1993) 22–40.

Niebuhr, Reinhold. *An Interpretation of Christian Ethics*. New York: Seabury 1979.

Papanikolaou, Aristotle. "Person, *Kenosis,* and Abuse: Hans Urs von Balthasar and Feminist Theologies in Conversation." *Modern Theology* 19.1 (2003) 41–65.

Reed, Robert Charles. "Decreation as Substitution: Reading Simone Weil through Levinas." *The Journal of Religion* 93.1 (2013) 25–40.

Russell, Bertrand. *Mysticism and Logic*. London: Allen & Unwin, 1911.

Saiving Goldstein, Valerie. "The Human Situation: A Feminine View." *The Journal of Religion* 40.2 (1960) 100–112.

Taylor, Charles. *The Ethics of Authenticity*. Cambridge, MA: Harvard University Press, 1991.

Thurman, Howard. *A Strange Freedom: The Best of Howard Thurman on Religious Experience and Public Life*. Edited by Walter E. Fluker and Catherine Tumber. Boston: Beacon, 1998.

Weil, Simone. *Gravity and Grace*. Translated by Emma Craufurd. London: Routledge and Kegan Paul, 1952.

———. *Waiting for God*. Translated by Emma Craufurd. New York: Harper Perennial Modern Classics, 2009.

5

Interiority as Freedom
Arendt and Stein

PETER NGUYEN

According to Hannah Arendt, totalitarianism emerges by exploiting alienated, lonely people in times of social and political polarization. Totalitarianism seeks to erode free association to the point of atomizing people. An individual's only possible relationship is with the totalitarian state and its ideology, which become the sole source of human purpose. Any individual can disappear in a mass movement, losing her freedom in the process. This abandonment of human particularity and freedom leads to an attenuation of individual moral responsibility, which ultimately makes mass murder possible. Because Arendt's chilling vision speaks to current social and political developments, this paper asks, "How does one resist becoming a 'mass person' and find true freedom?" To offer an answer, this paper proposes a dialogue between Arendt and her predecessor, Edith Stein.

Stein's work offers an account of interiority, or living from the depth of the soul, as a world of freedom unfettered by the outside world. For Stein, the main challenge for people in a totalitarian society characterized by mass dehumanization is to withdraw from the society's pervasive ideology and its everyday cruelty in order to nourish one's soul with a sense of friendship with God. The fruit of this intimacy with God is the recognition of others as one's neighbor and the radical giving of oneself to them.

ARENDT AND THE MASS PERSON

In *The Origins of Totalitarianism*, published in 1951, Arendt argues that totalitarianism is made possible by the development of a mass society that views distinct, unique individuals as superfluous. Mass consumption, mass unemployment, mass murder, and the decline of local communities, which result from the centripetal pressures of mass bureaucracies, all contribute to the loss of individual distinctiveness.

For Arendt, the totalitarian concentration camps of Nazi Germany and the Soviet Union were "laboratories" where one of the goals of totalitarianism—the destruction of the individual human and human individuality—was implemented. These camps not only sought to "exterminate people" but also to eliminate "spontaneity itself as an expression of human behavior" and to transform "the human personality into a mere thing, into something that even animals are not."[1] Dehumanization assumed various forms: imprisonment, forced labor, indiscriminate maltreatment, and finally, the anonymous death of extermination. As a result, the human being was cut off from reality and ceased to be an agent of spontaneous action.[2]

For Arendt, the concentration camps, as the laboratories of totalitarian regimes, sought to achieve three goals: the destruction of the judicial person, that of the moral person, and finally, that of unique personal identity. The first step in making human individuality superfluous was to eliminate the part of the person that depends on the law's enactment, its regular practice, and its constancy.[3] In a totalitarian state, the law was divorced from any clear and consistent pattern of judgment. Under this state of affairs, being a noncriminal did not guarantee freedom from police terror, from subjugation to forced labor, or from deportation to extermination camps.

Arendt argues that on the whole, totalitarian regimes aimed to "destroy the civil rights" of their own people, who eventually became "outlaws in their own country," like "the stateless and the homeless."[4] Just as the stateless lived outside the scope of the law, always transgressing it and always vulnerable to punishment simply as a result of existing, so the citizens of a totalitarian regime became strangers in their own homeland. In a system of arbitrary justice and punishment, the individual's life was an agonizing slog.

The second step in making the person superfluous was the destruction of the person's moral capacity. This, Arendt argues, can be illustrated by

---

1. Arendt, *Origins of Totalitarianism*, 437–38.
2. Arendt, *Origins of Totalitarianism*, 438.
3. Arendt, *Origins of Totalitarianism*, 447.
4. Arendt, *Origins of Totalitarianism*, 51.

the way the concentration camp made martyrdom almost unimaginable by eliminating the belief that protest to the point of death had any meaningful ethical significance.[5] Arendt offers the following quotation of David Rousset:

> How many people here still believe that a protest has even historic importance? This skepticism is the real masterpiece of the SS. Their great accomplishment. They have corrupted all human solidarity. Here, the night has fallen on the future. When no witnesses are left, there can be no testimony.[6]

As a result of the camps' reduction of human life to a profoundly impersonal, isolated, and disconnected state, it seemed that no act of compassion or courage could extend beyond the barbed wire and walls surrounding the barracks. From Arendt's perspective, a sacrifice "must have social meaning" to be worthwhile.[7] Unfortunately, this meaning was obliterated. The "anonymous" and impersonal extermination practiced in the camps seemed to have "robbed" "death of its meaning" and dignity.[8] Martyrdom thus seemed an empty gesture among the damned of Auschwitz.[9]

For Arendt, the camp's most terrible blow was forcing the internees to choose not "between good and evil, but between murder and murder."[10] The totalitarian systems implicated the entirety of their populations in their crime and blurred the line between persecutors and persecuted. The concentration camp acquired enough power not only to be the judge and executioner of every human being but also to turn every human being into the judge and executioner of every other human being. This moral chaos was the final goal; that is, the goal was to create a system in which conscience "ceases to be adequate and to do good becomes utterly impossible," and even the system's victims are viewed as bearing "the consciously organized complicity of all men in the crimes of totalitarian regimes."[11]

For Arendt, after totalitarianism had eliminated the judicial and moral person, the system's final obstacle—the remaining aspect of human identity that would distinguish people from animals herded to slaughter—was

---

5. Arendt, *Origins of Totalitarianism*, 451.

6. Roussett, *Other Kingdom*, 461, quoted in Arendt, *Origins of Totalitarianism*, 451.

7. Arendt, *Origins of Totalitarianism*, 451.

8. Arendt, *Origins of Totalitarianism*, 452.

9. Yet we know that religious persons in these camps performed courageous and compassionate acts of martyrdom. They became a small light of hope that reminded the people trapped in the camps that there was a world beyond that of the camps.

10. Arendt, *Origins of Totalitarianism*, 452.

11. Arendt, *Origins of Totalitarianism*, 452.

individual uniqueness and personality. An inner "persistent stoicism" was the last "refuge" for an individual seeking protection, even if she was about to die in a gas chamber.[12]

The totalitarian system waged war against human individuality in a variety of ways.

The destruction of individuality began when people were transported like animals in packed cattle cars and, once in the concentration camps, embarrassed, humiliated, stripped, shaved, dressed in standardized prison garb, and branded with numbers that replaced their names. These practices reduced people to "ghostly marionettes, which all reacted with perfect reliability even when going to their own death."[13]

This tragic image conveyed the ultimate goal of the totalitarian system: to create a being without initiative, deprived of any creative ability, who could be pushed and pulled apart at will because the destruction of "individuality" is the destruction of "spontaneity," of a person's "power to begin something new" from her "own resources, something that cannot be determined on the basis of reactions to environment and events."[14] Totalitarians sought to render the creative individual unnecessary. Totalitarianism's ultimate goal was not only despotic rule over people but also the creation of "a system in which [people] are superfluous." This system engaged in constant dehumanization to create a "world of the dying"—a reality of mounting absurdity and hopelessness for its denizens.[15]

For Arendt, "the chief characteristic of the mass man [in totalitarian society] is not brutality and backwardness, but his isolation and lack of normal social relationships."[16] Because Arendt views identity as an intersubjective product of human interaction, she concludes that this isolation necessarily leads to a crisis of identity. Isolated, the person loses her sense of individuality, of the uniqueness that constitutes what she alone can bring to the world. This loss breeds "the mass man's typical feeling of superfluousness."[17]

Toward the end of *Origins*, Arendt links the ideology and terror of totalitarianism to the modern phenomenon of loneliness. She argues that loneliness itself helps to create and sustain totalitarianism's conditions of possibility. Loneliness, according to Arendt, radically severs people from

---

12. Arendt, *Origins of Totalitarianism*, 453.
13. Arendt, *Origins of Totalitarianism*, 455.
14. Arendt, *Origins of Totalitarianism*, 455.
15. Arendt, *Origins of Totalitarianism*, 457.
16. Arendt, *Origins of Totalitarianism*, 317.
17. Arendt, *Origins of Totalitarianism*, 311.

INTERIORITY AS FREEDOM

one another. She describes loneliness as a wilderness in which a person feels forsaken by human companionship—even when surrounded by others:

> What makes loneliness so unbearable is the loss of one's own self, which can be realized in solitude but confirmed in its identity only by the trusting and trustworthy company of my equals. In this situation, man loses trust in himself as the partner of his thoughts and that elementary confidence in the world, which is necessary to make experiences at all. Self and world, capacity for thought and experience are lost at the same time.[18]

Loneliness is an unbearable experience, she argues, because it causes people to "lose confidence in themselves as partners in their thoughts and that elementary confidence in the world which is necessary"—to have any experience or agency at all.[19] Loneliness is not merely the absence of people; at a deeper level, it results in a lack of self-identity or individuality, which can be attained only through companionship and community.

Moreover, in a totalitarian society, people lose the freedom to evaluate ideas critically. Those who lack the confidence or space to think, Arendt warned, will be led astray because the turbulent impressions of the outside world easily overwhelm them and can thus lead to the dissolution of their individuality.

In her last major work, *The Life of the Mind*, Arendt states that the embodiment of the lonely mass man was the Nazi bureaucrat Adolf Eichmann, whose war crimes she reported in 1961. The dilemma was not that Eichmann was guilty but rather that his actions, which sent millions to their deaths, were not rooted in any great hatred or depth of evil.[20] Eichmann lacked any such depth of hatred. In fact, he lacked depth or interiority of any kind. She writes,

> I was struck by a manifest shallowness in the doer that made it impossible to trace the uncontestable evil of his deeds to any deeper level of roots or motives . . . the only notable characteristic one could detect in his past behavior during the trial and throughout as well as in his behavior during the pre-trial police

---

18. Arendt, *Origins of Totalitarianism*, 477.

19. Arendt, *Origins of Totalitarianism*, 477.

20. Contemporary research has shown that Arendt and many others who observed Adolf Eichmann at trial were misled by his performance. Eichmann deceived people into thinking he was a dull and thoughtless bureaucrat. In fact, before his extradition to Israel, he left behind papers in Argentina that revealed a deep-seated anti-Semitism. In Jerusalem, he acted like an unthinking functionary to save his own life. See Neiman, *Evil in Modern Thought*, 329–34.

examination was something entirely negative: it was not stupidity but thoughtlessness.[21]

At his trial, Eichmann seemed completely enslaved by the superficiality of clichés and platitudes.[22] He was susceptible to the ideologies of his time, a man who unthinkingly allowed himself to be led mindlessly from one idea to another.[23] In a word, he lacked the freedom found in interiority to accept or reject an idea.

Paradoxically, Arendt maintains that thinking in solitude produces free, ethical subjects. What Arendt calls thinking is an ongoing, "soundless" conversation between me and myself.[24] In *The Life of the Mind*, her exploration of the contemplative life in light of the problem of evil, she quotes a well-known saying of Socrates:

> It would be better for me that my lyre or a chorus I directed should be out of tune and loud with discord, and that a multitude of men should disagree with me than that I, being one, should be out of harmony with myself.[25]

This passage offers a view of the thinking subject as not one but "two-in-one."[26] This subject can talk, agree, or disagree with herself. Arendt implies that when we are engaged in thinking, we enjoy the company of another within us, even when the world is against us. Arendt writes,

> Thinking, existentially speaking, is solitary but not a lonely business; solitude is that human situation in which I keep myself company. Loneliness comes about when I am alone without being able to split up into the two-in-one, without being able to keep myself company.[27]

Like Socrates, Arendt believes that maintaining this company and conversation is essential to the self's integrity. Socrates's insight into the inner life points to the intrinsic reflexivity of the life of the mind. One can agree or disagree with oneself. The mind's inner duality enables questions to be posed, answers to be given, and an ongoing dialogue to ensue.

21. Arendt, *Life of the Mind*, 1:4–5.
22. Arendt, *Life of the Mind*, 1:5.
23. Perhaps a more accurate and compelling example of a mindless bureaucrat would be Rudolf Höss, the SS Kommandant of Auschwitz. His memoirs offer a portrait of a small-hearted, cold, functionary monster. See Höss, *Death Dealer*.
24. Arendt, *Life of the Mind*, 1:75.
25. Arendt, *Life of the Mind*, 1:181.
26. Arendt, *Life of the Mind*, 1:179–93.
27. Arendt, *Life of the Mind*, 1:185.

INTERIORITY AS FREEDOM

For Arendt, those who do evil will flee from their own company and abandon "silent intercourse" with themselves.[28] Consequently, there is little to prevent them from committing further crimes, because they "can count on it being forgotten the next moment. Bad people . . . are not full of regrets."[29] The person of the masses can commit crimes without remorse because she has long since ceased to carry on the internal conversation that would have allowed her to attend to and evaluate her own actions.

Arendt contends that this internal dialogue indicates that a person's existence is essentially plural. One's dialogue with peers in the public sphere is a continuation of one's inner dialogue. In this way, the freedom experienced through the public medium of language is born out of the dialogue within individuals. The very activity of thinking fosters an awareness of freedom by confirming or challenging the assumptions of the self. Because thinking in solitude is plural, it prepares the self for the experience of human plurality in the public sphere. It fosters an expanded mentality and a willingness to examine experiences with others on a shared and exchangeable basis.

In the second section of *The Life of the Mind*, Arendt examines the faculty of the will and its relation to freedom in the history of philosophy—an understanding of freedom that lies outside the arena of politics. She admits that she struggled to write this section, in large part because she could not reconcile her conclusion about the will and inner freedom with political freedom.[30] This section has received little scholarly attention, and some wonder if Arendt would have revised it if she had lived longer.[31]

In this section, Arendt emphasizes the importance of St. Augustine's elaboration of the concept of interior freedom. For Augustine, such freedom originates in the individual person in the form of a dialogue between me and myself, and it thus lies outside of public intercourse. For those excluded from the political realm, freedom consists of the self's ability to do what no one can stop it from doing.[32] That is, even imprisoned people can exercise an inner freedom that helps them maintain their convictions and strengthen their true selves. Dietrich Bonhoeffer and Alfred Delp, both of whom were imprisoned and martyred by the Nazis, held that individuals can retain their freedom even under totalitarian conditions.[33]

---

28. Arendt, *Life of the Mind*, 1:191.
29. Arendt, *Life of the Mind*, 1:191.
30. Fry, *Arendt*, 87–93.
31. McGowan, *Hannah Arendt*, 98.
32. Arendt, *Life of the Mind*, 2:79.
33. See Bonhoeffer, *Writings*; Delp, *Prison Writings*.

Arendt notes that Augustine understands the will as a source of action and the principle of individuation that gives people the interior freedom to initiate an action without being coerced by external forces. However, in her reading of Augustine, the will is not a conversational friend with itself but is in conflict with itself because when it wills God's law the desires of the body are aroused, making it difficult to follow God's law perfectly.[34]

Thus, although Arendt admires Augustine, she concludes that his account of the faculty of the will is incompatible with her own account of the faculty of reason. She argues that although thinking in solitude enables the person to engage the outside world, the will as understood by Augustine cannot be the basis for communal political action. For Arendt, the basis of a peaceful community cannot be a dialectical process in which a struggle within the self generates the power to act.[35] Extending this interior struggle to the political realm would increase strife, because indecision would hamper action on critical issues.

But Arendt does not minimize the importance of interior freedom. In her reading of Augustine, she recognizes that the will helps people form their identities, take initiative, and be creative. The will is the source of a person's character; following Augustine, Arendt asserts that it individuates people by distinguishing them from the common world of their neighbors.[36] But she wonders whether interior freedom is "relevant only to people who live outside the political community, as solitary individuals."[37]

STEIN ON INTERIOR FREEDOM AND THE COMMUNITY OF GOD

Edith Stein's 1919 treatise "Individual and Community," a phenomenological analysis of the kinds of experiences individuals in a community share, offers a response to this question.[38] She focuses on three kinds of experience: sensory, categorical, and affective. Sensory experience allows a person to interact with the material world. The experience of sensation depends on the physical body. The sensations arising from the material world are made "meaningful" by categorical acts, "which include predication, comparison,

---

34. It is unclear how much of Augustine's philosophy of the will Arendt embraced as her own. See Kiess, *Hannah Arendt and Theology*, 40.
35. Arendt, *Life of the Mind*, 2:93–94.
36. Arendt, *Life of the Mind*, 2:195.
37. Arendt, *Life of the Mind*, 2:199.
38. Stein, *Philosophy of Psychology*, 129–293.

judgment," and so on.[39] For Stein, meaning is a form of coherence we both draw from and place on experience. It is an orienting force that synthesizes the diverse characteristics of observed phenomena.[40] Our ability to make sense of an experience, to compare and contrast different experiences, or to make judgments about an experience enables us to value our existence, our relationships, and the world around us.

Affectivity, for Stein, is the deepest, most personal mode of experience because affective acts involve not only the individuation of the person but also the person's investment in the world of others around her. Affective acts "are stance-takings toward an allegedly factual material . . . they are reactions of the subject to the information of whatever kind which has been imparted to him."[41] The German for "affective acts" is *Gemütsakte*, which could also be translated as acts of feeling or temperament.[42] Stein maintains that affective actions are a profound way of engaging with the world and, as such, are intentional. They are not, as the popular use of English terms like "emotions" or "feelings" might suggest, private and contained within each person.[43] For example, to avoid responsibility to another person, someone might say, "These are my own emotions, and no one can tell me what to do!"—thus promoting hyperindividualism. We understand social and interpersonal reality on the basis of understanding both our own and others's affective acts.

Stein's approach to the affective life, according to Travis Lacy, reveals something about an individual's self: a person is a being who cares about and is invested in her surroundings and who not only thinks but also feels a certain way about her daily encounters.[44] The movements of the heart—the affective life—make freedom concrete in the sense that the person must think about the unfolding of her individuation and responsibility to the world.

Stein's vision of freedom in regard to a person's affective life is enhanced by her discussion of the interior life's sensitivity to values. According to Mette Lebech, "value is an objective motivating power" that can "motivate concretely" when it is "accepted as" one's own through an evaluation.[45]

---

39. Categorical acts help to give unity to our existence. See Lacy, "Interiority and Self-Gift," 620.
40. Stein, *Philosophy of Psychology*, 156–57.
41. Stein, *Philosophy of Psychology*, 157n41.
42. Stein, *Philosophy of Psychology*, 157.
43. Stein, *Philosophy of Psychology*, 157n41.
44. Lacy, "Interiority and Self-Gift," 621.
45. Lebech, *Philosophy of Edith Stein*, xv.

For Stein, there is a human capacity to respond to and discern values.[46] Each person's responsiveness to values constitutes her character and reveals something about her particular identity.[47]

Stein uses the word *Gemütsakte* to describe affective acts, and *Gemüt* refers to a person's capacity to receive and respond to value. *Gemüt*, depending on the context, can be translated as "mind," "feeling," "soul," or "heart."[48] When this faculty is active, a person is deeply and completely engaged in the activity at hand. *Gemüt*, the locus of a person's emotional life, is the faculty that integrates affective, aesthetic, and intellectual experiences. It enables a person to achieve unity and existential fulfillment. In this respect, Stein's philosophy of affective responsiveness to values is intrinsically linked to human individuation.

Moreover, Stein denies that we can simply "will" ourselves into a particular affection, including an affection for God and neighbor. Instead, the depth of affection depends on what Stein calls an individual's *Lebenskraft* (life power). *Lebenskraft* describes the fundamental vitality that empowers the human actions that give meaning to our existence and shape our character. *Lebenskraft* arising from a positive affective experience of certain values can open us to certain actions. On the other hand, *Lebenskraft* arising from a negative affective experience of certain values can close us off from certain actions. Stein gives an example of how our reception of beauty can remain underdeveloped if "we don't come into contact with values" that provide a positive experience of beauty.[49] Ultimately, *Lebenskraft* is an individual's energy that determines her capacity for an affective response, which enables her openness to experience and the values encountered in those experiences.

The connection between *Lebenskraft* and receptivity to value is crucial.[50] Receptivity is our ability to encounter and attend to values that engage or mobilize potential or undeveloped *Lebenskraft*. For Stein, as Lacy puts it, we can engage the world on the basis of actions that affect and shape our interiority.[51] For example, a person's values can be formed and developed by meeting a new, invigorating teacher who teaches a stunning novel filled with heroic characters. This teacher and the characters in the

---

46. In early-twentieth-century continental philosophy, the experience of values was called axiological experience.

47. Stein writes that in purely "intellectual activity, the true power of the intellect is not fully unfolded" (*Finite and Eternal Being*, 437).

48. See Boublil, "Stein's Perspectives on the Heart," 473–75.

49. Stein, *Philosophy of Psychology*, 199.

50. Lacy, "Interiority and Self-Gift," 622.

51. Lacy, "Interiority and Self-Gift," 622.

novel can provide a young person with a life power that affirms the student's uniqueness while opening her up to a larger world.[52]

For Stein, engagement with the world is based on actions and encounters that shape human interiority to some extent. It is through encounters that a person's values can be formed and developed. Stein's theory allows us to understand the importance of shaping people's affective responses, which are the basis of authentic actions in the world. A healthy community, then, has individuals who enter into relationships to give of themselves to one another and to be open to one another in order to maintain and nourish the integrity of the community.[53]

For Stein, a healthy community shapes people at the core of their being. People in authentic communities "live from their souls" rather than from superficial sensory experiences.[54] As such, Lacy argues, Stein's analysis of the relationship between the individual and her community provides a foundation for a theology of community. Stein's theology of community is based on a paradox: healthy communities engage people at the most interior and individuated level. Communities are made up not of the "least common denominator" but of the profundity of individuals who are shaped by community values in their particular and unique ways.[55] In Stein's philosophy, communities unfold in the lives of individuals who receive and live these values in unique ways.[56] Lacy beautifully underscores the crux of Stein's paradox: the "more individualized and developed" the members of a community, the stronger the community as a whole.[57]

This paradox brings us back to the problem of a mass society in which people are strangers to each other. Moreover, it sheds light on the conundrum at the end of Arendt's discussion of the will: can a damaged community—a community of the masses—be restored to health on the basis of individual freedom? Here, the presence of mistrust and alienation, both within and between people, can be addressed by a giving of self. Translating this idea into a Christian approach, it can be characterized as self-giving and becoming one with God in Christ. Christian self-giving involves a grace-filled, loving willingness to endure the pain caused by evil. The possibility of giving oneself to another in a mass society requires the cultivation of

---

52. Stein speaks of outsiders to a community or events within a community as sources of power for a community. See Stein, *Philosophy of Psychology*, 206–22.

53. Stein, *Philosophy of Psychology*, 206–7.

54. Stein, *Philosophy of Psychology*, 234.

55. Lacy, "Interiority and Self-Gift," 624.

56. Stein, *Philosophy of Psychology*, 261–63.

57. Lacy, "Interiority and Self-Gift," 624.

affective experiences over time, supported by an openness to Christ that allows Christ's self-giving love to nourish one inwardly.

It should be noted here that Stein's entry into the Carmelites in Germany in 1933 was an act of Christian self-giving love. When the Nazis took control of Germany in January 1933, Stein was removed from a teaching position in the Catholic Institute for Scientific Pedagogy at the University of Münster, where she had begun teaching in 1932. After being denied the opportunity to apply for a faculty position in philosophy because of her gender, and after teaching at an all-girls Dominican high school in Speyer from 1923 to 1931, Stein was given the opportunity to teach at the university level, though not as a professional philosopher. Unfortunately, her time and work at the university level lasted less than two years.

Because of the persecution of the Jewish people, Stein received an invitation to teach in South America. She considered the offer, but she also had a longing to enter the Carmelite order that had been with her since the time of her conversion and baptism in 1921. At that time, her spiritual directors advised her not to enter immediately, believing she would be a gift to the Church in the world as a teacher and scholar.

When she was removed from her university position, she initially exclaimed, "There is no more possibility for me in Germany."[58] On Good Shepherd Sunday, April 30, 1933, Stein went to St. Ludger's Church, in Münster, to seek clarity about her vocation. She wrote that she would not leave the church until she had "a clear assurance" of where God was calling her. After thirteen hours of prayer, she noted, "I had the assurance of the Good Shepherd."[59] Stein realized it was time to answer the call to enter the Carmelites. A possible key to interpreting Stein's decision may be the Good Shepherd passage from John's Gospel. Christ came as the Good Shepherd in the freedom of love to call his people to be with him and to lead them to a genuine, meaningful life amidst the threat of death. Following Christ's selfless love to the point of death is the way to union with God and the world.[60]

For Stein, the decision to enter the Carmelites in Germany instead of going to South America was an act of inner freedom. Such freedom involves the reception of Christ's love in prayer and a reciprocal response of love. In a time of crisis, Christ, the Good Shepherd, led her to remain in Germany. Joining the Carmelites in Germany in 1933 as a person of Jewish descent was the most personal and social act Stein could undertake. Her yes to Christ the Good Shepherd in 1933 revealed a freedom that meant accepting

---

58. Stein, "How I Came to Carmel," 18.
59. Stein, "How I Came to Carmel," 19.
60. Kelly and Moloney, *Experiencing God*, 219.

her call to be a Carmelite, a desire she had had since her conversion and entry into the Christian community in 1921. At the same time, she understood this identity as a most radical gift of self to the Church in Germany.

As a cloistered nun, Stein would fulfill the Rule of Carmel by prayerfully facing God in the Blessed Sacrament with her back to the world—the very world that opposed her. Yet, at the heart of her prayer was the world that needed her intercession. In this sense, Stein, the Carmelite, never left Germany, even as it was sinking into a mass movement that threatened community life as a whole and the human individual in particular. Although Stein's abandonment of worldly pursuits and her subsequent entry into the Carmelite convent in the midst of Germany's Nazi regime could be seen as an erasure of her identity, on another level, it was a form of Christian self-giving.

As Stein maintains in her 1928 text "Eucharistic Education," such receptivity to self-giving is the logic of the Church's sacramental life.[61] In the Eucharist, God descends freely and willingly and gives Himself up to humankind. The Lord opens Himself to us in the sacramental economy, and we, in turn, open ourselves to Him in our neighbor.[62] The communion between God and the human person thus restores and elevates human communities damaged by sin. Opening ourselves to God and giving ourselves to our neighbor make it possible to heal communities in decay.

Arendt's treatment of Augustine shows that she was aware of the importance of the will in the inner life and the life of freedom. Thinking and willing might prevent catastrophes perpetrated by shallow, unthinking individuals. She could not, however, reconcile how inner freedom could serve the public good. Perhaps a better way of framing the problem is to ask how one's freedom can be realized, especially in an ideologically driven society, as love and service. It is crucial that in her time of great discernment in Münster, Stein showed that the interior realm of the human person was the locus of the unique expression of her authentic personality and the locus of encounter with God and others.

The Church as Christ's Mystical Body, then, "is that community" in which "the deepest interiority" of humanity "is engaged because it is sustained by the highest sacrifice, that is, Christ's Passion."[63] If Stein is right to claim that the affective life of a community springs from its shared values, then contact with Christ's own self-giving, as Lacy maintains, incorporates

---

61. Stein, "Scripture, Prayer, and Eucharist," 160–63.
62. Lacy, "Interiority and Self-Gift," 626.
63. Lacy, "Interiority and Self-Gift," 626.

the baptized into a common body. Contact with Christ in the sacraments and prayer communicates a life force—a grace.[64]

The Church, for Stein, is bound together by the interiority of its members's responses to the prevenient self-giving of Christ.[65] If Stein's insights into the relationship between the individual and her community are correct, then the nature of the Church is revealed in the lives of the saints—its most exemplary members—those men and women who have made their interiority a dwelling place to encounter the love of Christ.[66] Such persons seek to share Christ's love with others, including their enemies, in order to weave them into the Mystical Body of Christ. In *Finite and Eternal* Being, Stein writes,

> Those saints who, trusting in this divine promise, resolved to practice heroic love of their enemies experienced the freedom of love. It may well be that a certain antipathy persists for some time, but it has no power to influence that basic attitude and those acts which are inspired and guided by supernatural love. In most instances the initial aversion will soon give way to the superior force of that divine love which fills the soul more and more. For love, as we know, is on the last analysis and its ultimate meaning a surrender of one's being and union with the beloved. Therefore, the one who does God's will learns to know the divine spirit, the divine life, and the divine love, i.e., that person learns to know God himself. For by doing what God demands of us with total surrender of our innermost being, we cause the divine life to become our own inner life. Entering into ourselves, we find God in ourselves.[67]

In Stein's writings and in the act of witness that was her life, the work of Christ's love transforms the person's soul, detaching her from the world for her sake and the sake of the world. Because of Christ's love, the capacity of people to deal with the plurality of the world lies in their recognition of the divine Other, who dwells in the depths of her being.

Stein's "Freedom and Grace," a text written in 1922, around the time of her conversion, sheds light on this divine indwelling.[68] She explores the Christian experiences she has undergone. She discusses the various

---

64. Stein, *Finite and Eternal Being*, 523.
65. Lacy, "Interiority and Self-Gift," 627.
66. Lacy, "Interiority and Self-Gift," 627.
67. Stein, *Finite and Eternal Being*, 446–47.

68. This text was originally dated in the 1930–1932 period. However, recent research has dated it in the 1920–1922 period, around the time of Stein's conversion. See Papa, "Implications of Stein's Early Christian Experience," 441–50.

dispositions of the human soul that can make it a host of God. Her early Christian experiences led her to propose two types of dispositions.[69]

The first type of disposition is characterized by a lack of freedom—in particular, inner freedom. The person with this disposition "receives impressions from the external world," is "triggered by these impressions," and is "not in control of" herself.[70] The person exhibits a lack of depth and a pronounced passivity, because she is a mere spectator who lacks the self-awareness necessary to respond discerningly. Such a person feels estranged from God instead of like a dwelling place for God.

A person with the second type of disposition is "guided from above," that is, guided by God rather than by external impressions of the world. And God dwells "from within" her inner being.[71] This soul is given the interior *habitus* of the children of God—the freedom of a Christian.[72] The person still receives impressions from the world, but because she receives them at a certain distance, they do not easily affect her soul. She judges them according to the resources of the deepest inwardness, which is guided by God's love.

Furthermore, the liberated person is no longer paralyzed by the anxieties of the world or even by the fear of her soul's fate but is liberated "to take responsibility for herself and for all others, even if she must do so alone." Such responsibility for self and others "is community building in the highest degree."[73] "That the individual," in Stein's view, "stands before God, by virtue of the juxtaposition and mutual coexistence of divine and human freedom, gives her the strength to stand for all—and this: 'One for all and all for one' is what defines the Church."[74] The more a person is filled with God's love at the core of her being, "the more" she can "represent" others.[75]

Strangely, in 1922, Stein seemed to intuit that taking responsibility for or representing others would be a prominent influence on her life. Without knowing how she would become a victim of the Nazis, Stein made herself available for Christ's atoning work on behalf of others. On June 9, 1939, she made her life an offering for the world:

> Even now, I accept the death that God has prepared for me in complete submission and with joy as being his most holy will

69. Stein, "Freiheit und Gnade," 16–19.
70. Stein, "Freiheit und Gnade," 16.
71. Stein, "Freiheit und Gnade," 16.
72. Stein, "Freiheit und Gnade," 16.
73. Stein, "Freiheit und Gnade," 31.
74. Stein, "Freiheit und Gnade," 32.
75. Stein, "Freiheit und Gnade," 32.

for me. I ask the Lord to accept my life and my death . . . so that the Lord will be accepted by His people and that His Kingdom may come in glory for the salvation of Germany and the peace of the world.[76]

Love for Christ is nothing less than a fundamental self-giving for the sake of others.

CONCLUSION

At the beginning of *The Life of the Mind*, Arendt, haunted by Eichmann's shallowness, identifies the problem of evil as a major motivation for undertaking the writing of the book. Evil becomes banal when it is part of the everyday reality a community of people occupy, a reality whose sheer facticity makes it incredibly difficult to imagine an alternative state of affairs. The banality of evil can create and sustain a terrible community precisely because it gives people a place, a role, and a set of tasks that carry them from day to day and that obscure any affective stirrings that would indicate things might be wrong.

An appeal to a person's inner world can be viewed as an invitation to an escape from the outer world's injustices, abuses, and tragedies, but for both Arendt and Stein, this position overlooks the importance of the inner world to the outer world. Having an inner life protects a person from being a person of the masses—a person lost in the constant swirl of noise and distraction. A life lived solely in or subjected completely to the external world will wither. It will lose depth, that is, its ability to act in the world. To regain the depth of one's interior life, to reemerge, and to participate with freedom in the public world, one needs solitude or contemplation. This may sound terrible, like an apparent denial of the world. But withdrawal from the public world is for the sake of the public world.

Arendt was under no illusion that such thinking was in itself a sufficient basis for ethical behavior. For those who, like Eichmann, had already become slaves to the bureaucratic routine of a totalitarian state, it offered little help. A radical event was called for, one that would awaken a people, introduce a new life force, and motivate people to abandon their contradictory atomistic-collectivistic existence. The challenge Arendt identifies is how to introduce such stirrings into a community awash in evil—a community that is not properly constituted but rather distorted into a mass of monadic individuals who are closed off from one another.

---

76. Stein quoted in Herbstrith, *Edith Stein*, 168–69.

I suggest that the best response to this challenge lies in the gifts of the saints and martyrs—people who sacrificed their lives in love to awaken their neighbors to the moral decay around them. Christian sacrifice is a deeply personal choice: the subject freely gives up her life for the sake of others. The self-sacrificial witness of the saint or martyr is the fruit of the surrender of the finite will to the guidance of God's love. The union of the finite and the divine wills creates the possibility of a gift of the finite self offered to restore a community that has lost the dignity of the human person or has perverted the common good. The surrender of the finite will to the divine will requires a contemplative or inner disposition. Ultimately, persons who possess and communicate their contemplative interiority are necessary for the salvation of men and women trapped in mass societies.

REFERENCES

Arendt, Hannah. *The Life of the Mind*. 2 vols. San Diego: Harcourt, 1981.
———. *The Origins of Totalitarianism*. New York: Harcourt Brace Jovanovich, 1973.
Bonhoeffer, Dietrich. *Dietrich Bonhoeffer: Writings*. Edited by Robert Coles, Maryknoll, NY: Orbis, 1998.
Boublil, Elodie. "Stein's Perspectives on the Heart at the Crossroads of Phenomenology, Anthropology, and Carmelite Mysticism." In *Edith Stein's Itinerary: Phenomenology, Christian Philosophy, and Carmelite Spirituality*, edited by Harm Kleuting and Edeltraud Kleuting, 471–79. Münster: Aschendorff, 2021.
Delp, Alfred. *Alfred Delp, SJ: Prison Writings*. Maryknoll, NY, Orbis, 2004.
Fry, Karin A. *Arendt: A Guide for the Perplexed*. New York: Continuum, 2009.
Herbstrith, Waltraud. *Edith Stein: A Biography*. San Francisco: Ignatius, 1992.
Höss, Rudolf. *Death Dealer: The Memoirs of the SS Kommandant at Auschwitz*. Edited by Steven Paskuly. New York: Da Capo, 1996.
Kelly, Anthony, and Francis J. Moloney. *Experiencing God in the Gospel of John*. New York: Paulist, 2003.
Kiess, John. *Hannah Arendt and Theology*. New York: Bloomsbury T&T Clark, 2016.
Lacy, Travis. "Interiority and Self-Gift: Edith Stein's Contribution to Ecclesiology." In *Edith Stein's Itinerary: Phenomenology, Christian Philosophy, and Carmelite Spirituality*, edited by Harm Kleuting and Edeltraud Klueting, 619–27. Münster: Aschendorff, 2021.
Lebech, Mette. *The Philosophy of Edith Stein: From Phenomenology to Metaphysics*. Oxford: Peter Lang, 2015.
McGowan, John. *Hannah Arendt: An Introduction*. Minneapolis: University of Minnesota Press, 1998.
Neiman, Susan. *Evil in Modern Thought: An Alternative History of Philosophy*. Princeton: Princeton University Press, 2015.

Papa, Joseph T. "The Implications of Edith Stein's Early Christian Experience as Reflected in 'Freiheit Und Gnade.'" In *Edith Stein's Itinerary: Phenomenology, Christian Philosophy, and Carmelite Spirituality*, edited by Harm Kleuting and Edeltraud Kleuting, 441–50. Münster: Aschendorff, 2021.

Stein, Edith. *Finite and Eternal Being: An Attempt at an Ascent to the Meaning of Being*. Translated by Kurt Reinhardt. Washington, DC: Institue of Carmelite Studies, 2002.

———. "Freiheit Und Gnade." In *Freiheit Und Gnade Und Weitere Beiträge Zu Phänomenologie Und Ontologie (1917 Bis 1937)*, edited by Beate Beckmann-Zöller and Hans Rainer Sepp, 14–51. Freiburg: Herder, 2014.

———. "How I Came to the Cologne Carmel: A Contribution to the History of the Carmel in Cologne." In *Edith Stein: Selected Writings*, edited by Susanne M. Batzdorff, 13–32. Springfield, IL: Templegate, 1990.

———. *Philosophy of Psychology and the Humanities*. Translated by Marianne Sawicki and Mary Catherine Baseheart. Washington, DC: Institute for Carmelite Studies, 2000.

———. "Scripture, Prayer, Eucharist." In *Edith Stein: Selected Writings*, edited by Marian Maskulak, 135–64. New York: Paulist, 2016.

6

The Freedom of Being Before God

The Sanjuanist Paradigm of Freedom in Edith Stein and Jean-Yves Lacoste

BENEDICT R. SHOUP

In this chapter, I explore the influence of the contemplative tradition on continental philosophy of freedom. Specifically, I demonstrate that Edith Stein and Jean-Yves Lacoste, two significant Catholic phenomenologists,[1] receive John of the Cross's mystical theology of the "dark night" in ways that lead them to formulate similar paradigms of freedom. And, although both thinkers present somewhat arcane theories, I would like to argue that their works still suggest concrete implications for Christian praxis.

That John influenced both Stein and Lacoste is well known. The two main texts under consideration here, Stein's *The Science of the Cross* and Lacoste's *Experience and the Absolute*, both acknowledge their debt to John.[2] That this influence brings Stein and Lacoste together over the topic of freedom, however, has not been explored. The effort to do so itself may

---

1. Stein's place in the canon of Catholic continental thinkers is well known. Lacoste's rise, especially in the anglophone world, has been recent but precipitous. For substantive introductions to his work, see Rivera, *Phenomenology and Experience*, 163–233; Schrijvers, *Lacoste*; Wardley, *Praying to a French God*.

2. Lacoste, *Experience and the Absolute*, 2–3. *The Science of the Cross* is itself an interpretation of John's life and writings.

come as something of a surprise. Lacoste does reference Stein, but while he admires her sanctity, he declares her work to be "mediocre."[3] Superficially, this does not invite comparison. But on a deeper level, I would like to propose that their receptions of the sanjuanist "night" configure a significant set of commonalities between their theories of freedom. My thesis is that, under the influence of John, both thinkers understand the night as a confrontation between divine freedom and human limitation which transforms freedom, leading the self from the confines of an immanent set of concerns into a more expansive horizon defined by a relation with God.

I open with an analysis of Stein's theory of freedom in *The Science of the Cross* in three parts: (1) the structure within which freedom operates, (2) the transformation of freedom wrought by the dark night, and (3) the implications of Stein's conception of freedom for practical action. I then examine Lacoste's theory of freedom in *Experience and the Absolute* according to three parallel points: (1) the structure of experience and knowledge, (2) the transformation of freedom through the night, and (3) the implications of this transformation for praxis. Throughout my engagement with Lacoste, I draw out similarities and differences with Stein's thought, before concluding the essay with a summary of the commonalities that obtain between both.

EDITH STEIN

Stein's relationship with John developed throughout her career, culminating with her last book, *The Science of the Cross*.[4] In one sense, this text served as an opportunity for Stein to introduce her religious sisters to John, who was still relatively unknown in the German-speaking world at the time.[5] This perhaps explains why much of the book functions as a kind of running paraphrase of John's four major prose commentaries, liberally studded with large quotations.[6] Towards the middle of the text, however, Stein inserts a substantial discussion in her own voice entitled "The Soul in the Realm of the Spirit and of Created Spirits."[7] In this section, Stein employs the fruit of her lifelong efforts to develop a personalist philosophy to address important questions raised by John's *Ascent* and *Dark Night* concerning freedom, interiority, divine union, and contemplation.[8] It is in this discussion that Stein

---

3. Lacoste, *Theological Thinking*, 25.
4. Payne, *Stein and John*.
5. Stein, *Science of the Cross*, vii.
6. Payne, *Stein and John*, 248, 250.
7. Stein, *Science of the Cross*, 53–185.
8. Payne, *Stein and John*, 252; Stein, *Science of the Cross*, 5.

uses the sanjuanist night to shape this final iteration of her conception of freedom.[9]

Structure: The Soul, Freedom, and Personal Types

Drawing on imagery borrowed from John, Stein begins the section by introducing a structural polarity between the interiority and exteriority of the soul. Exteriority and interiority refer to two domains of activity, insofar as they are governed by different sets of relationships. Thus, on the one hand, "exteriority" indicates the soul's ability to go "out through the activity of the senses" to the world around her *qua* material.[10] "Interiority," on the other hand, speaks of the soul's orientation towards union with "God in mutual, free, personal surrender," a surrender most fully achieved in this life through contemplation.[11] Here Stein cites John's own use of a similar polarity in *Flame* 2.32–3.[12] She concentrates especially on his claim in *Flame* 1.12 that God is the soul's "*deepest center.*"[13] For Stein, as for John, God so constitutes the interiority of the soul that the deepest center of the soul is not actually its "self," but the Trinity.[14] Stein, with resources from John, thereby sketches out a structural polarity that combines two metaphorical pairs—exteriority/superficiality and interiority/depth—such that the soul possess both an exterior orientation towards the corporeal (superficiality) and an interior orientation towards God (depth).

Stein argues that the human person inhabits this structure through what she calls the "I." Stein takes the I to refer to the soul's field of consciousness, which includes its awareness of itself and of the world around it.[15] For Stein this I is mobile, and therefore, so is the soul's field of consciousness. Stein explains that the I tends to set itself up in different positions within the soul's structure "according to the *motivations* that appeal to it."[16] She concretizes this idea by outlining different "types of persons."[17] The "sensual

---

9. On the development of Stein's theory of freedom across various stages in her work, see Beckmann-Zöller, "Stein's Theory of the Person"; Bello, "Freedom, Intentionality, and Trinitarian Love"; Borden, *Edith Stein*, 20–45; Calcagno, *Philosophy of Stein*, 81–97.

10. Stein, *Science of the Cross*, 153.

11. Stein, *Science of the Cross*, 154, 165, 178, 183.

12. Stein, *Science of the Cross*, 157n7.

13. Stein, *Science of the Cross* 154.

14. Stein, *Science of the Cross*, 179.

15. Beroch, "El Yo Steiniano," 123.

16. Stein, *Science of the Cross*, 162.

17. Stein, *Science of the Cross*, 163; *On the Problem of Empathy*, 113–16.

human being," to take one extreme, is the person who is motivated by sensual values.[18] Because she is motivated by these values, her I occupies the "place" in her soul which most proximately interacts with them. That is, she habitually acts in and through her senses and sensual desires, which are the kinds of operations that correspond to the goods that she values. This means that her I stands at the exterior end of her soul's structure.[19] Combining the ideas of both consciousness and mobility, Stein thus claims that the I is both "that in the soul by which she possesses herself" in conscious activity, and "that which moves within her as in her own *space*."[20]

The place that the I occupies in the soul's structure, in turn, determines her degree of freedom. To summarize the main points in advance, Stein understands freedom here both in terms of the individual's ability to "collect [*zusammenfassen*]" herself or take herself "in hand," and the horizon of knowledge and values according to which she makes her decisions.[21] To return to the sensual type, this individual only has her senses and sensuality recollected or in hand, and she habitually interacts with the world against the horizon of its ability to satisfy her sensual drives.[22] This horizon of activity effectively rules out faith in God on the one hand, and ethical treatment of neighbor on the other, which Stein thinks ultimately depends on our ability to treat each other according to "what is right in God's eyes."[23] It is possible for a sensual person to respond to a higher call to ethical (or religious) action, but her consistent concern for sensual values and the limited perspective this produces bridles her freedom to do so.[24]

We can contrast the sensual type with the person who inhabits the other end of the soul's structure, that is, the mystic.[25] The mystic is the one who occupies her own deepest center through a relation with the Trinity

---

18. Stein, *Science of the Cross*, 163.

19. Stein, *Science of the Cross*, 163.

20. Stein, *Science of the Cross*, 160. Stein offers an earlier take on the idea of the mobility of the I within the structure of the soul in an appendix to *Endliches und Ewiges Sein* devoted to Teresa of Avila's idea of the Interior Castle [*Die Seelenburg*]. In this essay, she writes: "Das Ich erscheint als ein beweglicher 'Punkt' im 'Raum' der Seele" [The I appears as a mobile 'point' in the 'space' of the soul] (524). For an extended discussion of the relationship between the I in *Science* and in *Endliches and Ewiges Sein*, see Beroch, "El Yo Steiniano."

21. Stein, *Science of the Cross*, 160; *Kreuzeswissenschaft*, 133.

22. Stein, *Science of the Cross*, 163.

23. Stein, *Science of the Cross*, 164–65.

24. Stein, *Science of the Cross*, 163–65.

25. Stein discusses a similar polarity in *Freiheit und Gnade*. See Nguyen's "Stein on Interior Freedom and the Community of God" in chapter 5 of this volume.

that is made possible by the Trinity's gift of contemplation.[26] This means, on the one hand, that she can hold her entire being in hand, from the bottom up, to use Stein's spatial image. As Stein puts it, "The deepest point is at the same time the place of her freedom: the place at which she can collect her entire being and make decisions about it."[27] The example of the mystical type thus clarifies that the I is free to dispose of the abilities of the soul at or above the "place" in the soul that it occupies.[28] But it is not (fully) free to act on the basis of the faculties or capacities "below" its habitual place. So, the sensual person is not free to consistently make rational, ethical choices, whereas the mystic is. Furthermore, the mystic can also "measure everything against . . . ultimate standards,"[29] that is, against the horizon provided by contemplative knowledge of the Trinity and of the world in light of the Trinity. The deeper the I goes, then, the freer it becomes, both in terms of its ability to take itself in hand, and in terms of the horizon against which it is able to make decisions. The mystic, who occupies her deepest center, is the freest person of all, because she can take her whole being in hand, and because she judges all things from God's perspective. Stein claims a close relationship with John on these points, asserting that there is a "most perfect agreement" between their common position that "the inmost region of the soul is the place of most perfect freedom."[30]

Thus far we have established a basic sense of Stein's model of freedom. Souls possess a structural polarity between exteriority and interiority. The human "I" has the ability to move through this structure, and it habitually occupies different places therein. The position the "I" takes determines the individual's freedom in terms of the capacities it has at its disposal and the standards against which it makes decisions. The sensual type and the mystic serve as the limit cases concerning the exterior or interior location of the I. The sensual type is the least free kind of person because her I occupies the most superficial stratum of her soul's structure. The mystic is the freest because she can take her whole being in hand and can judge all things against a divine horizon. But how does one arrive at mystical union? For Stein, this can only take place through the contemplative purgation of the dark night of the spirit.

---

26. Stein, *Science of the Cross*, 160, 162.

27. Stein, *Science of the Cross*, 160, 162, 165, 183.

28. Stein insists, though, that whoever acts according to sensual drives alone isn't "free" in any meaningful sense (*Science of the Cross*, 163–64).

29. Stein, *Science of the Cross*, 160.

30. Stein, *Science of the Cross*, 162.

Dynamism: The Nocturnal Journey

Stein develops her theory of the dark night of the spirit in the close reading of the *Night* that immediately precedes her more *sui generis* section on freedom. John divides his conception of the night into a series of phases.[31] Only the last and most intense, which he calls the "passive night of the spirit," concerns us here. As Stein explains, this specific purgative night results from a new gift of "mystical contemplation" which conforms the human person to the crucified Christ by temporarily overwhelming her normal rational operations and filling her with contrition.[32] Here Stein quotes John at length. The soul's relative immaturity means that she first experiences this illumination as the "annihilation" of her "faculties, passions, appetites, and affection" upon which her "experience and satisfaction in God had been based."[33] In the place of this experience, she now feel's "God's absence" and "the conviction that God has rejected her, and cast her into darkness with abhorrence."[34] But the interruption of her natural activities and her sense of divine loss result from the extreme difference between her normal operations and the divine operations given to her in contemplation (as well as her deepening contrition).[35] Therefore, as she adjusts to her participation in these divine operations (of knowing, loving, and remembering), the interruption of her faculties and the experience of absence begin to yield to something new.[36]

That is, the night gives way to the dawn of mystical union,[37] wherein the soul experiences the fullness of freedom in a foretaste of everlasting life. God's contemplative gift of self in mystical union gives "the inmost region of the soul . . . into the hand of the soul," along with the "freedom to dispose of it."[38] This makes sense, because the soul's deepest center is a place of "personal encounter with God," so only the "voluntary surrender" of God to the soul can open it up to her.[39] Furthermore, God intends this encounter to be mutual. This is why God also gives the soul the capacity to dispose of her inmost being in free self-gift back to God, a self-gift that Stein describes

---

31. See John of the Cross, *Collected Works*, 118–21.
32. Stein, *Science of the Cross*, 121–23.
33. *Dark Night* 2.4.2, quoted in Stein, *Science of the Cross*, 123.
34. *Dark Night* 2.6.2, quoted in Stein, *Science of the Cross*, 125.
35. Stein, *Science of the Cross*, 124.
36. Stein, *Science of the Cross*, 123–24, 130.
37. See *Ascent of Mount Carmel* 2.2.1.
38. Stein, *Science of the Cross*, 178.
39. Stein, *Science of the Cross*, 178.

as "the highest act of her freedom."[40] Here, Stein follows John to the heights of his theology of divinization. God's free self-gift to the soul is so complete that she gains the ability not only to dispose of herself, but to dispose of God as well.[41] Paraphrasing *Flame* 3.78, Stein explains how "the soul can now give God *more* than she is herself: she gives to God, God himself in God."[42] This, for Stein, constitutes a "foretaste" of eschatological life.[43] So the mystic becomes the paradigm of freedom. She has herself completely in hand as a gift from God and she makes all of her decisions from a divine perspective. She even has God at her disposal, to offer divinity itself back to God in the freedom of love.

John's night thus serves, for Stein, as the final passage that actualizes the fullness of freedom. God's gift of self in the night confronts the soul with the challenge of surrendering her accustomed operations and experiences for God's sake. This surrender allows her to acclimate to her participation in God's activities and God's horizon. In so acclimating, she makes the final transition from the limits of (exclusive) exteriority to an interiority wherein she takes possession of her deepest center and everything "above it" in mutual self-giving love with the Trinity. As the *passage* to this fullness then, the night plays a critical role in the shape of Stein's model of freedom more generally. The night reveals the gravity of the difference between the poles of exteriority and interiority, and the cost of traversing between them. It serves as a kind of core transitional space that illuminates the structures around it and the essence of the movement through them.

Action: The Freedom of the Martyr

Turning from theory to practice, Stein's own example translates her understanding of freedom into a pattern of life. In her dissertation, completed some six years before her conversion to Catholicism, Stein describes another personal type, the "*homo religiosus*." This type is the person who "sacrifices all his earthly goods to his faith."[44] Stein introduces the *homo religiosus* as an example of someone whose horizon of values may extend beyond our own (and probably extended beyond Stein's at the time).[45] Strikingly, about

---

40. Stein, *Science of the Cross*, 162.
41. Stein, *Science of the Cross*, 162.
42. Stein, *Science of the Cross*, 179.
43. Stein, *Science of the Cross*, 173.
44. Stein, *On the Problem of Empathy*, 115.
45. On the related question of religious consciousness, see Stein, *On the Problem of Empathy*, 117–18.

twenty-five years later, Stein herself becomes an exemplar *par excellence* of the *homo religiosus* through her martyrdom. Stein interpreted her sacrifice as a choice both for God and for solidarity with her own Jewish people. When offered a chance to escape to Switzerland in the midst of the war, Stein opted to stay with her sister who was unable to get a visa.[46] She saw her choice as an act of solidarity and the living out of her Christian vocation.[47] "Why should I be spared?" she asked, days before her arrest and deportation to Auschwitz.[48] "If I cannot share the fate of my [Jewish] brothers and sisters, my life, in a certain sense, is destroyed."[49]

Stein's choice to suffer with her people offers us a translation of the freedom of the night into the language of solidarity. Being with and for the suffering other: this can demand that we take our very lives in hand, and, at the expense of all of our abilities and experiences, give ourselves entirely over out of love. If Stein's witness translates the core logic of mystical freedom into that of martyrdom, it also suggests that we can further translate the logic of the martyr's freedom into less total acts of solidarity and resistance, acts like Stein's 1933 petition to the Holy See for the protection of Jewish people against the Nazis.[50] In these small acts too, which our own encounters with the suffering of others elicit, the sanjuanist night teaches us that the current limits of our power and experience are not the boundaries of our freedom, but rather the sacrificial offerings that we can surrender in order to discover ever-greater forms of loving solidarity and resistance.

JEAN-YVES LACOSTE

Lacoste performs his own transcription of the sanjuanist night by teasing out various domains of "nocturnal experience."[51] He works out these translations across a series of studies that culminate with his 1994 book *Experience and the Absolute: Disputed Questions on the Humanity of Man*.[52] In this work, Lacoste sets out to rethink the "humanity of man" according to humanity's potential encounter with the Absolute, and what this encounter

---

46. Nguyen and Roddy, "Performative Theodicy," 592.
47. Nguyen and Roddy, "Performative Theodicy," 592.
48. Nguyen and Roddy, "Performative Theodicy," 592.
49. Nguyen and Roddy, "Performative Theodicy," 592.
50. Nguyen and Roddy, "Performative Theodicy," 586.
51. Farley, *Lacoste on John*, 4.
52. *Expérience, evénement, connaissance*; *De la phénoménologie de l'esprit*; and *De la certitude au dénuement*. See Farley, *Lacoste on John*.

has to say about experience.[53] Pivotal to Lacoste's analysis of experience is his phenomenology of the "liturgy" and the liturgy's "nocturnal site."

By "liturgy," Lacoste does not mean concrete ritual practices in themselves, like the Mass or matins.[54] Instead, he gives the word a very specific, philosophical meaning. For Lacoste, the word "liturgy" stands for the summation of the whole logic that structures the encounter between humanity and God.[55] We will unpack the significance of this definition for Lacoste's understanding of freedom in a moment. But first, it is worth noting that his very formal, theoretical treatment of liturgy exemplifies his style more generally, which preferences highly conceptual discourse over the more narrative and "experientially eventful" phenomenology of someone like Edith Stein.[56]

It is with respect to the "nocturnal" dimension of Lacoste's conceptualization of liturgy that he turns most obviously to John of the Cross's night. He explicitly acknowledges his debt to John in the introduction to *Experience and the Absolute*.[57] But in the rest of the text he never cites him. His decision to leave John out functions not as a repudiation, but rather as a way of letting himself think freely with John, without claiming any interpretive authority over John's works in their own right.[58] However, while Lacoste's book lacks references to specific texts, a running comparison with Stein's densely textual engagement with John will make the sanjuanist nature of Lacoste's night clear. This comparison will also build out the set of commonalities between Stein and Lacoste that we will survey in the conclusion.

STRUCTURE: THE "EMPIRICAL I" AND THE "ESCHATOLOGICAL I"

Lacoste begins his analysis of experience with an exposition of Heidegger. As a general methodological point, Lacoste thinks that it is advisable to understand terms according to their normal, everyday usage.[59] For Lacoste, Heidegger has done a particularly effective job elucidating the underlying

---

53. Lacoste, *Experience and the Absolute*, 1.

54. He does, however, often appeal to liturgical or quasi-liturgical practices like reclusion, pilgrimage, and eucharistic devotion to exemplify his own philosophical understanding of liturgy. See Lacoste, *Experience and the Absolute*, 26–32, 92.

55. Lacoste, *Experience and the Absolute*, 2.

56. See Prevot, *Thinking Prayer*, 137, 160.

57. Lacoste, *Experience and the Absolute*, 2–3.

58. Lacoste, *Experience and the Absolute*, 2.

59. Farley, *Lacoste and John*, 7.

logic of "experience" as used in common parlance.[60] Of course, Heidegger is not so much concerned with the particularities of a given person's experience as with "the fundamental structures of experience such as they are everywhere, always and for everyone."[61] What Heidegger's identification of these structures offers is a basic delimitation of the a priori horizon of experience available to all. Lacoste uses the term the "empirical I [*le moi empirique*]" to summarize the self insofar as its mode or field of experience operates within these a priori limits identified by Heidegger.[62] In other words, the empirical I stands for the subject or the self of experience ordinarily understood.[63]

But if we define the self according to the limits of the empirical I alone, Lacoste thinks that we must admit certain religious and ethical consequences. On the one hand, Lacoste argues that God, defined minimally as "an Absolute who is someone,"[64] cannot be "experienced" in any evident way according to the Heideggerian parameters of experience.[65] That is, God simply does not "fit" within "experience" as Heidegger, and most of us, would generally understand the term. Thus, "Atheism is neither simply nor in the first place a theoretical problem: it is first what is a priori to existence."[66] Therefore, anyone who takes the empirical I as the full measure of human being basically precludes the possibility of a relationship with God. On the other hand, the empirical I also introduces ethical questions. For if ethics strives to establish an order wherein human beings are all related in good will as brothers and sisters, Lacoste thinks that it must first face the fact that we do not all actually and of necessity *experience* each other as brothers and sisters, at least according to the a priori logic of experience.[67] Therefore, even if ethics sets out to achieve the ideal of fraternal justice, the empirical I does not of itself have the resources to justify this ideal.[68] Even worse, we also contend with the consciousness that we have already violated this ideal by our own "pacts with violence and evil."[69] Any new attempts to do good and resist evil are therefore to some degree always already thwarted in

---

60. See Farley, *Lacoste and John*, 7.
61. Lacoste, *Experience and the Absolute*, 104.
62. Lacoste, *Experience and the Absolute*, 58, 60, 61, 62, 75, 80.
63. See Schrijvers, *Lacoste*, 73.
64. Lacoste, *Experience and the Absolute*, 21.
65. Lacoste, *Experience and the Absolute*, 102.
66. Lacoste, *Experience and the Absolute*, 105.
67. Lacoste, *Experience and the Absolute*, 74,
68. Lacoste, *Experience and the Absolute*, 72–75.
69. Lacoste, *Experience and the Absolute*, 93.

THE FREEDOM OF BEING BEFORE GOD

advance by our own moral ambivalence. The empirical I thus stands for a conception of the self as initially atheistic and morally compromised.

Lacoste opens up a way of considering the second major pole in the structure of human possibility through what he calls "liturgy." If Heidegger has outlined for us the initial parameters of experience, then the experience of *restlessness*, interpreted by what we have learned in history about an Absolute who is Someone, can cause us to call the limits of these parameters into question.[70] Lacoste argues that although they cannot experience God in the ordinary sense of the word, humans are nonetheless "free" both to affirm the existence of an Absolute who exceeds their experience, and to "choose to exist in his presence."[71] In other words, the human person has the ability to pray. And if Heideggerian "Dasein" or "being-in-the-world" represents the mode of human existence defined by the a priori logic of experience,[72] then Lacostian "liturgy" stands for "the logic that presides over the encounter between man and God writ large."[73] In effect, what this means is that humans can acknowledge the limits of experience according to the initial "givens of consciousness,"[74] i.e., the horizon of the empirical I, while also recognizing that they can define themselves against a wider horizon than these givens, the horizon of the possibilities implicit in a relation with the Absolute. Lacoste names the subject insofar as it is defined by the liturgical horizon the "eschatological I [*moi eschatologique*]."[75]

On the one hand, the eschatological I opposes the empirical I. This is because, to define oneself according to this second figure of the self, one must admit that humans can define themselves according to more than they can experience. That is, the eschatological I surpasses and contradicts the limits of the empirical I. Spelling out this contradiction, Lacoste explains that liturgical prayer consists in "the resolute and deliberate gesture made by those who ordain their being-in-the-world a being-before-God, and who do violence to the former in the name of the latter."[76] On the other hand, the eschatological I cannot actually separate itself from the empirical I in history. Just because we can live as if we relate to the Absolute does not mean that we can (necessarily) experience the Absolute. What we can do is

---

70. Lacoste, *Experience and the Absolute*, 146. On restlessness, see Schrijvers, *Lacoste*, 57–60.

71. Lacoste, *Experience and the Absolute*, 42.

72. Lacoste, *Experience and the Absolute*, 104–5.

73. Lacoste, *Experience and the Absolute*, 2.

74. Lacoste, *Experience and the Absolute*, 94.

75. Lacoste, *Experience and the Absolute*, 57–58.

76. Lacoste, *Experience and the Absolute*, 39.

superimpose or interlace the eschatological I over the empirical I,[77] which continues to dictate the parameters of experience conventionally understood. Thus, the eschatological I presents the opposite extreme of possible configurations of the self: the human person's ability to define herself and her actions not by experience, but by a relation with an Absolute who in principle transcends it.

Lacoste thus sets up a polarity between the empirical I and eschatological I that parallels, in certain formal respects, Stein's differentiation between exteriority and the sensual type on the one hand, and interiority and the mystical type on the other. To underscore some dissimilarities first, Lacoste's two figures of the ego do not represent personal types. Instead, they stand for two ways of defining the self which can coexist simultaneously in the same person. That is, all humans can be defined according to the empirical I. And the one who adopts the eschatological I cannot annul the empirical I, even if she learns how to bracket it in prayer. Neither do exteriority and interiority correspond directly with Lacoste's two Is. The empirical I includes higher forms of cognition and valuing than those proper to the sensual type. The eschatological I, for its part, stands for the human ability to define the self according to the possibility of a relation with the Absolute, whereas Stein's interiority refers to the capacity to *realize* this relationship personally and existentially.

But in a more abstract, formal sense, there are significant parallels between these polarities. The empirical I designates the self *qua* the limitations of an immanent set of concerns that effectively rule out a relation with God and prejudice the exercise of goodwill towards one's neighbor. Similarly, Stein's sensual type cannot participate either in a personal relation with God or in the ethically normed treatment of neighbor. Likewise, Stein's interiority denotes the dimension of human being that, like the eschatological I, is completely defined by a relation with God. The mystic is the person who lives out this total self-definition existentially through contemplation. In this way, both thinkers construct polar structures that differentiate between the ego as defined by the confines of immanent concerns, and the ego as defined according to its relationship with God.

Dynamism: Freedom in the Night

Lacoste clarifies the meaning of the liturgy and its relationship with freedom through the introduction of the theme of the "night" or "vigil."[78] As we

77. Lacoste, *Experience and the Absolute*, 57.
78. On the vigil, see Gschwandtner, "Vigil as Exemplary Liturgical Experience."

THE FREEDOM OF BEING BEFORE GOD

have already noted, Lacostian liturgy highlights the freedom that we have to define ourselves according to the horizon of a relation to the Absolute and to act accordingly. But if we define ourselves against this horizon, does that mean that the Absolute will show up in our experience? For Lacoste, this question leads back to the freedom of the Absolute itself. "Faced with an Absolute, whose freedom he recognizes," Lacoste explains, "the man who prays first learns that, although he exposes himself to this Absolute . . . his expectation of God can never compel God's condescension."[79] The simple act of defining oneself according to a relation with the Absolute does not mean God will necessarily rise to experience. Therefore, to live in relation to God, I have to give up or "do violence" to my native field of experience and any claim to its absolute significance, precisely in order to acknowledge the freedom of the one to whom I pray.

Lacoste underscores that this is not because the Absolute is unable to enter human experience. Quite the contrary: to deny God's ability on this point "would constitute an attack on [God's] freedom and . . . omnipotence."[80] But, Lacoste insists that if it is not God's good will to rise to experience of necessity or a priori, then the most basic logic of a relation with God demands that we *accept* this limitation to our experience. The liturgical relation with God thus unfolds in the "night" of "inexperience"[81] rather than in the diurnal field of consciousness proper to the empirical I. Human freedom does have the ability to organize life around a relation with the Absolute that it can rationally conceptualize. But God's freedom to not show up in our experience means that the "darkness" of inexperience defines the core "site" of this (new) life.

But the "bracketing"[82] of the native conditions of experience not only honors divine freedom, it also constitutes a deep affirmation of human freedom. Lacoste develops his insight on how the night makes us free in two directions, one negative and one positive. Negatively speaking, the "night" comes to stand for the necessity to surrender or displace different conceptions of experience and knowledge in general, and religious experience in particular, in order to relate to the Absolute. To "inexperience" as his nocturnal critique of Heidegger and of "every theory in which experience governs knowledge [*connaissance*] of God," Lacoste adds "nonvision" and

---

79. Lacoste, *Experience and the Absolute*, 47.
80. Lacoste, *Experience and the Absolute*, 143.
81. Lacoste, *Experience and the Absolute*, 147.
82. On Lacoste's unique deployment of phenomenological "bracketing," see Hart, "Poverty's Speech."

"nonfeeling" as critiques of Hegelian knowledge and Schleiermachian religious experience respectively.[83]

Lacoste does not think that we should become "overjoyed" by these subversions.[84] In fact, he is quick to highlight the disappointment and boredom that must accompany the act of letting inexperience speak to us of our liturgical liberation. He underscores the "disappointment occasioned when knowledge coincides with inexperience,"[85] a coincidence that undergirds Lacoste's subversions of Heidegger, Hegel, and Schleiermacher alike. And he argues that "Although liturgical inexperience [*L'inexpérience liturgique*] need not give rise to boredom [*ennui*], boredom is a constant and useful reminder to us that nonexperience [*nonexpérience*] is essential to the liturgical play—and that it can be intolerable to us."[86]

But while the "night" encapsulates our discomfiting liberation from ways of thinking and feeling that exclude or truncate a relation with the Absolute, it simultaneously reveals the full range of human freedom in a positive sense. By allowing the human person to take seriously her restlessness and the knowledge she has received about the Absolute, the "night" becomes the time in "which [the human person] can strive for what is most proper to him: to exist before the Absolute with which he is reconciled . . . Nowhere in the world does man reveal himself more truly."[87] In other words, the liturgical night frees the human person to engage with the whole domain of life that spreads out against the horizon of being-before-God. Therefore, "the act of keeping vigil appears to us . . . as the purest form of the self positing itself [*pure position de soi*], as the epitome [*compendium*] of an affirmation of our freedom."[88] The night thus sets us free to discover our identities, and ultimately to act, against the fullest horizon of human possibility.

So far, we have focused on the freedom that the night opens up in relation to God. But Lacoste also concerns himself with the freedom that the night makes possible in relation to our neighbor, that is, in the domain of ethics. Lacoste explains that the attention we pay to the Absolute in prayer takes on "the nocturnal character of the vigil in which, every ethical duty having been honored, man gives to the Absolute the time (and thus the

---

83. Lacoste, *Experience and the Absolute*, 146. As situated within the wider, nocturnal critique of Hegel and Schleiermacher, see Lacoste, *Experience and the Absolute*, 140–49.

84. Lacoste, *Experience and the Absolute*, 58.

85. Lacoste, *Experience and the Absolute*, 149.

86. Lacoste, *Experience and the Absolute*, 149; *Expérience*, 180.

87. Lacoste, *Experience and the Absolute*, 147.

88. Lacoste, *Experience and the Absolute*, 79; *Expérience*, 96.

being) he might otherwise have given to sleep."[89] Without denying the exigencies of justice, the vigil stands for the time we (non-abusively) take from our biological needs in order to attend to the Absolute.[90] This attention, in turn, makes it possible for the individual not only to judge herself, but also the world and her obligations to others in the world, in light of the Absolute.[91] In this way the vigil teaches us to see each other as brothers and sisters and to act accordingly. It thereby provides the grounding for ethics that the empirical I does not.[92] But it overcomes *this* limitation only by confronting the human person with another. If the vigil teaches the human person to long for a Kingdom, the place where we dwell with God and neighbor in eschatological fullness, it also forces us to realize that we can only accept the Kingdom as a gift from God. We cannot effect it ourselves, as if we could become the "*project managers of the definitive [les maîtres d'oeuvre du définitif]*."[93]

In a word, the vigil confronts us with our "'inoperativity [*désouvrement*],'" a term that captures the ethical valences of the symbol of the night, while linking it to the religious domain.[94] We are free to open ourselves to God in "hospitality," and we are free to strive to enact God's "design" for a world in which we treat each other as brothers and sisters.[95] But our efforts do not ensure the presence of the former or the realization of the latter. Thus, inoperativity marks the logic of both ethics and religious experience with respect to the Absolute. In both cases, liturgical inexperience frees us from the limits that the coordinates of the empirical I set on our relationships with God and neighbor. And if this inexperience comes at the cost of our obsessions with production and our self-concepts built upon it,[96] it also frees us to recognize all people as our brothers and sisters before God, and to act accordingly.

To return to our comparison, we can see that while Stein incorporates John's mystical "dark night of the spirit" directly into her theory, Lacoste borrows core notions of the night and applies them to the theoretical origins of a relation to God, rather than to its advanced purification. For Stein, the night involves the surrender of our experiential closeness with God and of

---

89. Lacoste, *Experience and the Absolute*, 78.
90. Lacoste, *Experience and the Absolute*, 79
91. Lacoste, *Experience and the Absolute*, 74.
92. Lacoste, *Experience and the Absolute*, 72–75.
93. Lacoste, *Experience and the Absolute*, 93 (emphasis original); *Expérience*, 113.
94. Lacoste, *Experience and the Absolute*, 78–80, 90–91, 145, 148, 156, 161.
95. Lacoste, *Experience and the Absolute*, 93.
96. Lacoste, *Experience and the Absolute*, 78, 156.

the normal operations of our spirits in order to allow trinitarian freedom to introduce us to a new depth of personal freedom and trinitarian relationship. Lacoste applies the same logic to the transition from the empirical I alone as the definitive figure of the self to the subordination of this figure to that of the eschatological I. In Lacoste's language, this transition depends on a confrontation with God's freedom in the form of inexperience and inoperativity. Furthermore, he insists that these challenges to human subjectivity as usual open up freedom to new horizons of action in relation to God and neighbor. Thus, although they deploy the sanjuanist night in different contexts to describe different transitions, Stein and Lacoste nonetheless share the same formal conceptions that the night denotes a confrontation with divine freedom in the form of inexperience and inoperativity, and that this confrontation yields a new horizon of relationality with God that increases our ability to act ethically towards God and our neighbors.

Action: Freedom at Work

I argued above that it is possible to enflesh Stein's theory of freedom by examining the freedom she herself manifested in the face of one of the most devastating programs of mass murder in human history. Lacoste, thankfully, has not faced the Nazis in his lifetime. But he does offer us some concise but telling intimations concerning the concrete implications of the liturgical vigil. First, whereas Lacoste insists that inexperience characterizes the vigil, he goes on to say that "It will certainly not be denied that the Absolute can be the subject of affective knowledge [*connaissance affective*], on condition that a somewhat precise hermeneutics of the latter (i.e., a 'discerning of spirits') can be undertaken."[97] In other words, while a proper relation to the Absolute depends on subordinating experience to knowledge, this subordination opens up a new kind of experience: namely, that which develops through the practice of the discernment of spirits. Through brief references to discernment of spirits, Lacoste effectively conjures up a highly developed and eminently practical Christian tradition. What we can say then is that, concretely, the freedom of the vigil looks like the freedom we gain to relate to God through discernment in all of its practical and embodied richness. On the ethical front, Lacoste's position is equally simple. The vigil teaches us to claim all people as our brothers and sisters. Therefore, although we cannot "bring about the *eschaton*" in history, our ability to see each other in light of the Absolute does "nevertheless shelter the paths that mark out

---

97. Lacoste, *Experience and the Absolute*, 142; cf. 49.

its inchoation."[98] What the vigil frees us for is not merely an abstract affirmation of possible communal love with God and neighbor, but an actual, and even experiential, life of love in history. Lacoste's exposition of the vigil thus directs itself towards the historical actualization of new relationships with God and neighbor through discernment and ethical action grounded in prayer.

CONCLUSION

But discernment and expanded ethical action do not exhaust the practical implications of Lacoste's vision. These may characterize the first fruits of the imposition of the eschatological over the empirical I. However, the liturgical vigil also makes it possible to think of something more extraordinary and no less concrete: namely, "the saint."[99] For the saint is the one for whom "being-before-God constantly subvert[s] his participation in the play of world and earth and the ambivalence that this play imposes on whoever participates in it."[100] Through a circuitous route, then, we can bring Lacoste's own theory back, at least implicitly, to Stein. The fact that Lacoste holds up Stein's outstanding *sanctity* means that he sees her life as a paradigmatic instantiation of his own theory of freedom, even as he criticizes her work of theorization.[101]

I would like to conclude by briefly summarizing the results of our comparison. Although they deploy the sanjuanist night in different contexts, Stein's and Lacoste's receptions of John lend their theories of freedom a surprisingly similar shape. They each give the night a central place in their articulations of freedom as a kind of confrontation between divine freedom and human inexperience and inoperativity. This confrontation brings about a transformation. Through a prayerful relation to divine freedom, human freedom opens up to the horizon of being-before-God, an opening that makes new forms of ethical treatment of our neighbor possible. The night thus brings about a kind of movement from one pole of human life, marked by the restrictions of an immanent frame of reference (i.e., the empirical I and the sensual type), to another pole characterized by the proto-eschatological amplitude of a life defined by a free relationship with God (i.e., the eschatological I and the mystical type). These commonalities emergent in Stein's and Lacoste's models of freedom embody the kinds of offerings that

98. Lacoste, *Experience and the Absolute*, 98.
99. Lacoste, *Experience and the Absolute*, 98.
100. Lacoste, *Experience and the Absolute*, 98.
101. Lacoste, *Theological Thinking*, 25.

John's contemplative theology of the night can offer to continental thought, while also pointing the way towards concrete modes of freely resisting evil through practices of prayerful discernment and solidarity.

REFERENCES

Beckmann-Zöeller, Beate. "Edith Stein's Theory of the Person in Her Munster Years (1932–1933)." *American Catholic Philosophical Quarterly* 82.1 (2008) 47–70.

Bello, Haddy. "Freedom, Intentionality, and Trinitarian Love in Edith Stein's Thought—The Need for a Phenomenology-Theology Dialogue to Have a Deeper Understanding of It." *Religions* 14.11 (2023) 1377.

Beroch, Maria Aracoeli. "El yo steiniano en Ciencia de la Cruz." *Teresianum* 70.1 (2019) 107–36.

Borden, Sarah R. *Edith Stein*. New York: Continuum, 2003.

Calcagno, Antonio. *The Philosophy of Edith Stein*. Pittsburgh: Duquesne University Press, 2007.

Farley, Matthew. "Jean-Yves Lacoste on John of the Cross: Theological Thinker Par Excellence." *Modern Theology* 32.1 (2016) 319.

Gschwandtner, Christina M. "The Vigil as Exemplary Liturgical Experience: On Jean-Yves Lacoste's Phenomenology of Liturgy." *Modern Theology* 31.4 (2015) 648–57.

Hart, Kevin. "'Poverty's Speech': On Liturgical Reduction." *Modern Theology* 31.4 (2015) 641–47.

John of the Cross. *The Collected Works of Saint John of the Cross*. Translated by Kieran Kavanaugh and Otilio Rodríguez. Washington, DC: Institute of Carmelite Studies, 1991.

Lacoste, Jean-Yves. "De la certitude au dénuement: Descartes et Jean de la Croix." *Nouvelle Revue Théologique* 113.4 (1991) 516–34.

———. *Experience and the Absolute: Disputed Questions on the Humanity of Man*. Translated by Mark Raftery-Skehan. New York: Fordham University Press, 2004.

———. *Expérience et Absolu: questions disputées sur l'humanité de l'homme*. Paris: Presses universitaires de France, 1994.

———. "Expérience, evénement, connaissance de Dieu." *Nouvelle Revue Théologique* 106.6 (1984) 834–61.

———. *From Theology to Theological Thinking*. Translated by W. Chris Hackett. Charlottesville: University of Virginia Press, 2014.

———. "De la phénoménologie de l'esprit à la Montée Du Carmel." *Revue Thomiste* 97.1 (1989) 5–37, 569–97.

Nguyen, Peter, and Nicolae Roddy. "Performative Theodicy: Edith Stein and the Recovery of Lamentation." *Modern Theology* 40.3 (2023) 572–99.

Payne, Steven. "Edith Stein and John of the Cross." *Teresianum* 50.1–2 (1999) 239–56.

Prevot, Andrew. *Thinking Prayer: Theology and Spirituality Amid the Crises of Modernity*. Notre Dame, IN: University of Notre Dame Press, 2015.

Rivera, Joseph. *Phenomenology and the Horizon of Experience: Spiritual Themes in Henry, Marion, and Lacoste*. New York: Routledge, 2022.

Schrijvers, Joeri. *An Introduction to Jean-Yves Lacoste*. Burlington, VT: Ashgate, 2012.

Stein, Edith. *Endliches und ewiges Sein: Versuch eines Aufstiegs zum Sinn des Seins; Anhang, Martin Heideggers Existenzphilosophie, Die Seelenburg*. Freiburg: Herder, 2006.

———. *"Freiheit und Gnade" und weitere Beiträge zu Phänomenologie und Ontologie*. Freiburg: Herder, 2014.

———. *Kreuzeswissenschaft: Studie über Johannes vom Kreuz*. Freiburg im Breisgau: Herder, 2003.

———. *On the Problem of Empathy*. Translated by Waltraut Stein. Washington, DC: Institute of Carmelite Studies, 1989.

———. *The Science of the Cross*. Translated by Josephine Koeppel. Washington, DC: Institute of Carmelite Studies, 2003.

Wardley, Kenneth Jason. *Praying to a French God: The Theology of Jean-Yves Lacoste*. Burlington, VT: Ashgate, 2014.

7

Divine Desire, Divine Freedom
Coakley and Lonergan on Prayer in Trinitarian Theology

JONATHAN HEAPS

INTRODUCTION

Bernard Lonergan describes theology as part of a community's "cultural superstructure," much like economics or political theory. It steps back to reflect, often in a theoretical way, on the practical enterprises of the community's common life.[1] If economics reflects on the business dealings of the community and political theory on its governance, then theology reflects on its religiosity. Of course, an economics professor might also run a business, or a political theorist stand for government office; and indeed, a theologian can benefit from an active life of religious faith. Still, Lonergan would caution that economists, political theorists, and theologians are primarily measured, at least within the cultural superstructure, on the quality of their scholarly reflection, not on their annual profits, policy wins, or personal sanctity, respectively.[2] In any case, Lonergan's distinction suggests that attempts to pursue both—practical enterprises and "superstructural reflection"—at the same time will lead to some confusion.

---

1. Lonergan, "Belief," 76–78.
2. Lonergan, "Belief," 76–78.

Is Sarah Coakley's argument, then, that contemplative prayer should be integrated into the very method of doing systematic theology an example of such confusion? Only superficially. This essay aims to develop Coakley's exhortation to silent prayer in the practice of systematic theology by showing how that practice transforms the horizon of the theologian in foundational and methodologically significant ways. Moreover, I will further argue that contemplative prayer can reconstruct his or her theological imagination for the sake of otherwise improbable advances in the field. To that end, I will begin (and, for reasons of space, *only* begin) to sketch out a new "analogy from freedom" for the processions of the Trinity that a dialogue between Coakley's and Lonergan's reflections on theological foundations might seed.

COAKLEY ON PRAYER AND "DIVINE DESIRE"

Sarah Coakley's *God, Sexuality, and the Self* makes a strong defense of systematic theology against its contemporary cultured despisers. Coakley's defense makes silent, "contemplative" prayer integral with her theological methodology—what she calls both "theology *totale*" and "theology *in via*."[3] Her book sets out a number of linked claims about this integration (that, for example, God's kindling and chastening of sexual desire will be part and parcel with the refinement of theological reasoning),[4] and a bevy of diverse evidences in support of them (ranging from patristic sources to contemporary sociological questionnaires).[5] But *God, Sexuality, and the Self* is, ironically, lighter on the sort of systematic or theoretical detail that might mediate between these evocative claims and myriad data. To bolster Coakley's account and fill in some of these speculative lacunae, I have turned to Bernard Lonergan's major methodological and trinitarian works.

What follows presents, albeit in a preliminary way, some of the lines of convergence between Coakley and Lonergan. Lonergan's highly technical theory of interiority helps differentiate the elements of desiring, reasoning, and liberty that seem to be at work behind Coakley's position. In return, Coakley's emphasis on the prayerful divinizing of eros through "trinitarian incorporation" suggests both a contemplative augmentation of Lonergan's "interiority analysis" and also a new psychological—even *existential*—analogy for trinitarian procession and so for the dynamics of divine life.

3. Coakley, *God, Sexuality, and the Self*, 15–20.
4. Coakley, *God, Sexuality, and the Self*, 12–15.
5. See, for example, chapter 4, in which Coakley engages in a small-scale sociological experiment with a charismatic Anglican congregation (Coakley, *God, Sexuality, and the Self*, 152–89).

In *God, Sexuality, and the Self*, Sarah Coakley broadly accepts three criticisms of systematic theology, but in a qualified way. She assents, in brief, that each names a persistent, but not unanswerable danger or challenge to systematic theology. First, she accepts that systematic theology can be "onto-theology," that "falsely, and idolatrously, turns God into an object of human knowledge."[6] Second, she accepts that it can be "hegemonic," "inappropriately totalizing, and thereby necessarily suppressive of the voices and perspectives of marginalized people."[7] Third, she accepts that it can be, in the idiom of psychoanalytic feminist discourse, "phallocentric," and so "ordered according to the 'symbolic,' 'male' mode of thinking which seeks to clarify, control, and master."[8]

Each of these criticisms unmasks systematic theology as, in one way or another, a form of motivated reasoning, and indeed, a mode of thinking motivated by an urge to master and dominate. Onto-theological reasoning desires to subject and subordinate the divine to the human. Hegemonic reasoning desires to circumscribe whose reasoning counts and so who gets to participate in public cooperation. Phallocentric reasoning desires to repress the destabilizing creativity that can arise from the "feminine" unconscious of psychoanalysis along with, ultimately, the women who embody it. Coakley further grants that, so motivated, systematic theology is commonly obtuse to (at best) or actively repressive of alterity (whether human or divine). It is also often obtuse to or repressive of human embodiment, especially under the related aspects of gender and sexuality.[9]

For Coakley, however, these criticisms are not insuperable. Again, they name persistent dangers for systematic theology, but she thinks they can be faced and mitigated. However, facing them requires the integration of theological method and procedure with particular, embodied, and graced habits of contemplative prayer.[10] Why can contemplative prayer empower systematic theology to face these criticisms but also move beyond them? First, contemplative prayer addresses the motivated character of theological reasoning by purifying its motivations insofar as the theologian offers up his or her desiring in general to God for progressive transformation in and through the practice.[11] Second, this transformative process occurs in and through an expressly *embodied* practice, which Coakley argues empowers it

---

6. Coakley, *God, Sexuality, and the Self*, 42.
7. Coakley, *God, Sexuality, and the Self*, 42.
8. Coakley, *God, Sexuality, and the Self*, 42.
9. Coakley, *God, Sexuality, and the Self*, 47–50.
10. Coakley, *God, Sexuality, and the Self*, 19.
11. Coakley, *God, Sexuality, and the Self*, 51–52.

DIVINE DESIRE, DIVINE FREEDOM

to transform both political and psychical gender and sexual dynamics. This empowerment is explicitly theological, insofar as it operates through prayer as colored by "the logic and flow of trinitarian, divine desire, its welcoming of the primary interruption of the Spirit."[12] Third, such contemplative practice is expressly organized around what is for Coakley the fundamental and paradigmatic "alterity" of divine desire to human desire:

> As one ceases to set the agenda and allows room for God to be God—the sense of the *human* impossibility of prayer becomes more intense (Rom 8:26), and drives one to comprehend the necessity of God's own prior activity in it. Strictly speaking, it is not I who autonomously prays, but God (the Holy Spirit) who prays in me, and so answers the eternal call of the "Father," drawing me by various painful degrees into the newly expanded life of "Sonship." There is, then, an inherent reflexivity in the divine, a ceaseless outgoing and returning of the desiring God; and insofar as I welcome and receive this reflexivity, I find that it is the Holy Spirit who "interrupts" my human monologue to a (supposedly) monadic God[.][13]

In this way, Coakley's titular concerns (God, sexuality, and the self) coalesce in her response to criticisms of systematic theology. But they also open upon her sub-titular topic, the Trinity. She writes: "Prayer (and especially prayer of a non-discursive sort, whether contemplative or charismatic) is the chief context in which the *irreducible* threeness of God becomes humanly apparent to the Christian."[14] Coakley strives to develop a vocabulary of "twoness" (between Father and incarnate Son, man and woman, perhaps even human and God) and "threeness" (where the Spirit is the third) as the linkage between desire, gender, and the Trinity in the context of silent prayer (and through that prayer, into systematic theology). Throughout *God, Sexuality, and the Self*, this way of speaking ("twoness" and "threeness") remains opaque. As I continue, I will introduce Lonergan's own methodological and trinitarian reflections in no small part as an effort to tease out and develop Coakley's evocative and promising, but ultimately mystifying locutions on the topic.[15]

Divine desire (and especially divine desire as experienced in contemplative practice) thus serves as both a grounding reality for systematic

---

12. Coakley, *God, Sexuality, and the Self*, 55.
13. Coakley, *God, Sexuality, and the Self*, 55–56 (emphasis original).
14. Coakley, *God, Sexuality, and the Self*, 55.
15. See, for example, the ostensibly conclusory sentence, "Twoness, one might say, is divinely ambushed by threeness" (Coakley, *God, Sexuality, and the Self*, 58).

theology beyond the accusations of its post-modern critics, but also an evidentiary basis for trinitarian theological speculation "on the merits." But Coakley's characterization of "divine desire," so central to her account of contemplative prayer's place in the future of systematic theology, might raise the eyebrows of classical trinitarians. After all, desire commonly implies both some good which is lacking and also some potency for desire's consummation, neither of which befits the infinite and immutable God of classical theism. Their concerns might be quelled when Coakley insists that divine desire (unlike creaturely desire) is not predicated on lack, but on "a plenitude of longing love."[16] Though, in classical trinitarian terms, this antithesis between the special character of divine desire and any kind of lack is properly asserted, Coakley leaves it unexplained. Matthew Levering, discussing Coakley's book, clarifies that Dionysian desire does not involve the implication of "lack" that St. Thomas Aquinas finds in the term, and that would lead one to predicate desire of God at most metaphorically.[17]

Coakley does, however, go on to characterize divine desire in trinitarian, principally pneumatological terms. It is, most generally, a matter of spiritual movement, going-out, or *ekstasis*. It can be paradigmatically predicated of God insofar as, in Pseudo-Dionysius's words, God is "yearning, on the move, simple, self-moved, self-acting, preexistent in the Good flowing out from the Good onto all that is and returning once again to the Good."[18] This perhaps clashes with psychological descriptions of desire as grounded in the projection of something absent or even fanciful to be acquired. But that is precisely the kind of association that the above antithesis is meant to avoid. Rather, divine desire is God on the move to move creatures to God. As Levering again puts it, "love goes out to the beloved ecstatically, so that the lover belongs to the beloved."[19]

Divine desire as loving movement is specified in contemplative practices by its function as a principle of what Coakley calls "incorporation," spurred by the Spirit through and into the Son to the Father.[20] Coakley specifically thematizes divine desire in Christian (Neo-)Platonist terms, both as a divinizing of the eros of human spirit and on the scheme of an exit from the One/God and then a reflexive course of return thereto.[21] Again,

16. Coakley, *God, Sexuality, and the Self*, 10.

17. Levering, *Doctrine of the Holy Spirit*, 39. Thanks to editor Benedict Shoup for directing me to this passage.

18. Pseudo-Dionysius, *Divine Names*, 4.14, cited in Levering, *Engaging the Doctrine*, 38.

19. Levering, *Engaging the Doctrine*, 27.

20. Coakley, *God, Sexuality, and the Self*, 67, 87, 113–14.

21. Coakley, *God, Sexuality, and the Self*, 8, 313–16.

DIVINE DESIRE, DIVINE FREEDOM

she retrieves Dionysius's identification of eros and agape, linking it not only to human *ekstasis*, but "preeminently" to God's. She quotes Dionysius on this point: "It must be said too that the very cause of the universe in the beautiful, good superabundance of his benign yearning for all, *is also carried outside of himself* in the loving care he has for everything."[22]

While these determinations are frequently supported with careful exegesis of tantalizing passages from patristic sources, I confess I have found them insufficient exposition of what Coakley has in mind. Coakley does much gesturing, implying, and suggesting with the aggregation and constellation of these passages, but never quite sets out a *theory* of contemplative prayer's place in theological method. How is the integration of contemplative practice with systematic theology supposed to work the way Coakley describes? She claims it can dissolve a series of false and stereotypical theological disjunctions, but *why* can it do so?[23] Again, she *describes* the evidence of the Spirit in prayer from the praying person's perspective (especially as recorded in Patristic sources), but does not provide a model for the reality the pray-er is experiencing.

Now, surely such models would need revision and complement in the course of things. Coakley's is a theology *in via*, after all. But for such a theology to get "on its way," it can and must venture such theories and models, not to set out the parameters of all future discussion, but as precisely that which is up for discussion. When I return to *God, Sexuality, and the Self*—as I frequently do—I find again and again that her proposal is very attractive, but also that I wish it were accompanied by more fully wrought psychology, metaphysics, and/or theological speculation, of the sort that would meet the exigence for system in a *systematic* theology.

LONERGAN'S PNEUMATOLOGICAL STARTING POINT

Bernard Lonergan is perhaps a surprising conversation partner for Coakley, but in his later work—*Method in Theology* especially—"religious conversion" and its place in theological method anticipates her on a number of these important points. From a high altitude, Lonergan's theological methodology is, for example, "incorporatively" or "reflexively" trinitarian in very much the way Coakley describes, wherein "the Holy Spirit is perceived as the primary means of incorporation into the trinitarian life of God, and as constantly and 'reflexively' at work in believers in the circle of response to the Father's call." On this approach, the "Holy Spirit is construed not simply

---

22. Coakley, *God, Sexuality, and the Self*, 314–15 (emphasis original).
23. Coakley, *God, Sexuality, and the Self*, xvi.

as extending the revelation of Christ, nor even merely as enabling Christ's recognition, but as actually catching up the created realm into the life of God (making it 'conformed to the likeness of his Son,' to use Paul's memorable phrase in Romans 8:29)."[24]

Lonergan does not render that underlying architectonic explicit in, for example, *Method in Theology* and, indeed, might not have noticed himself that it was operating tacitly. Still, readers may hold up the centrality of Romans 5:5[25] as well as Romans 8[26] for Lonergan's account of religious experience and faith, to say nothing of his threefold conversions (religious, moral, and intellectual—what he calls a "lifelong" task) in *Method in Theology*.[27] These, together with his earlier scholarly and teaching works on grace and the Trinity, offer ample materials with which to reconstruct his project's "incorporative" infrastructure. I hope some enterprising soul in Lonergan Studies might circle back from this essay to develop the point at length. In any case, in light of the relatively gestural quality of Coakley's position in *God, Sexuality, and the Self*, Lonergan's penchant for technical detail and apparatus offers a welcome set of clarifications to her account of "divine desire" in particular. At the same time and in the other direction, Coakley suggests a prayerful augmentation of Lonergan's own method in philosophy and theology, as well as a link between God's eternal liberty and the processes of human liberation.

In *Method in Theology*, Lonergan indicates that religious conversion—not to any particular religion, necessarily, but to a properly basic horizon that admits of transcendent meaning and value—is a being-in-love that has, in Christian scriptural terms, its source in the love of God poured into our hearts by the gift of the Holy Spirit.[28] "Though not a product of our knowing and choosing, it is a conscious dynamic state of love, joy, peace, that manifests itself in acts of kindness, goodness, fidelity, gentleness, and self-control (Galatians 5:22–23)."[29] But this being-in-love primarily manifests itself in

---

24. Coakley, *God, Sexuality, and the Self*, 111.

25. "God's love has been poured out into our hearts through the Holy Spirit, who has been given to us" (Rom 5:5 NABRE).

26. "In the same way, the Spirit too comes to the aid of our weakness; for we do not know how to pray as we ought, but the Spirit itself intercedes with inexpressible groanings. And the one who searches hearts knows what is the intention of the Spirit, because it intercedes for the holy ones according to God's will. We know that all things work for good for those who love God, who are called according to his purpose. For those he foreknew he also predestined to be conformed to the image of his Son, so that he might be the firstborn among many brothers" (Rom 8:26–29 NABRE).

27. Lonergan, *Method*, 101, 114, 223–30.

28. Lonergan, *Method*, 100–104.

29. Lonergan, *Method*, 102.

that commitment to self-transcendence that Lonergan argues is the essence of conscious human authenticity.[30] What religious being-in-love specifically contributes to our overall thrust for self-transcendence is an antecedent willingness to follow that thrust, that élan wherever it might lead. As a lover might say to a beloved: "For you? Anything."

But human authenticity is precarious, accomplished only in a devotion distracted across the aggregate moments of selfhood's vicissitudes, easily derailed by even a single instance of refusing the ecstatic call "beyond." It is furthermore beset in its development on all sides by the accretions, concretizations, structures, and powers and principalities of others' inauthenticity, of others' sinfulness. Lonergan called these the "objective surd," which is to say an irrationality that is nevertheless materialized in the common nonsense of a community and tradition.[31] We are so beset that commonly the pursuit of self-transcending authenticity occurs first and foremost in and through a withdrawal from the idiotic self-stifling of inauthenticity.

> So human authenticity is never some pure and serene and secure possession. It is ever a withdrawal from unauthenticity, and every successful withdrawal only brings to light the need for still further withdrawals. Our advance in understanding is also the elimination of oversights and misunderstandings. Our advance in truth is also the correction of mistakes and errors. Our moral development is through repentance for our sins. Genuine religion is discovered and realized by redemption from the many traps of religious aberration. So we are bid to watch and pray, to make our way in fear and trembling.[32]

Authenticity, very often, is dominated by the project of purging ourselves of the obstacles to self-transcendence before we ever begin to "reach out," so to speak, into new territory.

For Lonergan, the driver of authentic self-transcendence, both in its purgative and expansive modes, is an erotic desire for truth and value that, of itself, contains no principle of restriction.

> By the desire to know is meant the dynamic orientation manifested in questions for intelligence and for reflection. It is not [merely] the verbal utterance of questions... It is the prior and enveloping drive that carries cognitional process from sense and imagination to understanding, from understanding to judgment, from judgment to the complete context of correct

---

30. See Lonergan, "Self-Transcendence."
31. Lonergan, *Insight*, 652–53.
32. Lonergan, *Method*, 106.

> judgments that is named knowledge ... By demanding adequate understanding, it involves man in the self-correcting process of learning in which further questions yield complementary insights ... it prevents him from being content with hearsay and legend, with unverified hypotheses and untested theories ... it excludes complacent inertia; for if the questions go unanswered, man cannot be complacent; and if answers are sought, man is not inert.[33]

In conscious living, this eros is also the criterion against which our attention, our inquiry, our bright ideas and firm judgments, our moral and practical conundrums and our pathways of commitment are to be measured. Lonergan assures us that in every conscious person this eros is present and operative, whether one happens to notice it, thematize it, or make it a deliberate factor in one's living or not. It is itself a gift of divine light, a created spiritual participation in uncreated spirit.[34]

But precisely because it can be present and operative to our self-presence and conscious activity without necessarily drawing our attention or inquiry or understanding or commitment, its presence is ambiguous. Or, put another way, the pure unrestricted desire to know conceived as eros (which Lonergan himself does not often do, but I think reading Lonergan with Coakley's Christian Platonism invites) is a necessary but not yet a sufficient condition for human authenticity. The givenness of the desire to know is not, of itself, a marker of religious conversion's being-in-love. However, if I find that I not only have a desire for spiritual self-transcendence, but also the willingness to follow wherever that desire might lead, then the erotic charge of the human spirit is met by a corresponding agapeic empowerment, in this case as what Lonergan called an "antecedent willingness."[35] It will be experienced as a willingness to pay attention to what God would have me experience, to ask those questions it is given me to ask, to attest to such truths as in my judgment cannot be authentically denied, to commit myself to courses of action that I cannot in good conscience deny are my responsibility. And when this antecedent willingness evinces radical openness to whatever—*whatever*, without exception—is true, honorable, right, pure, lovely, good, excellent, and worthy of praise (Philippians 4:8), then one's being has become being in love by the gift of the Holy Spirit (Romans 5:5).

---

33. Lonergan, *Insight*, 372–73.

34. "The intellectual light itself which we have within us is nothing else than a certain participated likeness of the uncreated light" (Aquinas, *ST* I.Q84.A5C).

35. Lonergan, *Insight*, 645–47.

Philosophically, this account of the human spirit augments the earlier Lonergan's own more rationalistic, more narrowly Thomist theory of human freedom, one wherein acts are free when their effects depend on not just a being in act, but *rational* being in act.[36] On this theory, freedom is a mode or species of causal efficacy. In this mode, the necessary and sufficient conditions for some effect—i.e., some action—are a concept of the effect that follows from the agent's understanding and a decision to effect it. These, in Thomist terms, are called freedom of determination and freedom of exercise, respectively. Now, this account of freedom makes an advance beyond purely metaphysical accounts of freedom, where liberty is just unimpeded causal efficacy and is shared equally among conscious and unconscious agents. It is able to integrate the specific difference that makes a difference between agents with liberty and agents without it: the effects of free agents are produced as the term of an *intelligent* process, whereas as agents lacking liberty produce their effects as the term of a merely *intelligible process*.[37]

Now, that earlier theory remains valid and, as I will discuss more below, it continues to have analogical potential for clarifying how to understand trinitarian procession in God. Still, that intellectualist theory of freedom is decentered by a deeper modality of freedom: the antecedent willingness to affirm value—even transcendent value—in one's living *even though one has not first affirmed it in one's thinking*. This freedom does not follow on a word of judgment but is rather that more radical freedom and autonomy from out of which every true judgment, every responsible decision must emerge, including (to Coakley's methodological point) *theological judgments*. The later Lonergan's account of religious conversion keys this deepest, agapeic form of spiritual liberty to the mission of the Holy Spirit and, like Coakley, cites Romans 5 and 8 to support this linkage.

The (erotic) desire to know truth and affirm value orders the human spirit to what is really so in a word of factual judgment and what is really good in a word of practical judgment. This latent ordering becomes operative through lived, conscious conformity to our own native reasonableness and responsibility. But such conformity is subject to aberrations both exogenous and endogenous. One may be (and indeed likely is) formed in an inauthentic culture, saturated with greater or lesser evils and stupidities. But one also can become him or herself a principle of oversight, irresponsibility, and malice, and so one can betray a sound upbringing. One way or the other

36. See, for example, his discussion of rational self-consciousness in Lonergan, *Insight*, 625–28.

37. For an extremely detailed analysis of the role of rational, intelligent process in human liberty (as well as some consideration of its analogical significance for divine liberty), see Heaps, *Ambiguity of Being*, 177–210.

(and often both), one requires not only development in understanding, in morality, and in sanctity, but also purgation and repentance of those obstacles to each. But at the (agapeic) root of the entire psychological and existential process is the mission of the Spirit, ordering and propelling human liberty and human selves toward and through conformity to the Incarnate Word as the true and living way to the Father, *ho theos*.[38]

FROM COAKLEY TO LONERGAN: AN AUGMENTATION

Coakley's *God, Sexuality, and the Self* can provide two elements that Lonergan does not consider in *Method in Theology*. First, Coakley makes prayer integral to the theological specification of this incorporative process and its expression in theological reasoning. Though Lonergan only makes passing reference to contemplative practice (under the heading of what he calls the mystic's "mediated immediacy"), it seems that this would be a welcome addition to his perspective.[39] The first of Lonergan's transcendental precepts is "be attentive" and his mature theological methodology takes its stand on the fundamental significance of interiority. This makes it rather odd that Lonergan did not treat contemplative practices of interior attention (although his exercises in self-appropriation owe much to St. Ignatius of Loyola's spiritual exercises).[40] Such \ heighten our presence to self at that existential level where deep erotic desire operates. It is at that level that one might consciously, habitually get in touch with the guiding and governing pure desire for truth and goodness that Lonergan made the *sine qua non* of his project. Cultivating the power of attention cannot, then, be a happenstance or punctiliar exercise of will (a prospect that contains a number of mistakes folded together), but rather must be a kind of practiced devotion meriting its *own* attention. Though Lonergan did not develop this connection, I note that Coakley cites approvingly the work of Dom Sebastian Moore, who was a scholar of both Lonergan's work and spiritual theology.[41]

Second, Coakley suggests (if somewhat obliquely) a re-construal of our models of immanent trinitarian relations. She would have us analogize from the foregoing pneumatological priority in conscious Christian living

---

38. Lonergan, *Method*, 103n13.

39. Lonergan, *Method*, 75, 256.

40. The early pages of Patrick Byrne's *The Ethics of Discernment* develop this connection fruitfully, linking discernment and "self-appropriation." See Byrne, *Ethics of Discernment*, 23–35.

41. Coakley, *God, Sexuality, and the Self*, 342n2.

and away from "linear" models. Linear revelatory models of the Trinity give primary focus, according to Coakley, "to the Father–Son relationship, and the Holy Spirit becomes the secondary purveyor of that relationship to the church."[42] These linear models might imply the Spirit's subordination or superfluity to a putatively "more basic" dyad of Father and Son.[43] Coakley has speculative concerns that this produces a subordinationist theology and links these with the common feminist observation that subordination of the Spirit is suspiciously correlated with the subordination of women.

Now, the overtly-Thomist Lonergan of the Gregorian textbooks grounds his analogy for trinitarian procession, and so relation, in created intellectual emanation (the "psychological analogy," properly so-called for St. Thomas).[44] This approach begins from acts of understanding and/or judging and proceeds to the emanation of a "word." This *verbum mentis* may proceed either as a concept expressing understanding or the binary "yes" or "no" of a judgment of fact. These are the formal analogues of the procession of the eternal Word as being-in-act that proceeds not from some external being or internal potency, but from a consubstantial being-in-act internal to the Godhead—namely, the Father. Further, then, the proceeding of love (what Lonergan called a "judgment of value") from the prior word of understanding becomes the corresponding analogue for—in the Latin West anyway—the proceeding of the Spirit from the Father and from the Son.

Now, Lonergan's neo-scholastic trinitarian theology is quite explicit that the proceeding of love is not at all subordinated or superfluous to the proceeding of the Son from the Father, but nevertheless the model is plainly linear in the way that makes Coakley uncomfortable. Where rational control over the formal analogy—that is to say, strict logical inference and expression—might exclude such subordination or superfluity, nevertheless Coakley has a point, and one very much aligned with Lonergan scholar Robert Doran's emphasis on *psychic* conversion. For Doran, psychic conversion "is a transformation of the psychic component of what Freud called 'the censor' from a repressive to a constructive agency in a person's development."[45] "The habitual orientation of our intelligence and our affectivity exercises a censorship over the emergence into consciousness of the images" that will be the material of further, in this case theological, understanding. This

---

42. Coakley, *God, Sexuality, and the Self*, 111–12.

43. Coakley, *God, Sexuality, and the Self*, 111.

44. For Lonergan's synthetic presentation of a Thomist trinitarian theology founded in the psychological analogy, see Lonergan, *Triune God*. Lonergan did the exegetical spadework for that synthetic presentation in a series of articles originally published in *Theological Studies*, but now collected in Lonergan, *Verbum*.

45. Doran, *Theology and the Dialectics of History*, 59.

censorship can be constructive, hewing out irrelevances or red herrings, but it "is repressive when one does not want the [relevant] insight and so excludes from consciousness the images (needed)."[46] In this case, Doran thinks, one needs to undergo such psychic conversion to return the censor function to a constructive, rather than repressive role. Coakley makes a fair case that, at an imagistic, and so psychical level, such trinitarian linearity opens the door to admitting both pneumatological subordination and superfluity into the material conditions of ongoing theological reflection, even if we explicitly deny that this is our motivation. *God, Sexuality, and the Self*'s chapter on artistic depictions of the Trinity marshals a bevy of evidence for this thesis.[47]

FINAL PROPOSAL: AN ANALOGY FROM FREEDOM

Lonergan explicitly denies that there can be another analogy for procession beyond these two, from knowing and loving, respectively.[48] He also explicitly disqualifies any analogy that begins from the created participation in uncreated light that spurs all intellectual activity—i.e., the unrestricted desire to know *qua* desiring. He avers that "God does not ask questions, raise doubts, or deliberate, so conscious but spontaneous procession" such as that movement in us of the light of agent intellect, "is excluded."[49] Nevertheless, I want to take seriously the suggestion seeded by Coakley's provocations. I can, at this point, sketch out a hypothesis, but probably no more. Perhaps the intellectualist analogy from knowledge and love set out in St. Thomas and developed by Lonergan can be augmented. I would augment it with an arguably more primordial analogy from the agapeic eros for truth and goodness. It would be a primordial analogy from agapeic eros understood as freedom or liberty, but in Lonergan's sense of "antecedent willingness." Now, the Thomist analogies from knowing and loving are analogies for processions and, by extension, relations of eternal origin. Lonergan is quite right that this analogy from freedom could not *replace* those. But, following Coakley, it could perhaps shed analogical light on the *reflexivity* of those eternal relations and (here I venture even more tentatively) thereby deepen our understanding of the persons constituted by them.

I would argue, in fact, that Lonergan's trinitarian textbook does not *entirely* foreclose the prospect of such an augmentation. Indeed, while denying

---

46. Doran, *Theology and the Dialectics of History*, 59–60.
47. Coakley, *God, Sexuality, and the Self*, 190–261.
48. Lonergan, *Triune God*, 169–81.
49. Lonergan, *Triune God*, 181.

that there can be any other analogue for spiritual procession than these two (from knowledge and the love that follows knowledge), Lonergan makes a further, rather tantalizing specification. He asserts that the analogy from intellectual consciousness is best understood as an analogy from *existentially* intellectual consciousness, writing:

> It seems that the trinitarian analogy [for procession] ought to be taken from the exercise of existential autonomy. When one asks about the triune God, one is not considering God as creator or as agent, and so one is prescinding from practical autonomy. Nor is one considering God insofar as God understands and judges and loves all things, and so one is prescinding from speculative matters. But one is considering God inasmuch as God is in himself eternally constituted as triune, and so one takes one's analogy from the processions that are in accordance with the exercise of existential autonomy.[50]

Here Lonergan notes a point of dissimilarity between the created analogues for trinitarian processions. Human knowing and willing are fitting analogues because they are properly spiritual processes in which act proceeds from act. But they are not analogues for divine knowledge or divine decision, but rather for how God is "in himself eternally constituted as triune." They are, in other words, creaturely implements for gaining some imperfect but fruitful understanding of how God infinitely and eternally, knowingly and lovingly decides to be God. In other words, while we reach for understanding of God with intellectual and volitional analogues, what we reach *to* is the divine freedom itself—God's willingness to be God.

Hypothetically, then, I would have us attend to our own willingness to be our intelligent and responsible selves as an augmenting and accompanying analogue to the analogies from human knowing and loving. This is an analogy from freedom, not as achieved in determinate decisions, but as originating in us from beyond us. Thus the freedom in question must be understood as the agapeic willingness to cooperate with the erotic drive to self-transcending authenticity. And so my wager is that the psychological analogy can be made *both* to God's eternally rational and free affirmation that being God is truly good, but *also* and furthermore to God's free and loving willingness to be the God who knows and loves being God.

A systematic theology might follow Coakley's lead and put the accent on this latter, augmenting analogy from agapeically-erotic freedom, and so on God's infinitely eternal willingness to know and love being God. And this accenting is not only for the sake of multiplying the analogic means of

---

50. Lonergan, *Triune God*, 179.

imperfect, but fruitful understanding of the trinitarian mystery (to borrow Lonergan's formulation, rooted in the documents of Vatican I).[51] It could also—even especially—be for the sake of explicating Coakley's "non-linear" model of the immanent trinity. Coakley expresses her speculative concerns about linearity in theologies of the "immanent" or "ontological" trinity as follows:

> For God in Godself we must think more probingly about whether and how it is appropriate to parse the "Father" as "first" and as sole "source" of the other two "persons," as the biblical "economic" language in its linear mode clearly suggests. Even though we stand by the insistence that the economic Trinity is the "immanent (or 'ontological') Trinity," the latter (the "ontological") clearly cannot simply be reduced to the former (the "economic"): there must be that which God is which eternally "precedes" God's manifestation to us.[52]

Now, Lonergan speculates in *The Triune God: Systematics* that the "missions" or sending of the Spirit and the Son in the world are identical with the procession, but as related to an external, created term. And since it is the Father who sends the Son and the Spirit, it follows to treat of the processions on this basis in what Coakley calls a "linear" way. But if the Spirit has a prior "mission" evinced in the deep existential autonomy of all human persons, then one could generate on this basis an augmenting companion model that analogizes to divine existential autonomy. It would be a model where the Spirit is construed by analogy as what I might call a "non-primary co-source of processional circumincession." "Non-primary" because, as Coakley says,

> We would not only need to speak thus of the Son eternally coming forth from the Father "in" or "by" the Spirit (rather than the Spirit proceeding from the Father merely "and," or "through," the Son, as in classical "Western" and "Eastern" language); but, more daringly, we would also need to speak of the Father's own reception back of his status as "source" from the other two "persons," precisely via the Spirit's reflexive propulsion and the Son's creative effulgence.[53]

"Co-source," then, because of the reciprocal dependence of the Father for paternity upon not just the Son, but also the Spirit that timelessly kindles their freedom to be God. And the way in which this speculative

---

51. See Lonergan, *Triune God*, 19.
52. Coakley, *God, Sexuality, and the Self*, 332n33.
53. Coakley, *God, Sexuality, and the Self*, 333.

prioritization of the Spirit sends Coakley's language round in circles suggests the very "processional circumincession" with which the appellation concludes. It is the vitality of God's unending willingness to know and love being God. And though "non-primary co-source of processional circumincession" is, admittedly, an inelegant verbal construction, perhaps a certain rhetorical indirectness cannot be avoided if one is also seeking to avoid linearity. In any case, I think this construal can be developed in terms that do not violate the fundamental logic of Lonergan's Thomistic trinitarian theology, even if it moves into an existential key that the genre of that work (a Latin-language, scholastic manual) does preclude. At the same time, I do not think it impossible to develop this pneumatological appellation into a completely systematic trinitarian theology, although I fear it would likely prove a precarious feat of intellectual construction. But one might also, in a Pauline light, read this very theoretical weakness as a theological strength: perhaps such an intellectual instrument would be too delicate to serve as a cudgel of power and so contribute to defanging the criticisms of systematic theology that Coakley sets out (2 Cor 12:8–10)?

Finally, if we follow Coakley yet further, I would have us keep in mind that this mode of the psychological analogy would have both its existential and evidentiary ground in concrete experiences of existential transformation in prayer, especially of the silent, contemplative kind. The existential ground will be found in transformations of desire, as Coakley has it, but also of the agapeic antecedent willingness to go where that desire calls. These transformations will be lived before they are objectified in thought and objectified only "in retrospect as an undertow of existential consciousness, as a fated acceptance of a vocation to holiness, as perhaps an increasing simplicity and passivity in prayer."[54] The evidentiary ground, however, can only become available for marshalling and weighing with the interior subtlety developed through a habitual practice of interior attention. How else could one tease out in the unitary experiential flow of inner life this distinction between the eros of desiring and the agape of freedom? After all, what is given immediately is inherently indistinct. If one construes desire as propulsion the way Coakley does, then the operativity of desire will be found in the moving itself, but it can only take on theological significance as one makes a series of subtle distinctions. One must find oneself moved by another to move one's self, for that is the heteronomous source of creaturely autonomy. But also one must further distinguish the passive suffering of eros from the active expansion of agapic willingness that internally constitutes liberty.

---

54. Lonergan, *Method in Theology*, 226.

And then one must be able to affirm both the active and the passive as at once a gift and a participation.[55]

It may complicate the matter further, in practice, to find with such interior attention and subtle differentiations of experience, how the boundaries of prayer and the rest of life can nevertheless begin to blur. What antecedent willingness I discover in prayer can sustain itself beyond the silence of prayer, whether in the cognate silence of the library or in the clamor of the streets. I may find myself willing to entertain a new, challenging understanding of myself, or the world, or God. I may find myself willing to take on new endeavors and obstacles for the sake of the common good. I may find myself willing to suffer indignities and worse for the greater glory of God. As Coakley says, although the practices of silent prayer "are not primarily intended as acts of resistance to worldly oppression," she is confident "they will give courage for such" and although "nor are they therefore merely human strategies of resistance . . . they *are* acts of 'submission' to a unique power beyond human power" that alone can truly empower the powerless.[56] And it is in this way that both the transformation of human desire and the dilation of human willingness radically facilitate the ongoing, collaborative work of human liberation—in the Spirit, through conformity to the Word, to the Father.

REFERENCES

Aquinas, Thomas. *Summa Theologiae*. Translated by Fathers of the English Dominican Province. Benzinger, 1947.

Byrne, Patrick H. *The Ethics of Discernment: Lonergan's Foundation for Ethics*. Toronto: University of Toronto Press, 2016.

Coakley, Sarah. *God, Sexuality, and the Self: An Essay "On the Trinity."* Cambridge: Cambridge University Press, 2014.

Doran, Robert M. *Theology and the Dialectics of History*. Toronto: University of Toronto Press, 1990.

Heaps, Jonathan R. *The Ambiguity of Being: Lonergan and the Problems of the Supernatural*. Washington, DC: Catholic University of America Press, 2023.

Levering, Matthew. *Engaging the Doctrine of the Holy Spirit: Love and Gift in the Trinity and the Church*. Ada, MI: Baker Academic, 2016.

Lonergan, Bernard J. F. "Belief: Today's Issue." In *A Second Collection,* edited by Robert M. Doran and John D. Dadosky, 75–85. Toronto: University of Toronto Press, 2016.

---

55. For a highly detailed retrieval of Lonergan's Thomist metaphysics of divine and human cooperation, see Heaps, *Ambiguity of Being*.

56. Coakley, *God, Sexuality, and the Self,* 54 (emphasis added).

———. *Insight: A Study of Human Understanding*. Edited by Robert M. Doran and Frederick E. Crowe. Toronto: University of Toronto Press, 2000.

———. *Method in Theology*. Edited by Robert M. Doran and John D. Dadosky. Toronto: University of Toronto Press, 2017.

———. "Self-Transcendence: Intellectual, Moral, Religious." In *Philosophical and Theological Papers, 1965–1980*, edited by Robert M. Doran and Robert C. Croken, 313–31. Toronto: University of Toronto Press, 2004.

———. *The Triune God: Systematics*. Edited by Robert M. Doran and H. Daniel Monsour. Translated by Michael G. Shields. Toronto: University of Toronto Press, 2007.

———. *Verbum: Word and Idea in Aquinas*. Edited by Frederick E. Crowe and Robert M. Doran. Toronto: Toronto University Press, 1997.

PRACTICE

8

The Liberating Transformation of Mystical Eros

Amy Maxey

During a recent seminar on medieval women mystics, my students were challenged to examine their presuppositions about mysticism and its relationship to Christian discipleship. While they expected to find accounts of visions and directives for contemplation, my students were not prepared for the depth of these women's commitments to active lives of service, whether through quotidian living in intentional communities, tending plague victims and societal outcasts, or intervening in ecclesial and state affairs. My students were struck by the bold ways in which these women describe the dynamism of eros between their souls and God as the wellspring of their energies to be Christ in the world. In deed and in thought, these women integrated love of God and love of neighbor to develop authentic Christian spiritualities that resonate across the ages. As a constant refrain of our discussions, my students considered how these rich, practice-based theologies could be made more available for contemporary Christians who are seeking to relate their eros for God, as witnessed by the great mystics of the tradition, to the pressing demands of Christian discipleship in a contemporary world that hungers for justice and human flourishing.

Our semester-long conversations coincide with the concerns that have sparked the recent turn to contemplation in contemporary Christian theology. This trend reflects a renewed appreciation for the ways in which contemplative practices of prayer, in all their rich diversity, gradually transform the human person and open new possibilities for living in the world. The category of the "mystical-political" has proven generative for reflection on the intrinsic relation between contemplation and action while resisting the hierarchization of these categories as modes of life. Extricating the concept of mysticism from its modern associations with esoterism and paranormal religious experience allows more traditional connotations of contemplation and the encompassing spiritual life to reemerge as the salient dimensions of mysticism for Christian living.[1] Recent rehabilitations of the desirous, erotic dimensions of Christian mysticism emphasize the dynamic relationality between the divine and the human.[2] Typically in Christian mystical writings, the soul's eros for God is cast in individualistic terms such that a spiritually-sublimated eros enables the soul to transcend contingent sediments of human existence by ascending to union with the divine.[3] This Neoplatonic heritage has come under critique as theologians have reimagined the theological category of eros to affirm the materiality of Christian life and to expand mystical eros beyond a binary relation of contemplative-and-divine.[4] Bringing a revitalized understanding of mystical eros to bear upon the category of the "mystical-political" prompts theologians to consider how mystical eros transforms the Christian's freedom to act in the world.

In this vein, this contribution proposes an account of mystical consciousness animated by mystical eros which correlates the contemplative's interior transformation to the expansion of her freedom in a mystical-political register. In the first part of this chapter, I place historian Bernard McGinn's understanding of mystical consciousness in dialogue with womanist theologian M. Shawn Copeland's rehabilitation of eros to render a notion of Christian mystical consciousness as erotically motivated and intrinsically related to the social. I contend that contemplative practices mediate mystical consciousness to the subject so that she may self-consciously appropriate mystical eros. In the second part, I situate mystical consciousness and its accompanying contemplative practices within the development of Christian authenticity as articulated by theologian Bernard Lonergan. In continuing dialogue with Copeland, I argue that the transformations of mystical eros not only render a new horizon of values for the subject formed by contemplative praxis but also empower her to freely opt for the concrete good of others in *imitatio Christi* as an authentic disciple.

[1]. A classic modern account of mysticism is James, *Varieties of Religious Experience*. For a helpful contextualization of James, see Schmidt, "Making of Modern 'Mysticism.'"

[2]. For example, see Coakley, *God, Sexuality, and the Self*.

[3]. For a classic account of this Neoplatonic sense of eros, see Dionysius, "Divine Names," 81–83.

[4]. For a variety of such attempts, see Burrus and Keller, *Toward a Theology of Eros*.

MYSTICAL CONSCIOUSNESS AND EROS

Informed by a lifetime of study of Western Christian mystical traditions,[5] McGinn has heuristically characterized mysticism as the element of religion which concerns the preparation for, the attainment of, and the lived effects resulting from mystical consciousness of the mediated immediacy of the presence of God.[6] McGinn resources technical language and conceptual scaffolding from Lonergan's account of intentionality and "interiority"[7] which, in addition to affording precision to terms, "emphasizes the *entire process* of human intentionality and self-presence, rather than just an originating pure feeling, sensation, or experience easily separable from subsequent acts of thinking, loving, and deciding."[8] McGinn's understanding of mysticism commends itself to conceiving of contemplation and its accompanying practices as privileged conditions in which mystical consciousness arises, develops, and transforms the Christian subject. By constructively developing the latent erotic undertones of McGinn's framework in dialogue with Copeland, I will characterize mystical consciousness as animated by a dynamism of mystical eros between God and the human person which is intrinsically related to the manner in which the Christian lives out an embodied spirituality within her social worlds.

---

5. Spanning seven volumes, McGinn's *The Presence of God* constitutes a watershed history of Western Christian mysticism. For an overview, see Arblaster and Faesen, "Bernard McGinn's *Presence of God*."

6. This definition, as I have articulated it here, draws from McGinn's "General Introduction" to *The Presence of God* in McGinn, *Foundations of Mysticism*, xvii, and "Mystical Consciousness," 47–53.

7. Space precludes giving an exhaustive rehearsal of Lonergan's account of human knowing and interiority. In sum, he conceives of human knowing as a self-transcending, formally dynamic structure consisting of the concatenation of acts of experience, understanding, and judgment. Coming to know leads to choosing values to pursue in one's lived life and, upon the transformation of religious conversion, to discerning how to live in the love of God. This realm of human interiority is constituted by the spontaneous occurrence of such acts, but it can become known and its processes differentiated, which invites a person to affirm and appropriate herself as a knower. A full treatment of Lonergan's cognitional theory can be found in Lonergan, *Insight*. For a summary, see Lonergan, "Cognitional Structure." For a summary of the turn to interiority and differentiation of consciousness, see Lonergan, *Method in Theology*, 80–82.

8. McGinn, "Mystical Consciousness," 46.

Mystical Consciousness and Contemplation

In McGinn's account, mystical consciousness is a development of religious consciousness which is marked by a distinctive conscious intentionality and self-consciousness due to the presence of God.[9] Unlike the ordinary experience of consciousness—which entails both consciousness of intended objects and conscious self-presence immanent to the subject's operations of perceiving, knowing, and acting—mystical consciousness is "consciousness-*beyond*" ordinary modes of consciousness, or "meta-consciousness," a neologism McGinn takes from Thomas Merton.[10] In a dynamic manner, God's presence transforms every level of conscious intentionality, meaning that God is both immanently present to human intentional acts (in a way analogous to the subject's immanent presence in these acts) and present as the transcendent horizon towards which these acts are oriented.[11] McGinn utilizes Lonergan's terminology of "mediated immediacy" to specify the manner of God's presence to the subject in mystical consciousness. Typically, human subjectivity is immediate to subjective acts as an unthematized undergirding presence, but this immediacy of self-presence can be mediated inasmuch as the subject objectifies herself as an "I," that is, as a self-conscious identity overlaid with the mediating concepts that enable the subject to know herself as such.[12] Yet in discrete moments where the subject encounters the presence of God, the mystic "drops the constructs of culture and the whole complicated mass of mediating operations to return to a new, mediated immediacy of his subjectivity reaching for God," meaning that the immediacy of one's subjectivity is rendered perceptible through its thrust to the divine.[13] As McGinn develops Lonergan's term, because this experience of oneself as a transcendental subject is conscious it can "become known, but only in an indirect way as a tendency or drive, not as something capable of conceptualization, because of its unlimited and unrestricted nature."[14] Because God's presence is immediately entwined with the subject's conscious intentionality, the subject is aware of God's co-presence to her subjectivity inasmuch as she is self-aware, and her degree of self-awareness mediates the immediate co-presence of God. In McGinn's

---

9. For Lonergan's account of consciousness, see *Insight*, 344–52. For his account of religious consciousness, see *Method in Theology*, 96–120.

10. McGinn, "Mystical Consciousness," 47.

11. McGinn, "Mystical Consciousness," 47.

12. Lonergan, *Method in Theology*, 74–75.

13. Lonergan, *Method in Theology*, 30.

14. McGinn, "Mystical Consciousness," 51.

words, this experience "can be expressed as a state of loving attraction and mental awareness in the face of the divine mystery."[15]

Notably, "mystical consciousness" in McGinn's terminology does not relate solely to the intentional level of experience. It is not merely awareness of a novel perception of God as an "object"; neither is it a static state of consciousness conceived as some kind of subject-position to occupy. Rather, in McGinn's words, mystical consciousness is a graced elevation of consciousness which "restructures the subject's drive to understand, affirm, and live out the gift received," and these components collectively constitute the effects of mystical consciousness on the subject.[16] The mediated immediacy of the gift of God's love is pre-reflective and pre-conceptual, and though the subject is incapable of distinguishing knowing from loving at the empirical level of conscious intentionality,

> differentiation (not separation) between knowing and loving begins as the subject moves from the world of immediacy to the mediation of meaning by means of conscious acts of insight, judgment, and decision, acts that are self-conscious and therefore potentially open to self-reflection.[17]

Thus, mystical consciousness animates the mode of conscious intentionality that prompts the mystic to probe her "mystical experience" in order to arrive at a deeper understanding of it (as evidenced, for example, in Julian of Norwich's developed understanding of the Parable of the Lord and Servant to the "Long Text" of her *Showings*).[18] Moreover, mystical consciousness enables the subject to welcome the transformations God's grace engenders, appropriate as one's own a new horizon of ultimate values, and concretely live the Christian life of charity (as evidenced, for example, in Hadewijch of Antwerp's teaching of what it means to "live Christ in his humanity").[19] Mystical consciousness in its fullest realization is the subjective correlate to the intellectual and affective appropriation of God's presence through grace, involving both ordinary and transcendental acts of understanding, loving, and deciding.[20]

---

15. McGinn, "Mystical Consciousness," 50.

16. McGinn, "Mystical Consciousness," 50–51.

17. McGinn, "Mystical Consciousness," 52.

18. Julian relates that this "parable" was part of her original visionary experience, but she did not initially understand its meaning and did not relay it in the original "Short Text" of the *Showings*. After twenty years of reflection, she revised and lengthened her work to include both the parable and its meaning. See Julian, *Showings*, 269–70.

19. See Letter 6 in Hadewijch, *Complete Works*, 56–63.

20. McGinn clarifies that these acts are "transcendentalized" forms of understanding,

McGinn's framework for understanding mystical consciousness offers rich grounds for embedding mystical consciousness within contemplative practices. In a basic sense, contemplative practices prepare a person for mystical consciousness. Inasmuch as the practice of contemplation turns the contemplative's attention inwards, it enables the contemplative to attend to both her desire for God and its graced fulfillment, as well as to have insights into the divine and into herself as transformed by divine presence. Sustained attention to these realities is often stymied by the demands of living, but contemplative practice, by momentarily withdrawing the person from the dramatic flow of life, opens the space for these subterranean elements to come to conscious awareness. In Lonergan's phrasing, being drawn up into the divine life is immediate to the reality of being Christian, but the practice of prayer mediates this reality, modulating it from "being a sort of vegetative living to a conscious living" so that "this life of grace within us can become a habitual conscious living" in ways both spontaneous and deliberately chosen.[21]

In these terms, contemplative prayer mediates the contemplative's mystical consciousness to herself. Contemplative practices are not merely activities which provide space for encountering God; they are also the arenas in which the spiritually adept cultivate the inner intellectual and affective habits which increase the likelihood of grasping insights into the spiritual life and being transformed by them. McGinn's framework contextualizes and integrates discrete contemplative-mystical experiences and insights within an encompassing spirituality, that is, within the inherent dynamism of spiritual and personal development. Within this paradigm, the embodied, ritualistic, and culturally-conditioned dimensions of contemplative practices are not absolutely transcended upon reaching a rarefied "mystical experience." On the contrary, they become essential components of the mystic's mediation of God's immediate presence to herself, by which the phenomenon as a whole becomes, in a way, intelligible as an encounter with divine mystery and love which opens new possibilities for future Christian living.[22] Contemplation expands the mystical encounter with God to bear on the "everyday."

---

loving, and acting in that they "reflect the presence of the divine by way of what Merton called meta-consciousness" (McGinn, "Mystical Consciousness," 51).

21. Lonergan, "Mediation of Christ in Prayer," 179.

22. I say "in a way" to indicate that the intelligibility which emerges is not complete, as exhaustive knowledge of God exceeds the creature's capacities. I maintain with McGinn that there is a distinctive intentionality to this encounter which preserves divine mystery. He warns that if subsequent intellective acts "reduce God to a specific content of thought or object of love, that is . . . affirm the final validity of any idea of God, such a

McGinn's insistence on the interpenetration of the intellective and affective dimensions of mystical consciousness provides grounds for developing the erotic dimensions of mystical consciousness in a manner congruent with the ways in which mystical writings testify to the desire for God.[23] Although McGinn's account does not explicitly draw attention to the connection, Lonergan's cognitional theory is grounded in desire, as the "eros of the mind" drives conscious activity to know, which is enfolded within the broader self-transcendence of the "eros of the human spirit" ordered to vertical finality.[24] Upon conversion, religious consciousness engenders an erotically-motivated dynamism of love and knowledge: "From an experience of love focused on mystery there wells forth a longing for knowledge, while love itself is a longing for union; so for the lover of the unknown beloved the concept of bliss is knowledge of [God] and union with [God]."[25] The eros of the spirit is amplified rather than sated in mystical consciousness, as suggested by Gregory of Nyssa's characterization of *epektasis* as the unending desire for God.[26] This desirous dynamism "remains within subjectivity as a vector, a fateful call to a dreaded holiness."[27] Mystical consciousness elevates the subject's eros for God so that she may proceed unhindered into deeper intimacy with the divine beloved, and contemplative practices mediate this erotic intimacy in such a way that it transforms her conscious living.

Erotic Modulations from M. Shawn Copeland

To enrich this underdeveloped dimension of mystical eros in such a way as to open it to a mystical-political horizon, I turn to M. Shawn Copeland's theological rehabilitation of "eros" adapted from Black feminist essayist and poet Audre Lorde. Positively characterizing eros as "a resource within each of us that lies in a deeply female and spiritual plane," Lorde reclaims the erotic as "the power of our unexpressed or unrecognized feeling."[28] Patri-

---

move would abandon the realm of the mystical and threaten to subvert the very ground of its distinctive intentionality" (McGinn, "Mystical Consciousness," 52–53).

23. For overviews, see McGinn, "Love, Knowledge, and Mystical Union"; "Language of Love"; "Tropics of Desire."

24. On the "eros of the mind" and vertical finality, see especially Lonergan, *Insight*, 97, 497–99, respectively. On the "eros of the human spirit," see Lonergan, *Method in Theology*, 16, 228, 390.

25. Lonergan, *Method in Theology*, 106.

26. See, for example, Gregory, *Life of Moses*, 115–16.

27. Lonergan, "Self-Transcendence," 328.

28. It seems to me that Lorde's use of "female" is not intended in an exclusively biological sense. Rather, Lorde reclaims the term from patriarchal paradigms that have

archal society, fearing this power, denigrates the erotic by eliding it with the pornographic, which reduces eros to "plasticized sensation."[29] In Lorde's rehabilitation, erotic feeling mediates the subject to herself, becoming "the nursemaid of all our deepest knowledge" inasmuch as eros awakens the subject to her desire for her self-realization and the fullness of life.[30] Eros constitutes, in the words of Joy Bostic, an "epistemological reservoir" from which the subject affirms her passion for life.[31] Reclaiming her erotic feeling heightens the subject's self-awareness, and she is empowered to become a more conscious knower, lover, and actor who is able to join her self-empathy with empathy for the world.[32]

By enabling the human person to consciously claim herself, eros frees the subject from coercive self-narratives imposed from without which would make her impotent. Instead, she becomes "responsible to [herself] in the deepest sense" as she ceases "being satisfied with suffering and self-negation, and with the numbness which so often seems like their only alternative in our society."[33] Eros sets a horizon for the subject's becoming that is charged with ethical importance, "for having experienced the fullness of this depth of feeling and recognizing its power, in honor and self-respect we can require no less of ourselves."[34] Ultimately, by awakening a sense of responsibility to oneself, eros capacitates the subject for feeling a wider sense of communal responsibility, leading the self outside of a narrow narcissism to solidarity with others, as "our acts against oppression become integral with self, motivated and empowered from within."[35]

Copeland theologically appropriates Lorde's thought to articulate Jesus of Nazareth's eros as the energy and joy with which he "gave his body, his very self, to and for others, to and for the Other."[36] This christological gloss grounds Copeland's articulation of "eros as fully embodied spirituality," where eros "suffuses and sustains depth or value-laden experiences and relationships that emerge whenever we 'shar[e] deeply any pursuit [whether]

---

pejoratively associated the erotic with the feminine. Lorde's essay effects a valorization of both. Lorde, *Sister Outsider*, 53.

29. Lorde, *Sister Outsider*, 54.
30. Lorde, *Sister Outsider*, 56.
31. Bostic, "Flesh That Dances," 280.
32. Lorde, *Sister Outsider*, 54.
33. Lorde, *Sister Outsider*, 58.
34. Lorde, *Sister Outsider*, 54.
35. Lorde, *Sister Outsider*, 58.
36. Copeland, *Enfleshing Freedom*, 50.

physical, emotional, psychic, or intellectual with another person.'"[37] The eros of embodied spirituality prompts Christians to affirm the goodness of the other and empowers Christians to stand with those whose lives are stifled by the powers of the world which oppressively regulate the other.[38] Courtney Bryant characterizes this dimension of Copeland's thought as "erotic defiance" inasmuch as "the erotic arouses resistance" to "all that seeks to constrain the fullness of their being."[39] For Copeland, Christ's eros liberates the body and human desire from "cloying common-sense satisfaction, misuse, and disrespect," in order to cultivate authentic love.[40] Jesus mediates this embodied spirituality in word and in deed, for "in Jesus, God manifests an eros for us *as we are* in our marked particularity."[41]

Modulating Lorde's and Copeland's notions of eros into a Christian mystical key and integrating it with McGinn's understanding of mystical consciousness offers a holistic vision of the manner of erotic transformation engendered by the contemplative encounter of God's love. From Lorde comes a notion of eros that resists reduction to either an unreflective passion or entirely spiritualized affectivity. Rather, eros empowers a person to take account of herself as an actor in her world who has responsibilities to others. Crucially, for both Lorde and McGinn's Lonerganian infrastructure, eros is correlated with a feeling of heightened self-consciousness that must be appropriated in a decisive manner. For McGinn, this interior heightening of consciousness orients the person toward the divine while for Lorde it orients the person toward the embodied, historical, and social dimensions of human life, but for both thinkers, one orientation is not competitive with the other. By fusing their thought together, the transcendental orientation of mystical eros can be conceived of in terms that do not exclude the material, contingent, and communal dimensions of human living but instead invite the person transformed by mystical eros to enter deeply into her socio-historical reality. Copeland's christological appropriation of this notion explicitly expands the category towards the transcendental horizon of the good while maintaining a connection to the concrete relations among finite beings. Christ's eros for human beings both mediates God's mysterious eros for the world and models the ways in which the conscious self-appropriation of mystical eros orients human life to love of God and of neighbor (Matt 22:37–40). Mystical eros, informed by the depth of womanist reflection,

---

37. Copeland, *Enfleshing Freedom*, 50, quoting Lorde, *Sister Outsider*, 56.
38. Copeland, *Enfleshing Freedom*, 51–52.
39. Bryant, *Erotic Defiance*, 59.
40. Copeland, *Enfleshing Freedom*, 70.
41. Copeland, *Enfleshing Freedom*, 70.

deepens appreciation for the awe-inspiring gift of life, defies the powers of the world which seek to suppress human flourishing, and empowers the Christian who has appropriated this transformative eros to work for the liberation of the oppressed.

MYSTICAL CONSCIOUSNESS, CHRISTIAN AUTHENTICITY, AND FREEDOM

By melding McGinn's understanding of mystical consciousness with Copeland's rehabilitation of eros, I propose an account of mystical consciousness as erotically motivated and intrinsically related to the social. In sum, mystical eros animates the process by which the contemplative mediates her encounter with divine love to conscious awareness, self-consciously appropriates the values of divine love and liberation, and freely acts to realize these values in her social worlds. By situating this account within Lonergan's account of Christian authenticity, I will indicate how, in a mutually augmenting manner, contemplative practice expands the possibilities for the Christian to exercise her freedom, for new possibilities for authentically living a life of love emerge with deeper intimacy with God and more thoroughgoing transformations of mystical consciousness. Continuing in dialogue with Copeland's mystical-political vision, I argue that the transformations of mystical eros render expanded horizons for authentic Christian freedom enacted through Christian discipleship.

The Practice of Contemplation and Christian Authenticity

For Lonergan, authenticity is the human person's "deepest need and most prized achievement," as it is nothing less than the human person's concrete actualization of herself as a self-conscious, self-transcending subject oriented towards the true, good, and loveable.[42] Attained through the confluence of genuine attention, intelligence, reasonableness, and responsibility,[43] authenticity is always a precarious affair marked by a dialectical tension with inauthenticity, for development in authenticity brings to light ways in which the subject remains inauthentic, which spurs deeper self-discernment and reveals possibilities for attaining further degrees of authenticity.[44] The

---

42. Lonergan, *Method in Theology*, 238.
43. Lonergan, *Method in Theology*, 248.
44. Lonergan, *Method in Theology*, 106.

subject discovers her moral values and responsibilities through engaging concrete questions of how to act in the world, because in exercising one's freedom "one not only chooses between courses of action but also thereby makes oneself an authentic human being or an unauthentic one."[45]

Though finite and constrained by the given exigencies of the world, the human person's exercise of freedom in the course of her development as a rational, emotional, and conscientious person conditions how her development as a subject unfolds (either authentically or unauthentically) and which habits (or vices) are cultivated, thereby also conditioning the possibilities for her future exercise of freedom.[46] The moral questions faced by the human person are ineluctably concrete, regarding which actions benefit her social worlds and which choices contribute to her development of authenticity as the lived project of her life. Indeed, as one grows in age and agency, human freedom is given fuller reign in its "thrust toward authenticity," such that "we discover for ourselves that our choosing affects ourselves no less than the chosen or rejected object, and that it is up to each of us to decide for himself what he is to make of himself."[47]

To be authentically responsible as a moral subject, then, is to choose the good that is authentically discerned as such, regardless of any material loss or benefit one personally stands to receive, and to remain faithful to the choice. Upon religious conversion, the ordinary manner of achieving authenticity is elevated by the gift of God's love, which transfigures the conscious horizons of the subject's knowing and loving.[48] The gift of God's love, which can become a consciously appropriated, unrestricted, and permanent state of being in love with God,[49] opens new possibilities to respond to God's love by authentically and freely integrating one's patterns of life with the values of divine love and seeking to know the beloved.[50] Born of intimacy with God, Christian authenticity is lived out as "a love of others that does not shrink from self-sacrifice and suffering," for Christ is the model of authentic Christian living.[51]

Contemplation is a potent spiritual praxis for developing Christian authenticity, for by entering the space of prayer, the Christian encounters the

45. Lonergan, *Method in Theology*, 39.
46. Lonergan, "*Existenz* and *Aggiornamento*," 224.
47. Lonergan, *Method in Theology*, 225.
48. Lonergan, *Method in Theology*, 102.
49. See Lonergan, "Philosophy of God, and Theology," 193. See also Blackwood, *And Hope Does Not Disappoint*, which charts the development of Lonergan's later thought on the fifth level of intentionality.
50. Lonergan, *Method in Theology*, 112.
51. Lonergan, *Method in Theology*, 272.

divine beloved in an intimate, interpersonal, transformative manner which may develop into mystical consciousness. Inasmuch as contemplative practices mediate the gracious transformations of mystical eros, they enable the Christian to self-consciously appropriate the horizon of divine values and to choose to act in accord with the ultimate value of divine love. Contemplative practices provide time and space outside of the flow of dramatic living for the Christian to discern how to exercise her freedom in the concrete and unique circumstances in which her authenticity is to be realized. The response to God's grace is an exercise of freedom that is ineluctably personal, for no one can make such a choice on behalf of another.

Spiritual practices of self-discernment, such as the Daily Examen, prompt such discernment to proceed authentically in honest self-transparency such as that nurtured by the manner of erotic self-knowledge heralded by Lorde. With this embodied erotic valence, contemplation as a dynamism of eros is not oriented merely "inward" and "upward" but, additionally, "outward," extending to the ways in which the person lives in the world. In this vein, it is important to recover the insights from the mystical voices from the tradition who emphasize the intrinsic relation of contemplation and the virtuous life of Christian charity,[52] for these are the lived effects of mystical consciousness as indicated by McGinn's paradigm. Habitually practiced, contemplative prayer sustains the development of Christian authenticity and freedom. Attaining further degrees of authenticity deepens contemplative practice and expands the possibilities for freely choosing a life of self-sacrificial love.

Transformed Freedom and Embodied Christian Spirituality

Freely choosing to give mystical eros full reign in directing the development of Christian authenticity leads to concretely enacted Christian discipleship. Contemplative appropriation of mystical eros capacitates the Christian to make the decision to live a life of agapeic love. I return to Copeland's thought at the close of this essay to characterize how the contemplative increase of discerning self-knowledge makes the subject more consciously responsible for her actions in the world.[53] Copeland offers a vision of this "mystical-political way":

---

52. This dimension of Christian mysticism was underappreciated in modern accounts of mysticism that emphasized "mystical experience." For one example of mystical doctrine on virtue integrated with contemplation, see Ruusbroec, "Spiritual Espousals."

53. The return to Copeland is facilitated, in part, by her appropriation of Lonergan's

> To live as Jesus's disciple means to live at the disposal of the cross—exposed, vulnerable, open to the wisdom and power and love of God. Lived response to his call requires a praxis of solidarity and compassion as well as surrender to the startling embrace of Divine Love.[54]

Recalling Catherine of Siena's language of "infinite desire," Copeland affirms that, in its mystical dimension, the cross "hallows in the disciple a kind of infinite desire and capacity for life in and with God."[55] In other words, mystical eros expands the horizon of possibilities for authentically exercising one's freedom as a disciple. Meditating on Copeland's identification of the locus of discipleship as "standing at the foot of the cross" and Simone Weil's conception of prayer as attention, Nancy Pineda-Madrid observes that "standing requires attention suffused with desire for God."[56] In light of womanist conceptions of eros, this standing-at-attention is also suffused with desire for self-integrity and for human flourishing, both of which are desires of God, poured out in love at the cross.

Copeland insists that authentic Christian discipleship "calls not merely for planning, self-examen, sacrifice, and personal resolve but for love unmeasured, unstinting, overflowing, fearless, passionate."[57] The deeper one's intimacy with Christ, the deeper one's participation in the love which animated his embodied spirituality. Christ himself "incarnates the freedom and destiny of discipleship"[58] as "the measure or standard for our exercise of erotic power and freedom in the service of the reign of God and against empire."[59] As embodied erotic spirituality, standing with the crucified motivates the choice to stand with the crucified people of the world. Christian spiritual practices "till, nurture, and water the fragile soil of our souls" so that "authentic love reveals itself concretely in option and action" by engendering "the radical disposal of self for, on behalf of, and with the other and those others whom society tolerates, despises, and excludes."[60]

---

cognitive theory to give an account of womanist subjects. See especially Copeland, "Thinking Margin." For an overview of Copeland's use of Lonergan, see Gray, "Significance and Singularity."

54. Copeland, *Knowing Christ Crucified*, 109. For an overview of Copeland's understanding of discipleship, see Hinsdale, "Enacted Discipleship."

55. Copeland, *Knowing Christ Crucified*, 118. This theme prominently inaugurates Catherine's mystical writing. See Catherine, *Dialogue*, 25–27.

56. Pineda-Madrid, "Standing at the Foot of the Cross," 118.

57. Copeland, *Knowing Christ Crucified*, 118.

58. Copeland, *Knowing Christ Crucified*, 116.

59. Copeland, *Enfleshing Freedom*, 51.

60. Copeland, "Turning Theology," 772–73.

These marginalized others—Copeland's theology consistently identifies poor Black women—constitute the communities in which the social dimensions of erotic responsibility concretely take shape and in which Christian freedom is actually exercised. In a mystical-political vision, the dynamism of mystical eros continues to simmer even in "impasse" situations,[61] deepening self-knowledge and making possible the decision to work towards a future that one cannot anticipate in the face of seemingly insurmountable social structures of oppression such as patriarchy, racism, and global economies of extreme inequalities. On the voyage of life, we are invited, in Copeland's words, to "recognize, acknowledge, and accept God's great and gracious desire for us—the Divine Desire who lights the dark night of our world and guides our rowing to open arms of Holy Mystery."[62] For the Christian who stands in the face of divine love and mystery, there opens a broad horizon of freedom which makes concrete acts of love and resistance real options.

In the mystical-political paradigm I have proposed, the Christian transformed by mystical eros who self-consciously discovers this transformation through contemplative practice is invited and empowered to choose freely the path of Christian discipleship. Mystical consciousness is not the beginning of the spiritual journey, nor its ultimate telos, but rather a mode of conscious intentionality heightened through contemplation in which Christian authenticity is enacted, cultivated, and allowed to "seep into" the rest of Christian living like fertilizing nutrients. As such, this paradigm brings contemplation and freedom together to conceive of Christian spirituality as the erotically-motivated, freely chosen, and embodied working-out of Christian authenticity.

REFERENCES

Arblaster, John, and Rob Faesen. "Bernard McGinn's *Presence of God*: The Project That Made Mystical Theology Respectable." *Louvain Studies* 41.2 (2018) 173–95.

Blackwood, Jeremy. *And Hope Does Not Disappoint: Love, Grace, and Subjectivity in the Work of Bernard J. F. Lonergan, SJ*. Milwaukee, WI: Marquette University Press, 2017.

Bostic, Joy R. "'Flesh That Dances': A Theology of Sexuality and the Spirit in Toni Morrison's *Beloved*." In *The Embrace of Eros: Bodies, Desires, and Sexuality in*

---

[61]. See especially FitzGerald, "Impasse and Dark Night"; "From Impasse to Prophetic Hope." For FitzGerald's influence on Copeland, see the 2016 Mary Milligan lecture given at Loyola Marymount University, published as Copeland, *Discipleship in a Time of Impasse*.

[62]. Copeland, "Introduction," 14.

Christianity, edited by Margaret D. Kamitsuka, 277–95. Minneapolis, MN: Fortress, 2010.

Bryant, Courtney. *Erotic Defiance: Womanism, Freedom, and Resistance*. Minneapolis, MN: Fortress, 2023.

Burrus, Virginia, and Catherine Keller, eds. *Toward a Theology of Eros: Transfiguring Passion at the Limits of Discipline*. New York: Fordham University Press, 2006.

Catherine of Siena. *The Dialogue*. Translated by Suzanne Noffke. New York: Paulist, 1980.

Coakley, Sarah. *God, Sexuality, and the Self: An Essay "On the Trinity."* Cambridge: Cambridge University Press, 2013.

Copeland, M. Shawn. *Discipleship in a Time of Impasse*. Los Angeles, CA: Marymount Institute and Tsehai, 2016.

———. *Enfleshing Freedom: Body, Race, and Being*. 2nd ed. Minneapolis, MN: Fortress, 2023.

———. "Introduction: Rowing Toward God in an Anguished World." In *Desire, Darkness, and Hope: Theology in a Time of Impasse: Engaging the Thought of Constance FitzGerald, OCD*, edited by Laurie Cassidy and M. Shawn Copeland, 1–20. Collegeville, MN: Liturgical, 2021.

———. *Knowing Christ Crucified: The Witness of African American Religious Experience*. Maryknoll, NY: Orbis, 2018.

———. "A Thinking Margin: The Womanist Movement as Critical Cognitive Praxis." In *Deeper Shades of Purple: Womanism in Religion and Society*, edited by Stacy Floyd-Thomas, 226–35. New York: New York University Press, 2006.

———. "Turning Theology: A Proposal." *Theological Studies* 80.4 (2019) 753–73.

Dionysius the Areopagite. "The Divine Names." In *Pseudo-Dionysius: The Complete Works*, 47–131. Translated by Paul Rorem and Colm Luibhéid. New York: Paulist, 1987.

FitzGerald, Constance, OCD. "From Impasse to Prophetic Hope: Crisis of Memory." In *Desire, Darkness, and Hope: Theology in a Time of Impasse: Engaging the Thought of Constance FitzGerald, OCD*, edited by Laurie Cassidy and M. Shawn Copeland, 425–53. Collegeville, MN: Liturgical, 2021.

———. "Impasse and Dark Night." In *Desire, Darkness, and Hope: Theology in a Time of Impasse: Engaging the Thought of Constance FitzGerald, OCD*, edited by Laurie Cassidy and M. Shawn Copeland, 77–102. Collegeville, MN: Liturgical, 2021.

Gray, Susan L. "The Significance and Singularity of M. Shawn Copeland's Methodology." In *Enfleshing Theology: Embodiment, Discipleship, and Politics in the Work of M. Shawn Copeland*, edited by Robert J. Rivera and Michele Saracino, 167–83. Lanham, MD: Lexington/Fortress Academic, 2018.

Gregory of Nyssa. *The Life of Moses*. Translated by Abraham J. Malherbe and Everett Ferguson. Classics of Western Spirituality. New York: Paulist, 1978.

Hadewijch of Antwerp. *The Complete Works*. Translated by Mother Columba Hart. Classics of Western Spirituality. New York: Paulist, 1980.

Hinsdale, Mary Ann, IHM. "'Enacted Discipleship' as Christian Anthropology." In *Enfleshing Theology: Embodiment, Discipleship, and Politics in the Work of M.*

Shawn Copeland, edited by Robert J. Rivera and Michele Saracino, 97–113. Lanham, MD: Lexington/Fortress Academic, 2018.

James, William. *The Varieties of Religious Experience: A Study in Human Nature.* Edited by Matthew Bradley. Oxford: Oxford University Press, 2012.

Julian of Norwich. *Showings.* Classics of Western Spirituality. New York: Paulist, 1978.

Lonergan, Bernard. "Cognitional Structure." In *Collection*, edited by Frederick E. Crowe and Robert M. Doran, 205–21. Collected Works of Bernard Lonergan 4. Toronto: University of Toronto Press, 2005.

———. "*Existenz* and *Aggiornamento*." In *Collection*, edited by Frederick E. Crowe and Robert M. Doran, 222–31. Collected Works of Bernard Lonergan 4. Toronto: University of Toronto Press, 2005.

———. *Insight: A Study of Human Understanding.* Edited by Frederick E. Crowe and Robert M. Doran. 5th ed. Collected Works of Bernard Lonergan 3. Toronto: University of Toronto Press, 1992.

———. "The Mediation of Christ in Prayer." In *Philosophical and Theological Papers, 1958–1964*, edited by Robert C. Croken et al., 160–82. Collected Works of Bernard Lonergan 6. Toronto: University of Toronto Press, 1996.

———. *Method in Theology.* Edited by Robert M. Doran and John D. Dadosky. Collected Works of Bernard Lonergan 14. Toronto: University of Toronto Press, 2007.

———. "Philosophy of God, and Theology." In *Philosophical and Theological Papers 1965–1980*, edited by Robert C. Croken and Robert M. Doran, 157–218. 5th ed. Collected Works of Bernard Lonergan 17. Toronto: University of Toronto Press, 2004.

———. "Self-Transcendence: Intellectual, Moral, Religious." In *Philosophical and Theological Papers 1965–1980*, edited by Robert C. Croken and Robert M. Doran, 313–31. 5th ed. Collected Works of Bernard Lonergan 17. Toronto: University of Toronto Press, 2004.

Lorde, Audre. *Sister Outsider.* Berkeley: Crossing, 2007.

McGinn, Bernard. *The Foundations of Mysticism: Origins to the Fifth Century.* Vol. 1 of *The Presence of God.* New York: Crossroad, 1991.

———. "The Language of Love in Christian and Jewish Mysticism." In *Mysticism and Language*, edited by Steven T. Katz, 202–35. Oxford: Oxford University Press, 1992.

———. "Love, Knowledge, and Mystical Union in Western Christianity: Twelfth to Sixteenth Centuries." *Church History* 56.1 (1987) 7–24.

———. "Mystical Consciousness: A Modest Proposal." *Spiritus* 8.1 (2008) 44–63.

———. "Tropics of Desire: Mystical Interpretation of the Song of Songs." In *That Others May Know and Love: Essays in Honor of Zachary Hayes, OFM: Franciscan, Educator, Scholar*, edited by Michael F. Cusato and F. Edward Coughlin, 133–58. St. Bonaventure, NY: Franciscan Institute, 1997.

Pineda-Madrid, Nancy. "Standing at the Foot of the Cross." In *Enfleshing Theology: Embodiment, Discipleship, and Politics in the Work of M. Shawn Copeland*, edited by Robert J. Rivera and Michele Saracino, 115–28. Lanham, MD: Lexington/Fortress Academic, 2018.

Ruusbroec, John van. "The Spiritual Espousals." In *John Ruusbroec: The Spiritual Espousals and Other Works*, 54–66. Translated by James A. Wiseman. Classics of Western Spirituality. New York: Paulist, 1985.

Schmidt, Leigh Eric. "The Making of Modern 'Mysticism.'" *Journal of the American Academy of Religion* 71.2 (2003) 273–302.

9

Reclaiming Silence as a Spiritual and Political Practice of Freedom

Min-Ah Cho

Silence is fervently sought as a spiritual practice in our time, both inside and outside religious settings. Such popular practices of silence are valuable in themselves and beneficial for managing the anxiety and stress associated with daily living. Many of these practices, however, see silence simply as a momentary freedom from the realities of pain and loss and systemic violence that exist in our surroundings, especially for those in vulnerable life circumstances. This gentle perspective on silence presents a dilemma for individuals who recognize its significance but want to address societal issues that constrain people. In both the activist and academic circles I am involved with, questions are often asked about finding a balance between contemplation and action, between the need for silent solitude and impassioned participation with the world. Can we be both deeply connected to the world and committed to the need for introspection? Can the freedom we experience in silent practice respond to the imperative for political freedom, amplifying the struggle against oppressive forces that hinder the well-being of vulnerable communities and individuals?

My chapter investigates these questions by describing the significance of freedom rooted in contemplative traditions for reframing political freedom and by challenging the obsession with autonomy pervasive in modern politics. I argue that contemplative silence can free us from the desire to control and the inclination to seek quick solutions. This freedom

RECLAIMING SILENCE AS A PRACTICE OF FREEDOM

encourages us to engage more deeply with life's realities and cultivates a longing for communion with the silence of God and solidarity with those who are silenced.[1]

I begin this chapter by differentiating contemplative silence from coercive silence, and then unraveling the political forces underlying the negative perceptions of silence in everyday life. Second, I examine how silence can be utilized in political struggles for freedom, challenging the conventional dichotomy between speech and silence that often emerges in discussions about democracy and human rights. Third, in order to ground my discussion on the Christian practice of freedom through the lens of the Gospel, I draw from Canadian philosopher Paul W. Gooch's book, *Reflections on Jesus and Socrates*, which distinguishes Jesus's silence in two ways: the silence *of* Jesus that reveals the immorality of violence and the silence *in* Jesus that demonstrates trust in divine mystery. I will discuss how Jesus's silence is reflected and practiced within Christian liturgical contexts and explore how these ideas can be extended to the struggles of everyday life in the pursuit of freedom. In conclusion, I propose that silence beckons one towards a life balanced with contemplation and action, where liberation from the world's disruptive and destructive forces becomes attainable, enabling individuals to advance toward divine love.

RECLAIMING SILENCE FOR SPIRITUAL PRACTICE

The Christian tradition has revered silence as prayer *par excellence*. The practice of silence, namely contemplation, is to be taken foremost of all in the literal sense. It is considered a means to access the divine, develop self-knowledge, and live a more holistic life. God manifests the divine self in silence, as the Psalmist sings: "Be still, and know that I am God!" (Ps 46:10). The monastic traditions of the Christian East and West developed the spirituality of silence through practice and theology.[2] The Quaker tradition epitomizes the significance of silence in liturgy and community gatherings.[3] Contemplative silence in these traditions is neither a solitary experience nor

---

1. A portion of this chapter appears in a different form in my book, *The Silent God and the Silenced: Mysticism and Contemplation amid Suffering* (Washington, DC: Georgetown University Press, 2025).

2. For more references of silence in the Christian monastic traditions, see Laird, *Into the Silent Land*; *Sunlit Absence*; Williams, *Silence and Honey Cakes*; Davis, *Monastery Without Walls*; Arico, *Taste of Silence*; McColman, *Befriending Silence*; Bianco, *Voices of Silence*; Heuertz, *Mindful Silence*.

3. For more information about the implications of silence in the Quaker tradition, see Birkel and Sheldrake, *Silence and Witness*.

indifferent to suffering, unlike in popular practices of silence; rather, it is a shared experience and common journey among the people of faith, which opens them to recognize their deepest emotions and innermost pains.

However, in a world rife with violence, silence assumes different meanings compared to those in contemplative traditions. It is a complex and multifaceted phenomenon that demands meticulous attention and examination. As philosopher Paulo Freire, feminist scholar bell hooks, and postcolonial writer Gayatri Spivak argue, when silence manifests within the frameworks of gender, race, and class, it is frequently interpreted negatively as a symptom of oppression and a submission to structural violence that restricts one's freedom.[4] Individuals and groups in vulnerable circumstances are often silenced and unheard rather than choosing silence for themselves.

Silence is *gendered*. Assertiveness and confidence are discouraged in women during socialization because they are considered unfeminine.[5] Silence is also *racialized*. The histories of racism in the US and elsewhere have tied the bodies and tongues of persons of color. Silence is *classed* as well. Poverty keeps individuals from accessing the ability and means to communicate needs, ideas, and interests.[6] Religious settings are not exceptional. Silence is *segregated*. Although contemplative silence is not foreign to the communities of people of color, the practice of silence in their communities is either detached from their experiences or unrecognized due to negative connotations of silence. Having once been a member of a Roman Catholic religious community, I still deeply desire and habitually pursue contemplative prayer even after leaving the community. However, in seeking and joining both faith and non-faith communities focused on silence, I often felt despondent to find that the participants were predominantly white, intellectual, and middle class. Many Catholic parishes of color I have attended replace silent prayer with "saying aloud" the prayers of the Hail Mary, Our Father, and the Glorias.

This complex landscape of silence indicates that a meaningful discussion about the relationship between silence and freedom requires distinguishing the spirituality of silence from coercive silence. It is also crucial to recognize that the momentary freedom experienced through popular practices of silence is insufficient without critically examining the mechanisms that silence marginalized groups. The different forms of coercive silence can be summarized in the following ways: *forced* silence upon marginalized

---

4. For more information, see Freire, *Pedagogy of the Oppressed*; bell hooks, *Teaching to Transgress*; Gayatri Chakravorty Spivak, "Can the Subaltern Speak."

5. Rodriguez, "Un/Masking Identity," 1067–90.

6. Asare, "Social Media"; Martin, "Black LinkedIn Is Thriving."

groups and individuals, *neglectful* silence of the privileged negating the suffering of others, *complicit* silence to protect themselves at the expense of putting others in danger, and *evasive* silence to seek remote peace and avoid reality.[7] These forms of silence must be confronted and broken, and the work of activists, scholars, and ministers who encourage the voiceless to speak should not be undermined.

I join and support the initiatives to break coercive silence, yet I also believe that silence in the context of power imbalance and suffering needs to be examined carefully. Such negative perspectives on silence often come from the dichotomous understanding between speech and silence. In Western intellectual and liberal democratic culture, silence is commonly associated with passivity, lack of agency, powerlessness, complicity, and concealment of truth, while speech and testimony are regarded as instruments of truth and freedom.[8] Largely focusing on empowering voiceless individuals, the project of human rights often strives to liberate and activate agency in order to speak out freely and resist coercive silence. Confiding in the speech-centered tradition, such political thought generates a set of dichotomies such as "speech versus silence, memory versus forgetting, resistance versus complicity, or power versus powerlessness."[9] Consequently, silence is equated with submissiveness, passivity, timidity, deception, and oppression across academic discipline, progressive activism, and daily life.

The dichotomy between silence and speech contains numerous problems. What underpins this dichotomy is the notion of the autonomous self within liberal politics. The concept of the autonomous self is defined as one who speaks, embodying rationality, self-sufficiency, and independence, asserting agency through speech.[10] The freedom of this secular modern self often comes at the expense of the freedom of others, especially those who are vulnerable and silenced. Furthermore, it obscures the complex power dynamics of communication and fails to capture the multifaceted nature of silence. The binary can also invalidate the effectiveness of silence as a tool for resistance, authentic self-expression, and spiritual practice, in which

7. I explore the various forms of silence in my forthcoming book, *The Silent God and the Silenced*.

8. There have been various attempts to deconstruct such binary positions between silence and speech across disciplines. To name a few, see Farmer, *Saying and Silence*; Claire, *Organizing Silence*; Glenn, *Rhetoric Retold*; *Unspoken*. Bernard Dauenhauer presents silence as a phenomenon instead of the absence of sound in *Silence*.

9. Gates-Madsen, *Trauma, Taboo*, 8.

10. Many postmodern, postcolonial, and feminist scholars have criticized the concept of the autonomous self that is associated with speech-centered culture. Notable works include Derrida, *Of Grammatology*; Spivak, "Can the Subaltern Speak"; Butler, *Gender Trouble*.

diverse forms of expression converge, and multiple (un)speaking subjects, including the Divine, find their position to be present without words. The binary also leaves a mark on the Christian practice of silence, particularly in the midst of suffering. The dominant culture that is uncomfortable with silence is equally uncomfortable with the possibility that Divine incomprehensibility is synonymous with the silence of God.

To engage with these diverse dimensions of silence, we need a refreshed understanding of silence. I consciously refrain from defining silence as the absence of sound or speech. The contemplative tradition offers a helpful guide in this regard. Many mystics, both past and present, have referred to silence as a mode of divine existence, enabling one to engage with and listen to God. Following this tradition, I view silence as a particular type of presence—more precisely, a presence characterized by absence that becomes apparent when all other forms of sound and speech are negated. Silence exists both before any sound or word arrives and after all sounds and words have departed. Its unique nature lies in the fact that it is vastly open to embracing all meanings conveyed through sound and speech, yet none of them can define it. The mode of existence of silence emulates that of God, as expressed and experienced *via negativa*, which is central to the contemplative tradition.

Thus, contemplative silence cannot be equated with coercive silence in variations such as forced, imposed, neglectful, complicit, and evasive silence. Coercive silence isolates us from a relationship, but contemplative silence links us to the whole by allowing us to hear and see what remains unheard and unseen. Coercive silence takes and suppresses one's voice, but contemplative silence restores the voice by distancing it from the forceful demand of the words manufactured by the dominant. Coercive silence destroys one's self and erases one's presence, yet contemplative silence leads one to discover, examine, explore, and transform. Contemplative silence frees one from the relentless desires and power obsessions that fuel cycles of capitalistic competition and consumer culture, redirecting their focus towards the Divine, who embodies absolute freedom. Therefore, based on the insights gained from the contemplative tradition, we can explore the spirituality of silence and the possibilities it offers for resisting coercion that limits one's political and spiritual freedom. By embracing silence as a form of presence and prayer, we open up new ways to resist oppressive forces and cultivate a deeper sense of personal and communal liberation.

CONTEMPLATIVE SILENCE AND POLITICAL STRUGGLES

Albeit not classified as religious or spiritual, the use of silence in the context of suffering and particularly acts of resistance indicates such a renewed understanding of silence. For example, silence utilized in the political struggles of marginalized groups and individuals expresses manifold meanings at the intersection of power and agency. Furthermore, silence illuminates a spiritual and transcendental dimension that cannot be reduced to a mere political scheme. To name a few cases, the Day of Silence became a tradition in 1995 to spread awareness about the detrimental impacts of bullying and harassment of LGBTQIA+ individuals. X González, a survivor of the mass shooting at Marjory Stoneman Douglas High School in Parkland, Florida, solemnly paused for four minutes and twenty-six seconds of silence at the March for Our Lives 2018 as part of their address, denouncing gun violence and committing to "stop at nothing." During the 2020 Black Lives Matter movement, protesters across the world laid on streets for eight minutes and forty-seven seconds in silence to commemorate George Floyd's last breath before his death. In winter 2022, protesters in the major cities in China held up blank sheets of paper in silent protest to express their anger over COVID-19 restrictions. Blank paper was a statement about the silencing of dissent as well as a tactic used in part to evade censorship or arrest.

The sacrality of silence is evident in these political struggles, as it sets participants free from the prevailing culture of aggression. By fostering connections among strangers, silence instills inspiration in individuals, prompting introspection and revitalized perspectives. This spiritual potential of silence creates a "fluid, non-linear, internal, and sacred" space and provides a refuge for the vulnerable.[11] Nonetheless, the sacredness manifested here is not isolated from our time's urgent and profound needs but opens us toward a refreshed imagination amid suffering. This silence allows us to go within before we have to speak or act and prepares us to shape a ground that "connects the spiritual with the political."[12] In cases of political struggle, the use of silence disrupts the traditional dichotomy between speech and silence, fostering opportunities for both contemplative action and active contemplation.

In what follows, I aim to offer a theological reflection on the sacredness of silence as manifested in political protests. The spirituality of silence, especially when experienced amidst suffering, reveals a profound connection

---

11. Carrillo Rowe and Malhotra, *Silence, Feminism, Power*, 1–2.
12. Carrillo Rowe and Malhotra, *Silence, Feminism, Power*, 1–2.

between spiritual and political freedom. Jesus's silence manifested in the Gospels aids my pursuit to delve into the spirituality of silence as it resonates with the suffering of the silenced. This exploration finds resonance in Christian spiritual and liturgical traditions and provides support to the vulnerable as they navigate the quest for meaning amidst their pain.

Jesus's Silence and the Spiritual Practice of Freedom

The God of the Abrahamic traditions is a God who speaks. Yahweh communicates with people through words. However, although speech is at the center of the communication between Yahweh and the Israelites, silence is also an explicit theme in their relationship. Both the Hebrew Bible and the New Testament include stories of theophany intertwined with silence, especially in connection with the suffering of humanity. This God is the God who commands, "Be still, and know that I am God" (Ps 46:10).[13] This God, who reveals the divine presence through "sheer silence" (1 Kgs 19:12) also listens to their cries through silence as the stories of Abel, Hagar, and many other biblical figures illustrate.

The theme of silence in the Hebrew Bible appears dramatically in the Songs of the Suffering Servant in the book of Isaiah (Isa 42:1–4; 49:1–6; 50:4–11; 52:13–53:12), which became crucial markers for Christians, disclosing the identity of Jesus as the Passover lamb. In the Passion narrative, Jesus remains silent in his confrontation with the Jewish and Roman authorities. Surrounded by Caiaphas, the high priest, the scribes, and elders, Jesus was falsely accused of blasphemy, but he chose silence as his response to them (Matt 26:63). He stands before Pilate and once again is accused by the chief priests and elders; he does not answer (Matt 27:12). Pilate asks him, "Do you not hear how many accusations they make against you?" Jesus gives him "no answer, not even to a single charge" (Matt 27:14), which surprises the governor. Being led to Golgotha, Jesus continues to be silent amidst more clamors, angry shouts, and jeering. Without a word, Jesus is moved to the cross, where he is again targeted by mockery and humiliation. Finally, Jesus breaks his long and painful silence with a loud cry, uttering not his own words but a phrase in Psalm 22: "My God, my God, why have you forsaken me?" (Matt 27:46). He receives no answer.

In his reading of the Passion narrative in Matthew, Canadian philosopher Paul W. Gooch observes both the silence *of* Jesus and the silence *in* Jesus. By remaining silent in response to such violence, the silence *of* Jesus

---

13. Hereafter, all Bible translations will follow the NRSVue.

RECLAIMING SILENCE AS A PRACTICE OF FREEDOM

discloses the immorality and senselessness of the very attempt at his trial.[14] Jesus's decision to remain silent in the face of collective deception and malice is in itself an accusation, a powerful indictment of the sinister motives and wrongful intentions of those around him.[15] Jesus does not "take up the weapon of words in self-defense" nor does he "participate in a community of corrupted discourse."[16] Rather, he lets his silence speak for itself.

Meanwhile, the silence *in* Jesus, according to Gooch, is due to his faith in God's will, which prevented him from speaking because "there are neither words nor understanding" for God's will.[17] His trust in God breaks the law of economy and allows no logical explanation because it surpasses the limit of human understanding. It is a radical silence, and an attempt to articulate may create "false expectations about our abilities."[18] Because of his deep trust in Divine Love, Jesus knew that his entire being was to remain in tune with the will of God, and thus to express that love would fulfill love. The silences *of* Jesus and *in* Jesus reveal the fundamental characteristics of contemplation wherein individuals are liberated from the disruptive and destructive influences of the world, turning instead towards the Divine.

The Passion narrative is not the only place in the Gospels showing the significance of both the silence *of* Jesus and the silence *in* Jesus throughout his life and ministry. The Gospels repeatedly present Jesus's silence whenever he carries on his internal struggles. The temptation narrative exemplifies the silence *of* Jesus. Before Jesus started his public ministry, he went to the wilderness of Judea to be alone and prepare for his mission (Mark 1:12; Matt 4:1–11; Luke 4:1–13). He was there for forty days, tempted by Satan. While Mark, who features silence most significantly among the evangelists, keeps Jesus's wilderness experience in silence without offering any comments, Matthew and Luke interrupt his silence by voicing his internal dialogue with Satan, presenting specific moral and theological tests which he must face.[19] But even in their depictions, Jesus hardly engages in conversation with Satan. Instead, he stops the dialogue by simply replying to each of Satan's questions with a short quotation from the Tanakh.[20]

The silence *in* Jesus, too, frequently appears in the Gospels. All four Gospels hinge on a Jesus agonizing in solitary prayer and remaining in

---

14. Gooch, *Reflections on Jesus and Socrates*, 57.
15. Gooch, *Reflections on Jesus and Socrates*, 59.
16. Gooch, *Reflections on Jesus and Socrates*, 78.
17. Gooch, *Reflections on Jesus and Socrates*, 79.
18. Gooch, *Reflections on Jesus and Socrates*, 79.
19. MacCulloch, *Silence*, 37.
20. MacCulloch, *Silence*, 37.

God through silence.[21] He retreats from people to a solitary place seeking silence whenever needed. One of the most striking examples of silence *in* Jesus is his prayer in the Garden of Gethsemane before being arrested (Mark 14:32–42; Matt 26:36–46; Luke 22:39–46). Approaching the last hours before crucifixion, Jesus takes his disciples with him—Peter, James, and John in Mark, and his disciples as a whole in Luke—to the garden and tells them: "My soul is deeply grieved, even to death; remain here, and stay awake with me" (Matt 26:38). He continues to move "a little further" away from them so that he can pray alone with God, allowing the disciples to join him at a distance. Mark provides his prayer: "Abba, Father, for you all things are possible; remove this cup from me; yet, not what I want, but what you want" (Mark 14:36). Matthew and Luke also do so despite slightly different wording (Matt 26:39; Luke 22:42). Jesus prays the same prayer three times in anguish, and "his sweat became like great drops of blood falling down on the ground" (Luke 22:44). In the descriptions provided by the three Synoptic Gospels for the entirety of Jesus's prayer, God remains silent. And Jesus neither argues with God nor adds more words to the prayer of his agony. The evangelists avoid verbalizing the silence in Jesus and yet portray Jesus as listening to God's incomprehensible will and consciously following it. Jesus's silence as depicted in the Gospels allows us to reflect on how his will is transformed into unhindered freedom to carry out God's will without losing any of the intensity or integrity of his struggle.

The themes of Jesus's silence in the Gospel narratives eventually converge into the greatest silence of all: the event of his empty tomb, the vanishing of the Word of God before his resurrection. The silence *of* and *in* Jesus reveals that silence can be a powerful resource for political resistance for freedom: the silence *of* Jesus manifests as an expression of denial, resistance, and non-participation in violence, while the silence *in* Jesus exemplifies a means for deeper introspection, enhancing our receptivity for new insights. In the following section, I would like discuss Jesus's silence further by focusing on the Christian liturgy and prayer centered on the Passion of Jesus, where silence is powerfully expressed as an act of *imitatio Christi*, the imitation of Christ. Exploring how Jesus's silence is manifested and experienced in liturgy will help us translate contemplative silence into an active pursuit of freedom amidst political struggles.

---

21. The Gospel verses indicating Jesus's silence include Mark 1:12, 35, 45; 2:13, 23; 3:7, 13; 4:1; 6:31–32, 45–46; 7:24; 8:27; 9:2; 14:32; 15:25, 33; Luke 6:12–13; 9:18; 11:1; 22:39; 23:46; Matt 5:1; 13:1–3; 14:22–23; 15:29; John 7:10; 8:1–2; 10:39–41.

The Significance of Contemplative Silence in Liturgy

Silence in liturgy is not simply a pause.[22] From the Roman Catholic tradition, the General Instruction of the Roman Missal indicates specific roles of silence in liturgy to prepare the participants with a "devout disposition" toward God, to recollect themselves, meditate upon the Word of God, and praise God in their hearts.[23] In Quaker worship, the belief that God communicates with each one of the spirits through "a direct and living in-breathing" of the Divine life underpins all speech and actions, with silence serving as the cornerstone of these practices.[24] In order to hear the Divine voice speaking to us, one needs to be still.[25] The purpose of silence in Christian liturgy is to listen to God who speaks in silence. Or, more specifically, to listen to "what no eye has seen, nor ear has heard, nor the human heart conceived, what God has prepared for those who love him," as the Apostle Paul writes in his first letter to the Corinthians (1 Cor 2:7–9).

Silence in Christian liturgy, above all, orients participants to the meditation of the life, death, and resurrection of Jesus. The liturgy of Tenebrae offers a tangible example of how silence powerfully witnesses the Passion of Jesus, while also inviting us to experience both the silence *of* Jesus and *in* Jesus throughout the narrative. Tenebrae, which is Latin for "darkness," "shadows," or "gloom," is the name for three prayer services located within the Christian liturgy in the last three days of Holy Week. Before the Tenebrae service begins, the reading of the Passion narrative allows the participants to engage in the liturgical drama of the Triduum, attesting the unjust and unlawful trial of Jesus and joining his silent protest against the forces of evil. Following the unbearable cacophonies of the collective wrongs recorded in the Passion narrative, the Tenebrae liturgy begins with words taken from St. Epiphanius's sermon for Holy Saturday, recognizing the mystery of the silence of the night Jesus was buried: "Something strange is happening—there is a great silence on earth today, a great silence and stillness. The whole earth keeps silent because the King is asleep."[26] Then the service proceeds with the mournful Psalms and the chanted lamentation of Jeremiah, and

---

22. Ratzinger, *Spirit of the Liturgy*, 209.

23. The four specific moments of silence in the *General Instruction of the Roman Missal* are in the sacristy before Mass, the Penitential Act and the period after *Oremus*, meditation after the homily, and post-communion. See ICEL, *General Instruction of the Roman Missal*, paras. 45, 51, 54, 56, 164, 165, 271.

24. Jones, "Rethinking Quaker Principles," 179–82.

25. Bronx, *Silence*, 20.

26. Epiphanius, "Ancient Homily for Holy Saturday."

the diminishment of candles one by one until a single candle remains to symbolize Christ.

At the end of the service, a loud noise rings in the space in darkness, emblematizing the earthquake before Jesus died, and the last candle is hidden. Then everyone departs in silence as the silence fuses with the darkness and becomes indistinguishable from it. Words and music rest in silence, making themselves part of the tacit and ongoing whole. Silence at last becomes a spatial whole that radically orients us toward the unfathomable divine mystery, inviting us to wait for the Resurrection.

While liturgy encompasses the significance of silence in a profoundly beautiful way, reflection on the significance of silence manifested in liturgy should not be restricted to the context of liturgy alone. The patristic adage *lex orandi, lex credendi*—"the way we pray determines the way you believe"[27]—underscores the importance of exploring liturgical silence beyond the confines of the liturgy itself.[28] The spirituality of silence manifested in liturgy must be organically connected to everyday life, instilling distinctive attitudes and values into the believer, which the believer can then make known beyond the confines of the church.[29]

As mentioned above, the Tenebrae liturgy is a powerful reminder of Jesus's silence. The liturgical silence exemplifies a space of freedom to listen to the God of silence as Jesus did, both externally in the sanctuary and internally in our hearts. Similar to the manner of the silence *of* Jesus in the Passion narrative, liturgical silence invites us to pause ourselves from engaging with the noise created by our own and others' discriminatory impulses and egocentric desires. Meanwhile, similar to the silence *in* Jesus, the personal and solitary space of internal silence experienced in the liturgy draws us into the divine mystery, leading us to wait for a deeper connection with the Divine and others. With this in mind, we might ask: what insights does the Tenebrae liturgy provide in understanding the role of silence at the intersection of spirituality and political struggles in pursuing freedom?

Jesus's silence, as manifested in liturgy, offers insights into how we can respond to the struggling reality of life's margins—areas where death is contained and accountability is demanded. Firstly, while liturgical silence does not signify deliberate ignorance or avoidance of the brutality of the Cross that testifies to the unjust reality of the suffering world, it prompts reflection and understanding of these realities, which can then prevent us

---

27. McGrath, *Christian Theology*, 142.

28. Derived from the fifth-century letter attributed to Prosper of Aquitaine, a disciple of Augustine of Hippo, *Lex orandi, lex credendi* underscores the force of liturgy to affect belief. See Wainwright, *Doxology*, 225–26.

29. Cavanaugh, *Theopolitical Imagination*, 92–93.

from reacting rashly or letting ideologies of dominance and abrasive political agendas take them over. In this context, attentive listening emerges as the primary and essential requirement. Spiritual insights arise when we free ourselves from the tendency to find a quick fix and instead attune ourselves to listening. Silence resists external interruptions and allows us to listen to the Divine and others. Rather than being driven to action by impulse, we become capable of embracing the potential for transformative moments that unfold organically and unexpectedly, free from the limitations of personal agendas. Silence guides us towards a state of contemplative awareness, where God takes the lead in initiating, sustaining, and revitalizing the bedrock of our perception. Here, we can bear witness to the transcendent and pave the way towards a more just and equitable world.

Secondly, understanding the significance of liturgical silence also encourages us to consider the complementary relationship between silence and speech. Silence in liturgy is by no means a simple absence of words or the opposite of sound. In liturgy, we witness the simultaneous intensification of words and silence, culminating in a reflection on the meaning of the Cross. When the words break silence, and silence soothes the words, the two engage in a mutual relationship with no hierarchical distinction. Silence creates the condition for the words and music to permeate the minds and hearts of the participants, just as darkness was the fathomless ground of light during the Creation described in Genesis. In turn, the words and music exhaust themselves to the farthest extent in the mode of imitating the God who emptied the Divine self and died on the Cross. Then, silence gives rebirth to words and music that humbly honor the mystery beyond their capabilities to comprehend. Words and music in liturgy must acknowledge that their roles are to evoke wonder and awe instead of conquering and dominating the mind.

The interplay between silence and words in liturgy prompts us to reconsider the conventional dichotomy between words and silence based on the concept of the autonomous self. Unlike the individual autonomy within liberal politics, which reinforces the dichotomy between speech and silence and pursues freedom without considering those deprived, liturgical silence presents a more nuanced approach to freedom. By inviting us to engage with the silence *of* and *in* Jesus as manifested in the Passion narrative, liturgical silence acknowledges the unspeakable aspects of suffering and the complexities of lives entangled with such unspoken aspects. This acknowledgment is especially relevant for those in vulnerable circumstances, whose autonomy is often suppressed, preventing them from expressing and practicing their full agency. True freedom involves more than personal freedom and autonomy; it requires a collective responsibility to understand and address the varied challenges that arise from people's unique identities and experiences, which may not always be voiced. This approach to freedom calls for a conscious effort to discern and pursue paths that not only liberate the individual but also contribute to the freedom of others. It acknowledges that our lives are intertwined with myriad factors, including race, gender, socioeconomic status, and more, creating a rich but sometimes challenging mosaic of human experience.

Thirdly, complementing prophetic engagement in political struggles through words and actions, contemplative silence encourages us to practice unsaying and adopt a state of receptive anticipation in our pursuit of freedom, as demonstrated by Jesus in the Passion narrative. This approach can help us reconsider entrenched conventions of thought and practice, thereby paving the way for the emergence of new insights and renewed relationships with others. It teaches us to relinquish external and internal impulses that seek to control our own lives and the lives of others based on our habits. Such a call to "wait" in attentive silence resists the illusion of freedom created by liberal politics. The built-in expectation for effective and clear communication can be set aside during this waiting period, as the earnest desire to genuinely see and listen often requires considerable time to be fulfilled. In this call to "wait" in silent listening, our shared vulnerability becomes an occasion to understand the freedom of both myself and others. Genuine solidarity with the voiceless who fight for freedom can only be achieved when the observer's mind is attuned to listening to their pains and struggles. Therefore, we witness silence stretching outward toward engagement with transformative social action and becoming a resource to prepare our hearts to resist together against the forces that silence us and close our ears.

CONCLUSION: BRIDGING CONTEMPLATIVE SILENCE WITH POLITICAL STRUGGLES IN THE PURSUIT OF FREEDOM

Thus far, I have explored the significant role of silence in both spiritual practices and political activism, emphasizing how the spirituality of silence can be translated into practice in political struggles pursuing freedom. I described how Jesus's silence in the Passion narrative, as reflected in liturgical practices, serves as both an antidote to the challenges of modern politics and as a transformative force in the pursuit of freedom within political struggles. Silence underpins the pacing of speech and action by imbuing intervals with significance, sharpening focus on the incomprehensible, and heightening receptivity to new inspirations. These moments can free us from our obsession with the autonomous self and the desire to control, reminding us of our deep connection with the divine and with others.

This discussion reveals that silence is not simply a passive retreat or momentary escape but a dynamic tool for introspection and social change, fostering a life where contemplation and action are intertwined. The synthesis aims for true freedom, rooted in Divine Love and expressed in solidarity with the oppressed, driving us towards deeper reflection and transformative action in the pursuit of both spiritual and political liberation.

The spheres of one's spiritual pursuit and political engagement are hardly separable because they are interconnected culturally, historically, and ideologically, influencing and shaping each other. Whether consciously or not, spirituality influences how Christians participate in politics. While prophetic engagement in political struggles for freedom is crucial, silence can also serve as a complementary approach to witnessing and countering various injustices often accompanied by hateful and hurtful speech and rhetoric.

Silence in political struggles does not offer an immediate solution. In our culture of violence, marked by immeasurable loss, there is a relentless demand for effectiveness and productivity. Within this framework, silence can be perceived as weak, ineffective, useless, and passive. Such pressing demands forcefully trivialize the necessity to pause and open ourselves to the unknown, unspoken, and unheard that leads us to freedom on a deeper level. It is important to exercise caution when we feel ethically obligated to "act immediately," as this approach can be hasty and overlook important considerations, potentially leading to unintended consequences. Silence trains our ears and minds to free ourselves from the urge to control and rearrange our relation to the whole by offering a heightened awareness of the silence of God as well as a deeper awareness of the silent presence of others. It invites us to recognize our dependence on God and others, while freeing us from the ideologies of dominance and abrasive political agendas. It can foster a practice conducive to political freedom, serving as a continuous critique of the oppressive voices of the powerful and as a conduit for amplifying the voices of the weak and vulnerable.

Therefore, I suggest that theology and spirituality in our time must take silence more seriously and the task of listening more strenuously in order to advance genuine accountability. Theology ought to muster the courage not only to speak but also to unspeak to renew its language. I vouch that theology is not only a matter of speaking about or to God, but a matter of listening and attending to God, who reveals the Divine self through silence. In other words, the observance of silence allows us to reflect upon the layers of uncertainty and ambiguity that remain unsolvable, irrelevant, and obtrusive in everyday life, while attuning us toward the reality of suffering others. It fosters a commitment to empathy and listening to others through God, ensuring that freedom is inclusive and equitable, recognizing that individual well-being is deeply intertwined with the well-being of society as a whole.

REFERENCES

Arico, Carol J. *A Taste of Silence: Centering Prayer and the Contemplative Journey.* New York: Lantern, 2015.

Bianco, Frank. *Voices of Silence: Lives of the Trappists Today.* Norwell, MA: Anchor, 1992.

Bronx, Jane. *Silence: A Social History of One of the Least Understood Elements of Our Lives.* Boston, MA: Mariner, 2019.

Butler, Judith. *Gender Trouble: Feminism and the Subversion of Identity.* Milton Park, UK: Routledge, 2006.

Carrillo Rowe, Aimee, and Sheena Malhotra, eds. *Silence, Feminism, Power: Reflections at the Edges of Sound.* New York: Palgrave Macmillan, 2013.

Cho, Min-Ah. *The Silent God and the Silenced: Mysticism and Contemplation amid Suffering.* Washington, DC: Georgetown University Press, 2025.

Claire, Robin P. *Organizing Silence: A World of Possibilities.* Albany, NY: State University of New York Press, 1998.

Dauenhauer, Bernard. *Silence: The Phenomenon and Its Ontological Significance.* Indianapolis: Indiana University Press, 1980.

Davis, Bruce. *Monastery Without Walls: Daily Life in the Silence.* Bloomington, IN: iUniverse, 2001.

Derrida, Jacques. *Of Grammatology.* Baltimore, MD: Johns Hopkins University Press, 2016.

Epiphanius of Cyprus. "An Ancient Homily for Holy Saturday." *Institute of Catholic Culture*, n.d. https://instituteofcatholicculture.org/articles/7476-2.

Farmer, Frank. *Saying and Silence.* Logan: Utah State University Press, 2001.

Freire, Paulo. *Pedagogy of the Oppressed*, London: Bloomsbury Academic, 2018.

Gates-Madsen, Nancy J. *Trauma, Taboo, and Truth-Telling: Listening to Silence in Post-Dictatorship Argentina.* Madison: University of Wisconsin Press, 2016.

Glenn, Cheryl. *Rhetoric Retold: Regendering the Tradition from Antiquity through the Renaissance.* Carbondale, IL: Southern Illinois University Press, 1997.

———. *Unspoken: A Rhetoric of Silence.* Carbondale: Southern Illinois University Press, 2004.

Gooch, Paul W. *Reflections on Jesus and Socrates: Word and Silence.* New Haven, CT: Yale University Press, 1996.

Heuertz, Phileena. *Mindful Silence: The Heart of Christian Contemplation.* Downers Grove, IL: InterVarsity, 2018.

hooks, bell. *Teaching to Transgress*, Milton Park, UK: Routledge, 1994.

International Commission on English in the Liturgy (ICEL). *The General Instruction of the Roman Missal*. 3rd ed. Washington, DC: ICEL, 2002. https://www.vatican.va/roman_curia/congregations/ccdds/documents/rc_con_ccdds_doc_20030317_ordinamento-messale_en.html.

Jones, Rufus. *Rethinking Quaker Principles*. London: Pendle Hill, 2014.

Liard, Martin. *Into the Silent Land: A Guide to the Christian Practice of Contemplation*. Oxford: Oxford University Press, 2006.

———. *A Sunlit Absence: Silence, Awareness, and Contemplation*. Oxford: Oxford University Press, 2011.

MacCulloch, Diarmaid. *Silence: A Christian History*. New York: Penguin, 2013.

McColman, Carl. *Befriending Silence: Discovering the Gifts of Cistercian Spirituality*. Notre Dame, IN: Ave Maria, 2015.

McGrath, Alister E. *Christian Theology: An Introduction*. London: Blackwell, 2007.

Ratzinger, Joseph Cardinal. *The Spirit of the Liturgy*. San Francisco: Ignatius, 2000.

Rodriguez, Dalia. "Un/Masking Identity: Healing Our Wounded Souls." *Qualitative Inquiry* 12.6 (2003) 1067–90.

Spivak, Gayatri C. "Can the Subaltern Speak." In *The Postcolonial Reader*, edited by Bill Ashcroft et al., 24–25. New York: Routledge, 1997.

Wainwright, Geoffrey. *Doxology, the Praise of God in Worship, Doctrine, and Life: A Systematic Theology*. New York: Oxford University Press, 1980.

Williams, Rowan. *Silence and Honey Cakes: The Wisdom of the Desert*. Oxford: Lion, 2004.

10

On Care for Our Common Gnome

Eco-Spirituality and Freedom in Maximus the Confessor

Kathleen McNutt

INTRODUCTION

How might a deeper understanding of the relationship between contemplation and freedom enrich our capacity to see and to act in ways that contribute to healing the ecological destruction that threatens creation? I will argue that Maximus the Confessor's detailed distinction between what he calls *gnome* or gnomic will, on the one hand, and natural will, on the other, entails valuable insights for the outworking of our freedom in the complex and ambiguous situation in which we find ourselves.[1] As the subtitle of Pope Francis's environmental encyclical *Laudato Si': On Care for our Common Home* indicates, the ecological crisis is an enormous challenge to our ability to dwell together on the planet and to the religious and spiritual dimensions of human life.

In our capitalist, consumerist culture, the notion of "freedom" often implies nearly unimpeded action toward a nearly unrestricted choice of objects. In everyday practice, many of us define ourselves and work out

---

1. *Gnome*, or gnomic will, is an inclination or deliberative desire which can be swayed by opinion, whereas natural will is consistent and rational. See Thunberg, *Microcosm and Mediator*, 211; Blowers, *Maximus the Confessor*, 122.

our fundamental freedom through our choices between ever-proliferating alternatives. In *Fratelli Tutti*, Pope Francis has critiqued a contemporary understanding of freedom that is both too narrow and too broad. For Francis, too many value freedom of markets over freedom of persons, and we too often take a limited view of freedom, which "becomes an illusion that we are peddled, easily confused with the ability to navigate the internet."[2] At the same time as human freedom is narrowed and curtailed in these ways, it is also absolutized: "A kind of 'deconstructionism,' whereby human freedom claims to create everything starting from zero, is making headway in today's culture."[3] This creates a situation where we feel as though our lives are totally within our own power, and yet our capacity to freely and creatively imagine possible futures is profoundly restricted, channeled to the options readily at hand.

A certain kind of consumeristic ecological consciousness has adapted itself to this situation, so that we are often encouraged to use our freedom as economic actors to make more ecologically sound *choices*: paper rather than plastic straws, Meatless Mondays (or Fridays), biking rather than driving. I am not arguing against any of these actions, but rather exploring the notion of free choice inherent in this paradigm itself. For one thing, the kinds of action and choice that are typically within our individual purview are, we recognize, not enough. We feel powerless to effect change at the scale needed to stave off ecological disaster. Our freedom to make these choices is also constrained by our social and economic circumstances: infrastructure affects our individual transportation choices, while lack of time and resources affects our habits of eating and purchasing. As Francis writes in *Laudato Si'*, the kinds of small actions we may take as individuals and families do not change the world, though they do give us hope and shape our habits and values in important ways.[4] In addition, we are met frequently with false choices, like the choice between one product and another when no product would be better. Though we are encouraged to be eco-conscious actors and consumers, as Orthodox theologian John Chryssavgis has pointed out, "it is our 'acting'" (and, I would add, consuming) "that got us into this mess in the first place."[5]

In his work championing the ecotheological teachings of the "Green Patriarch" Bartholomew of Constantinople as well as in his recent book, *Creation as Sacrament: Reflections on Ecology and Spirituality*, Chryssavgis

2. Francis, "*Fratelli Tutti*," 50.
3. Francis, "*Fratelli Tutti*," 13.
4. Francis, "*Laudato Si'*," 212.
5. Chryssavgis, *Creation as Sacrament*, 175–76.

draws on the Greek Patristic tradition to encourage contemplation rather than action alone as the foundation for building ecological consciousness in our day. Chryssavgis writes of the ecological crisis, "The image of God in creation has been shattered; the face of God on the world has been distorted; the integrity of natural life has been fragmented. Yet, it is precisely in this shattered world that we are called to discern the caring nature of the Creator and discover the sacramental nature of creation."[6] These two fundamental realities—the image of God in the world and its fragmentary and hidden nature—frame the human condition in such a way that our task is not only to do but to discern. This requires stopping, slowing down, and genuinely seeing or contemplating (*theoria*).

This essay argues that the alternative understanding of freedom and free will articulated by seventh-century monastic and theologian Maximus the Confessor provides a fuller and more nuanced account of how our God-given free will works itself out under the conditions of human existence, characterized as they are by dis-integration, and how this gift of freedom in turn allows the re-integration of human persons and communities toward fellowship with God. For Maximus, contemplation and practical action flow into one another, seeking to perform this task of re-integration through the right use of human freedom. Freedom is served, for Maximus, by contemplation. For Maximus, as we will see, free will does not consist in choosing between alternatives but in enabling rational desire for the good. In the person who is deified (since the goal of all Christian life for Maximus is *theosis*, deification or union with God), freedom is union with and voluntary assent to God's freedom which wills the good.

MAXIMUS, HISTORICAL CONTEXT, AND THE NATURAL AND GNOMIC WILLS

Many scholars have commented that Maximus the Confessor fleshes out a full conception of the will for the first time in Greek Christianity, analogous to Augustine's "invention" of the will in the West.[7] Though his terminology and some of the nuances of his ideas changed over the course of his life, Maximus ultimately developed a rich account of the will. Free will plays a crucial role in his theological system because the free motion of human persons toward God is the integrating, mediating, divinizing impulse of the whole cosmos (the universe as an ordered whole). The human person stands at the center of creation as a microcosm of all its disparate parts. For

---

6. Chryssavgis, *Creation as Sacrament*, 4.

7. McFarland, "Theology of the Will," 518; Louth, *Maximus the Confessor*, 60.

Maximus these "parts," or the "divisions of being" according to which the universe is differentially structured, are the uncreated and the created, the intelligible and the sensible, heaven and earth, paradise and the inhabited world, and male and female. The task of human beings is to unify these extremes.[8] This mediation is ultimately accomplished in Christ's incarnation, life, death, and resurrection, but we participate in this unifying action by sharing in Jesus' divinized mode of human life. In Maximus's theological anthropology, the will is a fundamental aspect of what it means to be a human being. The capacity for self-determination is a natural one; that is, in Maximus's language, it pertains to shared human nature as such and not to the particularities of any individual person. Crucially, this natural capacity for self-determination is ultimately instantiated fully in Jesus Christ, who exhibited the truest form of freedom, in which he spontaneously and freely desired and willed the good.

Maximus distinguishes, especially in his later work, between the "natural" will (*thelema physikon*), which is "rational desire" that arises from our nature, and our lived experience of free will. Free will as we actually experience it has the character of *gnomic* will (*thelema gnomikon*). Maximus lays out the distinction between these in one of his last works, *Opusculum 3* (a fragment of a letter to the priest Marinus), in which he defines the natural will as "the power that longs for what is natural," or "the natural appetency of the flesh endowed with a rational soul."[9] To will something means to desire or to long for it, and what is desired is determined by the nature of the desirer: this natural appetency "possesses the natural power of the desire for being, and is naturally moved and shaped by the Word towards the fulfilment of the economy."[10] Therefore, the natural will always desires God and the good.

By contrast, Maximus defines the gnomic will as "the longing of the mind of a particular man moved by an opinion." Particularity is important, since the natural will belongs to human nature, while the gnomic will belongs to a particular instantiation of that nature, or *hypostasis*.[11] While *gnome* is a multivalent term in Patristic and even in Maximus's own theology, it has the overall meaning of a habituated inclination[12] or a type of desire that has been deliberated over.[13] Unlike the natural will, which always inclines,

---

8. *Ambiguum 41*, in Maximos, *On Difficulties in the Church Fathers*, 1305.
9. Maximus, *Opusculum 3*, in Louth, *Maximus the Confessor*, 193.
10. Maximus, *Opusculum 3*, in Louth, *Maximus the Confessor*, 193.
11. Maximus, *Opusculum 3*, in Louth, *Maximus the Confessor*, 193.
12. Thunberg, *Microcosm and Mediator*, 211.
13. Blowers, *Maximus the Confessor*, 122.

without deliberation, toward the good (that is, God), the gnomic will is ambiguous and literally ambivalent: it can turn either way. This deliberative will can choose between a multitude of objects of desire and can be influenced by sensation, passion, habit, misuse of reason, and any number of other experiences and flaws. *Gnome* implies deliberation, consideration, choice, and opinion, unlike the spontaneous desire of the natural will. The multitude of potential objects of choice here is emphatically not a marker of the gnomic will's freedom; rather, it is a symptom of the gnomic will's tendency toward dis-integration. To put this in other characteristically Maximian terms, gnomic will relates to one's *tropos* (mode of existence) and not to one's *logos* (principle of being). This distinction is important in Maximus's theology because it enables him to separate the pattern according to which creatures are formed—the *logoi* which participate in the one Logos—and the way or mode (*tropos*) in which creatures use their freedom, for good or ill.

The distinction between natural and gnomic will is deeply consequential for Maximus. Indeed, his position on the will was condemned at the Council of Cyprus in 636 and ultimately led to his exile. Though his views were posthumously vindicated, earning him the title of "Confessor," his insistence on the importance of Christ's two wills in upholding Chalcedonian Christianity was highly contested in his lifetime and rejected by imperial decree. The nexus of issues surrounding Christ's will or wills is known as the Monothelite controversy, and in the latter portion of Maximus's life this controversy, along with complex political maneuverings, threatened to divide the church. A position known as monenergism, the idea that Christ's *energeia* (activity or operation) was one and not two, was espoused as a possible resolution to the split between Chalcedonian Christians, who affirmed that Christ had two natures, and anti-Chalcedonian Christians. When discussion of one or two *energeia* was banned, the debate shifted ground to whether Christ had one or two wills.[14]

Maximus's position was that to uphold an orthodox teaching on Christology the church needed to affirm not only two natures in Christ, but also that these two natures logically entailed two operations (dyenergism) and two wills (dyothelitism). In *Opusculum 3*, Maximus defends his dyothelite position by arguing what we have said above: that the will arises from one's nature rather than from an individual *hypostasis*. Therefore, if Christ is truly said to have two natures (a doctrine upon which his whole understanding of our salvation and deification rests, since, to quote Gregory of Nazianzus's maxim, "what is not assumed is not saved"), he must also have two wills, one human and one divine, one deified and one deifying.

14. Allen, "Life and Times of Maximus," 307.

Yet, as Maximus's opponents surely knew, the idea of two wills coexisting within one person raises a new set of questions: does this imply internal contradiction in Christ? How are we to understand the difference or distinction between the divine will and human will? The *Ekthesis*, promulgated by Emperor Heraclius in 636 or 638, which upheld the Chalcedonian definition of Christ's two natures but presented a Monothelite (one will) interpretation, stated, "How is it possible that those who confess the correct faith and glorify one Son . . . also accept . . . two contrary wills in him?"[15] Maximus's key disagreement here is with the word "contrary." Two wills need not imply that these wills are in opposition to one another.[16] Indeed, the consonance of the divine and human wills in Jesus is a key part of Maximus's soteriology.

Maximus turns to an important scriptural locus for this question: the agony in the garden, in which Jesus says to the Father, "not my will but yours be done" (Luke 22:42 NRSV). In this event, Jesus's human will, or his desire, is to avoid suffering: a deeply human impulse, and in fact, according to Maximus, a fully natural and good one that does not inherently contradict Jesus's mission: "For it was not primarily in order to suffer, but in order to save, that he became a human being."[17] Jesus's submission of his human will to the divine will of the Father is not the loss of a battle but rather the rational inclination toward the greater good. Faced with the prospect of death, Jesus' natural desire is to avoid it, but he also inclines toward the divine will, which will ultimately result in the defeat of death. Ian McFarland further points out that the drama of Gethsemane is in Jesus's response to his particular vocation, a response that does not contradict his natural inclination but does go beyond and transcends it.[18] "The Savior therefore possesses as a human being a natural will, which is shaped, but not opposed, by his divine will."[19] In Maximus's mature thought, Christ's will is a fully natural will and not a gnomic one—though earlier in his career, before the Monothelite controversy, Maximus had attributed to Christ a gnomic will that was simply fully conformed to God because it was always deified.[20]

---

15. *Ekthesis* 1:214–15, quoted in Blowers, *Maximus the Confessor*, 48.
16. Blowers, *Maximus the Confessor*, 49.
17. Maximus, *Opusculum 3*, in Louth, *Maximus the Confessor*, 194.
18. McFarland, "Theology of the Will," 526–27.
19. Maximus, *Opusculum 3*, in Louth, *Maximus the Confessor*, 194.
20. Blowers, *Maximus the Confessor*, 236.

FREEDOM, SIN, AND SPIRITUALITY

McFarland contrasts Maximus's understanding of the freedom of the will to both the dominant libertarian understanding of our own time and the Greek rationality of Maximus's own. For both of these understandings, the freedom of one's will consists in the power of choice; that is, I have free will if I have the ability to deliberate and choose between options: I can desire or act under my own power, and I also have the ability to do otherwise. This state of things, however, is characteristic not of our natural will for Maximus but only of our gnomic will. Yet it is only the natural will that is completely free. In his letter to Marinus, Maximus writes,

> The will (*thelema*) is a rational and willing desire, but choice (*proairesin*) is a deliberative desire for things within our power. Therefore willing (*thelesis*) is not choosing, for willing is a simple desire ... but choice is a confluence of desire, deliberation, and judgment ... Willing depends solely on what is natural, but choice on those capacities that belong to us and operate through us.[21]

If the freedom of the will does not consist in the availability of deliberative choice, in what does it consist? McFarland writes, "Even as God does not choose the good, but wills it naturally, so the goal of human existence is to be so united to God that by grace we, too, will the good without any deliberation."[22] Freedom here implies lack of coercion and the presence of a rational agent; an "I" who genuinely wills and desires. It does not require options; it rather implies single-mindedness in pursuit of the good.

How do we attain such single-minded freedom? Sin consists not in the operation of a gnomic will but in the *opposition* of the gnomic will to God's will.[23] As with all our capacities and desires, Christians are to make use of our *gnome* in enacting love for God and neighbor. In the *Four Centuries on Love*, Maximus writes, "Just as God who is by nature good and free of passion loves all in an equal way as his creatures but glorifies the virtuous man for having become his friend through his intention (*gnome*) and has mercy on the wicked ... so also does the one who is good and without passion through his intention love equally all men."[24] In this work on love, or charity, Maximus emphasizes the perfection of love through the *apatheia* obtained through the spiritual life. Being "without passion" means that we do not

---

21. Maximus, *Opusculum 1*, quoted in McFarland, "Theology of the Will," 523.
22. McFarland, "Theology of the Will," 517.
23. Maximus, *Opusculum 3*, in Louth, *Maximus the Confessor*, 197.
24. *Four Centuries on Love* 1:25, in Maximus, *Selected Writings*, 38.

let this thing and that grab our attention or desire and move us away from our good inclination. *Apatheia* is the fruit of the virtuous life, the crowning achievement of which is love for all. For Maximus, our *gnome*, or habits of desire, are trained precisely through ascetic struggle and acquisition of virtue. In an ecological key, if we let our desires for wealth and goods take priority over love for the neighbor, that is a bad habit. Desire is a good capacity, as we have seen, but can be misdirected.

Elsewhere, in *Ambiguum 7*, Maximus writes again about the positive use of gnomic will: "If, then, rational creatures are created beings, then surely they are subject to motion, since they are moved from their natural beginning in being, toward a voluntary (*gnomen*) end in well-being."[25] Maximus continues, "I am not implying the destruction of our power of self-determination, but rather affirming our fixed and unchangeable natural disposition, that is, a voluntary surrender of the will."[26] This surrender ends in divinization. Maximus's assertion that motion (*kinesis*), understood as causal relationship, is an inherent, good part of creaturely existence cuts against the Origenist assumption of some of his contemporaries that motion is a defect. Against the Origenist understanding of creaturely life as a fall from rest into creation and motion (*stasis-genesis-kinesis*), Maximus argues that our beginning sets in motion a journey toward rest in God (*genesis-kinesis-stasis*).[27] This triad corresponds to another triad: the movement of creatures from being, to well-being, to ever-well-being. Each of these types or modes of being allows rational creatures to participate in God in a different way; in the middle term, well-being, creatures participate most actively through training our desire and will.

Understanding our own will as a gnomic will in process of being deified, I argue, reframes the issues of choice, deliberation, desire, and inclination that we encounter as persons attempting to act for good in the world. Maximus's understanding of our gnomic will is a realistic one, recognizing the powers of appetite, deliberation, and choice as always already conditioned by our particular circumstances, while maintaining our own responsibility for forming habits of virtue that make our exercise of our gnomic will in line with the will of God. On the one hand, no one of us has a merely natural will; the gnomic will is *the* condition under which we enact our capacity for self-determination. On the other hand, the gnomic will is by definition ambiguous and ambivalent; only by the process of deification

---

25. *Ambiguum 7*, in Maximos, *On Difficulties in the Church Fathers*, 1073C.

26. *Ambiguum 7*, in Maximos, *On Difficulties in the Church Fathers*, 1076B.

27. *Ambiguum 7*, in Maximos, *On Difficulties in the Church Fathers*, 1073B. see also McFarland, "Theology of the Will," 519.

does it more closely resemble a purely natural will, that is, a will that desires what God desires. McFarland notes,

> Insofar as we are inclined to understand freedom in terms of a liberty of indifference, we invariably view the will as the locus of that freedom, as the source of our identity, so that it is by our "free" acts we make ourselves who we are. The problem is that the more we become aware of the ways in which our choices are, on the one hand, constrained and conditioned by a variety of psychological and social forces, and, on the other hand, broken and sinful in their execution, the more hopeless our situation appears. By placing the will at the center of our sense of who we are, we condemn ourselves to a task of self-construction that is impossible, in which we always and inevitably fall short. Over against this overburdening of the will with impossible expectations, Maximus's doctrine roots our identities in God in a way that allows the will to assume a real but restricted place in our overall make-up.[28]

With such an understanding of the will, we can see how ascetic struggle, contemplation, and theology are each part of a larger spiritual project of forming and transforming our wills to participate in the divine will, which, in turn, entails the flourishing of all of creation. Below, I suggest two implications of this understanding of freedom for a spirituality of ecological healing.

Contemplation and Freedom in Eco-Spirituality

For Maximus, the natural will spontaneously desires the good without deliberation. Part of our gnomic situation is that we do not always immediately discern the good because of what Chryssavgis calls the "shattered image" of God in creation.[29] Contemplation, therefore, is a crucial part of training our desiring will, because the contemplation of natures (*theoria physike*) leads to our seeing their *logoi*. As mentioned above, *logoi* are, for Maximus, the principles, blueprints, or patterns of created things. All *logoi* participate in the one Logos, the Word of God incarnate in Christ. The *logoi* are intelligible; contemplating them allows one to apprehend the Logos in them. To contemplate the *logoi* of things is to see their beauty, unity, structure, and ultimate relation to God. Through sin, not only has our ability to see things clearly been distorted, but so has the order and beauty of nature itself.

28. McFarland, "Theology of the Will," 530.
29. Chryssavgis, *Creation as Sacrament*, 4.

As we have seen above, Maximus, like many spiritual writers of his day, thinks in threes; and the development of the spiritual journey he narrates consists of three stages. First is the practical life, involving the development of virtue and the conquest of the passions; next is the contemplative life; and the final stage is the mystical life. These correspond with the five mediations of the divisions of being discussed above: uniting male and female and paradise and the inhabited world are the work of virtue; uniting heaven and earth and the intelligible and the sensible are the work of contemplation. Mystical love unites the created and uncreated.[30] Unlike some of his predecessors in mystical theology, however, Maximus does not separate practical, ascetic struggle and contemplation as two distinct chronological stages of the spiritual life but moves between them, since the role of the human being is to make manifest the intelligibility of the unity of creation—and for that we need to both see and do. The active and contemplative life mutually interpenetrate and need one another.[31] Moreover, the divine initiative makes possible the entire process. Incarnation, as the very center of the cosmos, makes possible not only mystical union with God but also the practical and theoretical components of the spiritual journey.

Norman Wirzba articulates how a *theoria*, or way of seeing, also entails an *ethos*, or way of life, and an *askesis*, or form of discipline.[32] For Wirzba, the ecological crisis is also a "crisis of seeing" and thus "we are in need of a new *theoria*, a new way of seeing the world that might better enable people to cherish the world and live more faithfully within it."[33] He details the difference between seeing the world as nature and seeing it as creation, arguing that Christian *theoria* attempts to see the world as God sees it: as God's beloved creation. Christian *askesis* purifies our ability to see like Christ through living like Christ, particularly through the purification of the passions that, when detached from the Logos, yield a selfish attachment to things that aims to acquire, consume, and cling to them rather than to seek their good. Christian *theoria* thereby enables us to love like Christ loves, in a cruciform and life-giving way.

In *Laudate Deum*, Pope Francis's urgent apostolic exhortation that recapitulates the themes of *Laudato Si'* eight years after its publication, he returns to the theme of individual climate action. He offers a realistic but hopeful appraisal of the status of individual action in the global climate movement:

30. Thunberg, *Microcosm and Mediator*, 331–32.
31. Thunberg, *Microcosm and Mediator*, 336.
32. Wirzba, "*Theoria Physike*," 213.
33. Wirzba, "*Theoria Physike*," 216–17.

> Efforts by households to reduce pollution and waste, and to consume with prudence, are creating a new culture. The mere fact that personal, family and community habits are changing is contributing to greater concern about the unfulfilled responsibilities of the political sectors and indignation at the lack of interest shown by the powerful. Let us realize, then, that even though this does not immediately produce a notable effect from the quantitative standpoint, we are helping to bring about large processes of transformation rising from deep within society.[34]

Understanding freedom in the way that Maximus understands it can help Christians to make sense of the struggle to see and act in a way that benefits the planetary community. Sin and the "shattered image" of God in a hurting creation necessitate certain practices that make it possible to see the world as God sees it. Thus our actions for sustainability, conservation, and ecological restoration are not only an outworking of our free will under our historical limitations; they are also a way of life and an *askesis* that further purifies our vision. Our small actions are not the endpoint; they are the formation of habits that enable us to further participate in the life of God. They are not the sole expression of our freedom; they are practices that lead us into more freedom and better vision. These efforts can purify and clear our moral vision so that the status quo becomes starkly unacceptable. Hence, though our actions are limited, they can lead us in the right direction on the way to "well-being."

Freedom, Community, and the Common Good

Lars Thunberg observes, "Since *gnome* is always of an individual character, the separation [of God and human beings through sin] immediately also concerns inter-human relations. Thus . . . the fallen *gnome* as it were *cuts the common human nature into pieces,* since it divides men from each other because of their different opinions and imaginations, which again instigate contrary actions."[35] Reintegration through the virtues, then, is also reintegration into human community and desire for the common good. "The individuality of the human freedom of *gnome* is fulfilled in a *free relationship to a common goal.*"[36] Rightly used, then, our will acts in communion with others for a shared higher purpose. Pope Francis speaks in *Laudato Si'* of the importance of the civic, political, and social aspects of love, manifested not

---

34. Francis, "*Laudate Deum*," 71.
35. Thunberg, *Microcosm and Mediator*, 227.
36. Thunberg, *Microcosm and Mediator*, 228.

only in direct political activity but also in community organization and solidarity at various levels.[37] We must remember that there are dimensions of human life between the micro realm of our households, where our actions can transform us but do not make much of a dent, and the macro realm of global politics, where action is so desperately needed but so contested and embattled. Mediating institutions, voluntary associations, and "third spaces" seem to be on the decline, at least in the United States, yet such experiences of community are necessary expressions of social love that can train us in the practice of engagement and ecological responsibility.

Maximus's theological work is situated within a deeply monastic and liturgical context. His *Mystagogy* reflects on the themes of unity and diversity within the Church and on the role of the liturgy in communicating and shaping the Christian religious consciousness.[38] His understanding of the ascetic life and of contemplation are thoroughly rooted in relationships and community; growth in the spiritual life is not an individual achievement. The natural will is common to all human beings, but the gnomic will, as we have seen, can lead to division based on the inclinations and opinions of individuals. Enabling the right use of freedom must then be a communal effort, not to be undertaken alone. Healing divisions, for Maximus, does not entail eliminating differences, but rather strives to unite the disparate parts of the universe into one whole. The mediating role of the human being in the cosmos is also a model for interpersonal and communal relationships that can enhance the freedom and growth of all creation.

CONCLUSION

Human freedom is paramount in the struggle for the well-being of our planet, yet our individual capacity for choice often seems hopelessly limited. I have shown how Maximus the Confessor draws a distinction between free will as we experience it—that is, gnomic will—and the natural will possessed by Jesus as a fully divinized human being. Gnomic will is inherently limited in its freedom, not despite but because of its capacity to choose among options. I have argued that this distinction helps us to frame the ambiguity of our free will in terms that might help us to integrate this ambiguity meaningfully into an ecological spirituality. Though our freedom is limited and fragmentary, often dividing us from each other and from the common good, it is also, according to Maximus, the very way in which we are called to reunify both ourselves and the cosmic community. Through

37. Francis, "*Laudato Si*," 231–32.
38. Maximus, *Church's Mystagogy*.

the right use of freedom, trained through contemplation of nature, we begin to put the pieces back together.

The role of the free will in an ecological spirituality, then, is to form the habit of desiring the good of the planetary community. Particular choices and actions follow from that desire rather than being made piecemeal. Because of the distortions of personal and structural sin, we will not always see the fruit of our will and desire immediately. We can, however, rid ourselves of some of the traps in thinking and action that come from a view of freedom and will that limits the meaning of human self-determination to a mere choice between objects. An expanded vision of freedom can help us to reject the consumeristic paradigm that seeks to both constrain and absolutize choice.

REFERENCES

Allen, Pauline. "Life and Times of Maximus the Confessor." In *The Oxford Handbook of Maximus the Confessor*, edited by Pauline Allen and Bronwen Neil, 3–18. Oxford: Oxford University Press, 2015.

Blowers, Paul M. *Maximus the Confessor: Jesus Christ and the Transfiguration of the World*. Oxford: Oxford University Press, 2016.

Chryssavgis, John. *Creation as Sacrament: Reflections on Ecology and Spirituality*. New York: T&T Clark, 2019.

Francis. "*Fratelli Tutti*: On Fraternity and Social Friendship." Encyclical Letter given October 3, 2020. https://www.vatican.va/content/francesco/en/encyclicals/documents/papa-francesco_20201003_enciclica-fratelli-tutti.html.

———. "*Laudate Deum*: To All People of Good Will on the Climate Crisis." Apostolic Exhortation given October 4, 2023. https://www.vatican.va/content/francesco/en/apost_exhortations/documents/20231004-laudate-deum.html.

———. "*Laudato Si'*: On Care for our Common Home." Encyclical Letter given May 24, 2015. https://www.vatican.va/content/francesco/en/encyclicals/documents/papa-francesco_20150524_enciclica-laudato-si.html.

Louth, Andrew. *Maximus the Confessor*. London: Routledge, 1996.

Maximos the Confessor. *On Difficulties in the Church Fathers: The Ambigua*. Edited and translated by Nicholas Constas. Vol. 1. Cambridge, MA: Harvard University Press, 2014.

Maximus the Confessor. *Selected Writings*. Translated by George C. Berthold. New York: Paulist, 1985.

McFarland, Ian. "The Theology of the Will." In *The Oxford Handbook of Maximus the Confessor*, edited by Pauline Allen and Bronwen Neil, 516–32. Oxford: Oxford University Press, 2015.

Thunberg, Lars. *Microcosm and Mediator: The Theological Anthropology of Maximus the Confessor*. 2nd ed. Chicago: Open Court, 1995.

Wirzba, Norman. "Christian *Theoria Physike*: On Learning to See Creation." *Modern Theology* 32.2 (2016) 211–30.

11

Lectio Divina and Freedom
The Prayerful, Poetic Witness of Christophe Lebreton

Michael Rubbelke

INTRODUCTION: PRAYER, POETRY, AND FREEDOM

Andrew Prevot reflects on the deeply interwoven character of material and spiritual conditions of unfreedom. He writes, "All that is materially wrong in the world is a sign of a deep spiritual crisis, a radical unfreedom of the will that we seem incapable of overcoming by ourselves."[1] Human freedom remains ever elusive so long as the material and spiritual conditions of oppression remain in place. This diagnosis prompts a poignant question: "What would an abolitionist movement against spiritual slavery look like?"[2] In Prevot's view, two components prove necessary. The first is prayer, the human being's "communion with the infinite freedom of God" which "makes one want to witness [the world's] liberation."[3] The other is poetry, "because freedom must be sung before it can be achieved."[4] Which witnesses of prayer and poetry can offer resources to contemporary spiritual abolitionist movements?

1. Prevot, "Elusive Freedom," 16.
2. Prevot, "Elusive Freedom," 16.
3. Prevot, "Elusive Freedom," 16.
4. Prevot, "Elusive Freedom," 16.

Blessed Christophe Lebreton (1950–1996), OCSO, serves as a striking exemplar for such a movement. One of seven Trappists martyred in Algeria, Christophe lived a life radically dedicated to God, his brethren, and his Muslim neighbors amid the violence and oppression engulfing his country in the 1990s. His final prayer journal poetically reflects how Scripture informs his sense of freedom in the deeply unfree Algerian context. These writings emerge from Christophe's sustained practice of *lectio divina* (sacred reading). Emphasized in Benedictine, Cistercian, and Trappist monastic life, *lectio divina* brings the human being into meditative and desire-provoking encounters with God through Biblical texts. As Christophe demonstrates, this spiritual practice gradually capacitates pray-ers to understand freedom and their world differently. *Lectio divina* roots them in a stable practice of deep listening to God and others. It helps them to embrace solidarity with the marginalized. It opens the one praying to a share in Christ's freedom.

To explore Christophe's witness, one must first understand how *lectio divina* has traditionally been understood. Guigo II's *Ladder of Monks* will provide the classic four-step definition of *lectio divina* as "the spiritual exercise" of monastics. Second, the context of Christophe's prayer journal and his practice of *lectio divina* will be explored. Third, an examination of Christophe's reflections on John 6:67–68 will reveal how he uses *lectio divina* to reflect on his situation of extreme violence and to choose to remain in Algeria. From these encounters with Scripture, Christophe's prayer and poetry empower him to choose freely in unfree circumstances and provide a poignant and enduring example to ponder as we face the challenges of our own troubled era.

WHAT IS LECTIO DIVINA?

As religious orders returned to their roots after the Second Vatican Council (1962–1965), Benedictines, Cistercians, and Trappists emphasized anew the importance of *lectio divina*. This process of slowly and meditatively reading sacred Scripture allows the reader to listen carefully for God's voice and to respond in prayer and delight. One of *lectio divina*'s foremost proponents, Jean Leclercq, understood it as an experience-based practice which distinguished "monastic theology" from other theological styles.[5] As Leclercq noted, "Christian reading of Scripture is not primarily an intellectual exercise resulting from the correct use of a scientific method. . . . These alone will never result in *lectio divina*, a Christian reading, a reading in the Spirit,

5. Leclercq, *Love of Learning*, 190–228.

a reading of Christ and in Christ, with Christ and for Christ."[6] *Lectio divina* reconnects with the authentic spirit of Benedict, unhindered by later methodical styles of spiritual reading. Since the mid-1980s, this ancient monastic practice has gained popularity for lay Catholics and Protestants. It has also received positive attention in Catholic ecclesial documents like the *Catechism of the Catholic Church* and Pope Benedict XVI's 2010 apostolic exhortation, *Verbum Domini*.[7]

For Saint Benedict, sacred reading is an essential component of monastic life. In chapter 48 of his *Rule*, Benedict enjoins his brethren to maintain "specified periods for manual labor as well as for prayerful reading" by arranging the daily schedule to prioritize work and *lectio*.[8] According to some commentators, Benedict devotes at least three hours of every monastic's day to reading.[9] However, he does not offer details about *how* this reading should be done.

The classic description of *lectio divina*'s process comes from the *Ladder of Monks* by the twelfth-century Carthusian monk Guigo II. Guigo understands *lectio divina* as a four-stage "spiritual exercise" which he defines at some length:

> *Reading* is the careful study of the Scriptures, concentrating all one's powers on it. *Meditation* is the busy application of the mind to seek with the help of one's own reason for knowledge of hidden truth. *Prayer* is the heart's devoted turning to God to drive away evil and obtain what is good. *Contemplation* is when the mind is in some sort lifted up to God and held above itself, so that it tastes the joys of everlasting sweetness.[10]

For Guigo, *lectio divina* is dynamically oriented toward discovering hidden depths of scriptural meaning. It also elicits new desires for divine goods. Reading explores a particular group of scriptural words and concepts; meditation searches for hidden connections among scriptural passages; prayer asks for the goods which become known from these connections; and contemplation receives new joys to orient the pray-er toward eternal life.

---

6. Leclercq quoted in Studzinski, *Reading to Live*, 191. Studzinski's book offers the most comprehensive overview of *lectio divina*'s evolution in English as well as its contemporary interpretations in phenomenology and theology.

7. Polan, "Lectio Divina," 650–51; Studzinski, *Reading to Live*, 194–95; Benedict XVI, "*Verbum Domini*" nos. 83, 86–87.

8. Benedict, *Rule*, 69.

9. Polan, "Lectio Divina," 650.

10. Guigo, *Ladder*, 68 (emphasis added).

Guigo walks his reader through the process of *lectio divina*, using Matthew 5:8 as his reading ("Blessed are the pure in heart, for they shall see God").[11] In the description of meditation, Guigo focuses the pray-er's attention on the verse's meaning through scriptural associations. He connects the passage with the Psalms and the figure of Job to describe purity of heart. He then meditates on what "seeing God" means, connecting these words to an encounter with the risen Christ through a dense tissue of scriptural allusions. He concludes by emphasizing how the passage kindles a desire to see the risen Christ. This one brief passage's words and concepts have opened to new perspectives through meditation. As Guigo writes, "Do you see how much juice has come from one little grape, how great a fire has been kindled from a spark, how this small piece of metal . . . has acquired a new dimension by being hammered out on the anvil of meditation?"[12] In this view, *lectio divina* expands rather than reduces what Scripture means. It creates new meaning for the pray-er by connecting previously isolated texts (and experiences) in new and unexpected ways.[13]

Guigo links this expansion of meaning with an affective response. *Lectio divina* uncovers a new facet of good to be desired. From meditation, the soul "is consumed with longing, yet it can find no means of its own to have what it longs for; and the more it searches the more it thirsts. As long as it is meditating, so long is it suffering."[14] Aware of her own incapacity, the reader prays for what she desires, boldly asking the Author of Scripture to give the goods which meditation has discovered. Guigo models such prayer as he passionately writes, "All the while in my meditation, the fire of longing, the desire to know you more fully has increased. When you break for me the bread of sacred Scripture, you have shown yourself to me in that breaking of bread, and the more I see you, the more I long to see you, no more from without, in the rind of the letter, but within, in the letter's hidden meaning."[15] In response to prayer, the Lord occasionally grants contemplation—"a little taste of how sweet and delightful" the Lord is—yet this unmerited gift cannot remain long. Contemplation disposes the soul to

---

11. Scriptural texts in this chapter are from the NABRE.

12. Guigo, *Ladder*, 71.

13. For Guigo, meditation is not limited to scriptural texts. This expansive and allusive intellectual process describes an essential aspect of the act of reading, whether in *lectio divina* or otherwise: "The good and the wicked alike can read and meditate; and even pagan philosophers by the use of reason discovered the highest and truest good" (Guigo, *Ladder*, 72).

14. Guigo, *Ladder*, 71.

15. Guigo, *Ladder*, 73.

persevere in meditation and prayer.¹⁶ As the *Ladder of Monks* indicates, *lectio divina* prompts a dynamic intellectual and affective transformation. This change depends upon an encounter of divine and human freedom through Scripture's words, and it leads the pray-er onward to eternal life.

If Saint Benedict emphasizes the importance of *lectio divina* and Guigo highlights how it operates in a transformative way, we must explore more concretely what happens when understanding and desire expand the meaning of a scriptural text. One might object that Guigo's description of *lectio divina* may be used as a tool to restrain freedom, particularly if it results only in private insight, not social liberation. Moreover, on Guigo's account, *lectio divina* encourages the reader to desire heavenly goods, which some would argue can function as an "opiate for the masses" rather than a spur toward freedom. The witness of Christophe Lebreton's prayer journal answers these objections. For Christophe, *lectio divina* functions as an essential tool for discerning freedom amidst uncontrollable violence in Algeria in the 1990s. To understand Christophe's work, his context must be explored, so that one can investigate his concrete insights from this spiritual practice.

FRAMING CHRISTOPHE LEBRETON'S PRAYER JOURNAL

Throughout the 1990s, Algeria was a site of profound spiritual and material unfreedom. The long-standing socialist government canceled the legislative elections of 1991 due to its fear that Islamist candidates would prevail. As a result, widespread violence from groups like the Groupe Islamique Armée (GIA) consumed the country and claimed thousands of lives. This undeclared civil war found an especially deadly outlet against foreign-born residents associated with France's colonial legacy.¹⁷ These include the nineteen martyrs of Algeria who were beatified in 2018. Killed between 1994 and 1996, these members of religious orders chose to remain with the Algerian people in this time of terror rather than return to Europe.¹⁸

Among the martyrs, the Trappist monks of Our Lady of Atlas in Tibhirine offer a particularly vibrant witness to freedom. Algeria's violence directly affected their community. A group of twelve Croatian construction workers who frequented Tibhirine for Mass were murdered on December 15, 1993. Nine days later, on Christmas Eve, the monastery itself was raided by GIA fighters. This sparked a debate among the monks about whether

---

16. Guigo, *Ladder*, 78.
17. Kiser, *Monks*, 113–30.
18. Georgeon and Vayne, *Simply Christians*, viii–ix.

they ought to stay or leave. Led by their prior, Christian de Chergé, the community resolved to stay as long as it did not put the surrounding townspeople in danger. That resolve eventually led to the monks' martyrdom. On March 27, 1996, seven of the monks were kidnapped and held hostage for a prisoner exchange which never took place. The GIA announced their death on May 21.[19]

The youngest monk at Tibhirine, Christophe Lebreton, was a poet, and his prayer journal creatively and beautifully records the unfolding of his relationship with God in community over decades. As a young man, Christophe went to minor seminary but left to explore other romantic and political options as a law student in Tours in the late 1960s. He first encountered the Trappists of Tibhirine during his government-required time teaching in Algeria. This sparked his sense of vocation with the Trappists. He made solemn profession at Tamié in France in 1980, then transferred his vow of stability to Tibhirine in January 1989, where he was ordained on January 1, 1990. At Tibhirine, Christophe was responsible for tending the monastery's garden with local villagers as well as acting as novice master for the community.[20] His final prayer journal begins four months before the GIA's visit, and its last entry is written only a week before the monks' kidnapping.

To read Christophe's journal is to enter his own practice of *lectio divina*. Part diary, part *florilegium*, part chronicle, the journal is a site where Christophe records, listens, and responds to multiple voices. In addition to personal spiritual reading, the journal contains verses from the Psalms of the Divine Office, scriptural readings from the lectionary, selections from meal readings, discussions in monastic chapter meetings, letters, and conversations with monks and villagers. As Christophe's confrere, Jean-Pierre Schumacher, notes, the journal "discreetly reveals the interior of the life of one applying himself, like a diligent and interested pupil, to write in living letters the great history that is written by the very hand of the Master of History."[21] In this journal, we find divine and human freedom encountering each other through the medium of Scripture. Its prayer and poetry point to the possibility of a new world.

Christophe's journal illustrates several features of *lectio divina* in practice. First, while rooted in the Biblical text, *lectio* does not remain a solely textual or associative exercise. Rather, careful attention to Scripture elicits a broader listening to the rest of life, generating new meaning and desires in dialogue with the scriptural word. We can see one example a few weeks after

19. Kiser, *Monks*, 124–43, 145–55, 220–33.
20. Kiser, *Monks*, 64–66, 72–74, 79–82.
21. Schumacher, "Foreword," xxiv.

the GIA's incursion into the monastery. Here, Christophe mingles Jesus's words with the prior's and one of his coworkers in the garden:

> The eyes of the poor appeal to your authority in us. Christian said to M., Ali's son: "You know, we are a bit like the bird on the branch." And he answered: "But look: You are the branch. We are the bird. And if they cut off the branch . . ." There is a Gospel authority here that is recognized as doing more good than the Law: If you were to leave: Tibhirine would [be] finished, there would be nothing but quarrels. . . . We have to draw from the source of your authority, from the love with which you are loved. I must promote your authority in M., "my second-in-command" [!]. In each one of those with whom I work. To recognize it and rejoice in it: "I bless you Father for hiding these things."[22]

This text represents the diversity of voices finding expression through Christophe's scriptural meditations. It also indicates one way Christophe reflects on the Bible. As here, Scripture sometimes acts as the touchstone which reveals the deeper meaning of Christophe's everyday events. At other times, Christophe acts as commentator, recording interactions and other quotations as reflections on lines of scriptural text. He will also frequently take one line of Scripture and repeat it, weaving other reflections and quotations to ruminate upon it. For Christophe, the spiritual practice of *lectio divina* forms an essential process for sense-making in his daily life. It allows him to connect everyday events to salvation history, giving them deeper significance.

Second, *lectio divina* reveals and deepens the meaning of key experiences or texts from the pray-er's personal narrative. Far from giving straightforward literal injunctions from the Lord's mouth, *lectio divina* connects scriptural passages with significant moments in the pray-er's love story with God. These moments and the meanings they generate will be unique to each reader. In this way, *lectio divina* incorporates pray-ers' life-stories into the ongoing drama of Scripture. Christophe continually refers his meditative prayer back to two scenes that have been central to his own life drama.

First, Christophe experienced Christ's "I love you" in a powerful way. After declaring "I love you" to a lover and being met with silence while a law student in Tours, Christophe experienced Christ speaking these words back to him in the silence.[23] This "I love you" returns repeatedly in Christophe's journal—both in writing and his drawings—as a way of marking

22. Lebreton, *Born*, 31–32.
23. Lebreton and Minassian, "Frère Christophe," 498.

Christ's presence and guidance throughout his journey. As he writes near the journal's beginning: "Your *I love you* appeared to me one day. I have not recovered from it. . . . On one All Saints' Day I signed on the official sheet your *I love you* [referring to his solemn profession in 1980]. What takes place here is a hidden story, it is a game of love or nothing at all."[24] This experience serves as an anchor-point, informing Christophe's experience of violence and orienting his scriptural meditation.

For instance, in Christophe's entry on May 8, 1995, he is meditating on Jesus's words in the Good Shepherd discourse of John 10:1–10, the Gospel for Mass that day. He writes:

> To be your disciple means to be here, in Tibhirine—on this very morning: through you and out of you. I have come into Algeria through this gate. We have great freedom to go at our own speed, like you. You have come that all may have life, and have it completely. The point is being here like people who have their life from you, to the extreme of shedding all self-interest. To come to Algeria through you is a movement of infinite and precise love: God, love this people, be the servant of my *I love you*.[25]

Christophe remains close to the scriptural text, emphasizing Christ as the gate as well as Christ's goal of giving life abundantly in verses 9–10. At the same time, he applies these words directly to his life at Tibhirine, reflecting on what his response to Christ's "I love you" spurs him to do in a time of violence. He orients his meditation through the grounding words he had received years before. Christ's "I love you" mediates scriptural meaning for Christophe. So too *lectio divina* orients the reception of Scripture for readers according to the unique "salvation history" recounted in their own lives.

Christophe also frequently invokes John's account of Christ's crucifixion. This multivalent scene expresses several realities for Christophe simultaneously. The cross most fully expresses the "I love you" of Christ for all human beings.[26] It is the place where the Church is born from the side of Christ and the Spirit is breathed out at Jesus's last breath. Calvary is also where Christophe remains close to Mary, to whom he had consecrated himself and maintained an intense devotion throughout his life.[27] This scene forms a sort of leitmotiv to his other scriptural meditations.

---

24. Lebreton, *Born*, 6 (emphasis original).
25. Lebreton, *Born*, 151 (emphasis original).
26. See, e.g., Lebreton, *Born*, 71.
27. Olivera, "Behold," 221–25, 227–29.

For example, on December 13, 1994, Christophe is meditating on how the community ought to respond to the possibility of being forced to leave Algeria. To make this discernment, he brings the monastic community to the foot of the cross:

> A community is not called to secure survival for itself at all costs, but rather to give birth, to give life through the grace of the Spirit. "Woman, here is your Son . . ." It's unexpected: the Gift enters the Church at that very hour of Calvary. It seems to me we cannot exclude possible separations among us if there is a compulsory departure. Perhaps we ought to discuss that. Compulsory separations if one or/and another . . . is murdered.[28]

Set before the cross with Mary, breathing the gift of the Spirit, the Tibhirine community can discern its ultimate future, even in the face of death, failure, or separation. If life can emerge from the cross in unexpected ways through Mary and the Spirit, so too the possible end of the Atlas community can give new life. One notices that *lectio divina* leads Christophe to question rather than reinforce the status quo of the community. It encourages an active and Spirit-driven response to their concrete circumstances, especially in a fraught and unfree context.

Christophe's reading of Scripture does not tend toward a rigid "literalization" or one-sided application of any text. Rather, he receives new insights and applies them to his experiences in expansive and multifaceted ways. This reflects the general dynamism of *lectio divina*, which views as suspicious any insistence on there being only one "right" way to interpret a text. The literal sense of Scripture opens through meditation and prayer to vast depths of meaning and value beyond the letter. These meanings and values hold the potential for open-ended enrichment with further conversation partners as well as for leading to new encounters with the same text.

Having framed Christophe's context as well as some general features of his practice of *lectio divina*, one can now fruitfully explore his reflections on freedom. Given the vast array of possible examples in his writing, focus will be restricted to his use of John 6:67–68. Using this passage, Christophe engages the concrete question of freely staying at Tibhirine after the GIA's raid on the monastery, and his insights contain broader relevance for questions regarding freedom.

---

28. Lebreton, *Born*, 124–25.

FREEDOM IN CHRISTOPHE'S LECTIO DIVINA

The journal returns repeatedly to John 6:67–68. These verses at the conclusion to the Bread of Life discourse contain an important question and answer for Christophe: "Jesus then said to the Twelve, 'Do you also want to leave?' Simon Peter answered him, 'Master, to whom shall we go? You have the words of eternal life.'" Three extended examples of Christophe's meditation and prayer on this passage reveal how it shapes his reflection on freedom over the course of a year.

On April 11, 1994, following Easter, Christophe reflects on the community's decision to stay in Algeria. This decision still feels provisional, given that other circumstances or orders from the papal nuncio may change it. He probes the community's choice more deeply in light of Peter's question:

> "Where would we go, Lord?" The question is permanently being asked within us. It keeps going right through us ever since the encounter. We live with it, I think, pretty well, each one according to his temperament. What Peter says—there, standing before you—remains inseparable from the same question experienced in reality: "To whom would we go, Lord?" Your word here makes us live for ever [sic]. Your word makes us live always[:] your Word in us goes out to others, and your word in them comes forth to us. To whom would we go . . . it's almost a decision to leave, but it's been put off until later: Your word makes us live here so we stay, we abide. Come, Lord—O You!—here.[29]

The verse from John is repeated three times, and Christophe engages the passage progressively. First, he notes that Peter's question is not simply "past," but inseparable from the monk's contemporary dilemma. As a result, the monk's question can be further illuminated by Peter's answer, which Christophe explores in the second repetition, "You have the words of everlasting life" (John 6:68b). For Christophe, this eternal life is rooted "here," at Tibhirine, and it opens an exchange of Christ's Word between the monastic community and its neighbors. Both monks and neighbors are equally necessary for this dialogue in Christ. In the final repetition, Christophe notes the indecisive character of the decision to stay, but again roots the community in Jesus's word of life to them. Listening to and receiving the Word—not only described but enacted—thus stabilizes Christophe's desire to remain.

Christophe reflects on this passage again on Sunday, August 21, 1994. John 6:60–69 serves as the lectionary's daily Gospel reading. In this passage,

---

29. Lebreton, *Born*, 74. In this and the following passages, I have added punctuation in brackets where verse breaks originally separated Christophe's phrases.

Christophe notes that the ultimate decision is not between staying or leaving Tibhirine but about remaining on the way who is Jesus Christ:

> "And you, do you want to go away?" To go away. Jesus knows what it is: to go against the Father who gives us to Him, to go against the Gift that draws me to You, and in You I go to the Father. "To whom would we go?" To be here in order to go to you. This is beyond a choice between different possibilities. We are not at the convergence of different roads, but before you, who are the Way that opens out. And I am caught up in the event: drawn by your freedom as Son as if by your inhaling breath. To believe becomes the only locomotion that is worthwhile: going to You. A way that is almost obligatory but that does no violence at all to myself and invites me to keep on moving on that path, precisely on this way where your hand leads me[,] a way opens up and at the same "time"[,] an impulse runs through me[:] I can back down or consent.[30]

Christophe brings Peter's words together with Thomas's in John 14:5: "Master, we do not know where you are going; how can we know the way?" Jesus's answer, "I am the way and the truth and the life. No one comes to the Father except through me" (John 14:6) opens a new perspective. The ultimate choice is not leaving or staying but remaining in and with Christ, which may entail relinquishing knowing what the right option is in advance. Bringing these two Johannine texts together reveals that the community ultimately faces a choice for a person—Jesus—who shares divine freedom with the monks and capacitates them to take the next step in faith and in freedom, though they do not know where they are going. This choice is foundational, but it must also be renewed daily, knowing that one can "back down" from making it.

One final reflection on John 6:67–68 occurs on the Feast of the Chair of St. Peter (February 22) in 1995. A reading at supper the previous evening referenced Jesus's words in John 6:67, and this moves Christophe to meditate on the passage once more:

> "And you, don't you want to go away?" (John 6). Such probing by the Gospel deeply touches me. Without judging the departure of any of the others, for myself to go away from this place would mean to stop walking with you, in your steps, committed as they are to this land of Algeria. I also hear this question as coming from my neighbors, from Moussa, from Mohammed and from Ali: Do you want to go away, to leave us? But the question comes

---

30. Lebreton, *Born*, 102.

from You and keeps me free in the Gift of the Father, binding me to you here. Will we have to leave one day? Until then, never let me be separated from you. "Lord, to whom would we go?" You speak of living for ever [sic].[31]

Christophe reflects on these words in three movements. First, he describes what they mean personally, without judging how his monastic brethren would respond. For him, leaving Algeria would be to leave Christ's presence in this place. Second, Christophe imagines Christ's question on the lips of his coworkers in the garden (Moussa, Mohammed, Ali), who are concrete signs of the Lord's presence in Algeria. This signals the importance of his commitment to his Muslim neighbors. Finally, the question refocuses Christophe on Jesus, allowing him to see that it is a question asked of him on the way to the Father in the Spirit *at Tibhirine*, the place where Jesus desires him to be. It is a question which invites and spurs his free response, allowing him to forgo the certainty of a permanent commitment ("Until then . . ."). Christophe renews his resolve to stay in the words of Peter, following Christ freely here and now.

These examples show how Christophe's practice of *lectio divina* informs his understanding of freedom in concrete circumstances. One scriptural passage incorporates everyday life into the story of salvation history. This prayer practice functions as a crucible of associations and desires. Christophe's everyday experiences are purified here, and he receives the gift to see differently and to resist the fear and violence engulfing Algeria. Such a gift ultimately bears fruit in "the gift of one's own life for Christ and his gospel," an ending which demonstrates why Christophe's journal has become a "treasured [portion] of [the Trappist's] spiritual patrimony," in the words of Dom Bernardo Olivera.[32]

CONCLUSION: LEARNING TO PRAY AND SING FREEDOM WITH CHRISTOPHE

Though many lessons emerge over the occasional and unplanned course of Christophe's journal, three important components regarding freedom emerge. First, freedom is rooted for Christophe in a stable form of listening. One year after the GIA's visit to the monastery, Christophe reflects on the stability which true freedom entails: "Elizabeth's 'No!' before the whole clan impresses me: 'No, he shall be called John.' In order to truly come, Jesus'

---

31. Lebreton, *Born*, 139.
32. Olivera, *How Far*, 121.

'Yes!' (to his Father) needs various freedoms that are determined, firm, unshakable, without being obstinate, because at bottom what is involved is obedience in the Breath."[33] The acceptance of freedom requires the rejection of options which lead to unfreedom. Elizabeth's "no," for instance, opens up a new future by refusing to continue the custom of naming her son after her husband. So too, the one who listens to the Word of God in *lectio divina* must refuse any customary options which would prohibit a free "yes" to the Father.

Additionally, in listening to the voice of Christ attentively from every possible source, Christophe discerns with his community how to say "yes" to divine freedom. It is this listening, this obedience which is essential. Prolonged encounter with the scriptural Word of God produces a sensitivity in the pray-er to the possible presence of that Word in every word. As Christophe writes, "When it's a question of being monks here, this body [of Christ's presence] . . . would be characterized by . . . its wide-open ears, its gaze, its Nazarene-Trappist accent: and its child's size. The Father is GREATER."[34] This openness to the Word requires humility in the face of every temporal circumstance to listen, look, and speak as a beloved child of the Father in Christ. *Lectio divina* functions as an essential, daily practice to enact this stable form of listening.

Second, particularly in situations of seemingly unchangeable political difficulty like Algeria's in the 1990s, freedom must be defined as liberative solidarity with "the little people."[35] Christophe describes the monks' freedom as "the freedom of hostages: not the freedom to escape but the freedom of the person who goes beyond it all, breaking through the imprisonment imposed by all forms of violence."[36] Such a freedom promotes neither a martyr's identity nor resignation to an inherently violent situation, but enjoins Christophe to change the root causes of material and spiritual unfreedom. It refuses to settle with an unjust status quo out of fear.

Moreover, this freedom is oriented to change for those groups most affected by violence, even when there is no concrete or easily discerned path forward. Christophe notes, "Christian talked to me about us as hostages. Yes, but we must live this experience identified with the little people, with a view to LIBERATION and with the very FREEDOM of Jesus Christ: 'No one can take my life.'"[37] Only by identifying with the villagers and townspeople

---

33. Lebreton, *Born*, 125.
34. Lebreton, *Born*, 67 (emphasis original).
35. Lebreton, *Born*, 145.
36. Lebreton, *Born*, 67.
37. Lebreton, *Born*, 82 (emphasis original).

of Algeria can Christophe imagine his freedom being expressed, even in the gift of his own life. In concrete situations of uncontrollable violence, solidarity with the marginalized is the measure of true freedom, even as it can be expressed in different ways based on relationship to these beloved ones.[38] As *lectio divina* sensitizes the reader to God's overwhelming love for "the least of these" in Scripture, it unveils the hidden reality of Christ within these poor and vulnerable ones.[39]

Finally, Christophe understands his own freedom as a concrete enactment of Jesus Christ's freedom here and now. Freedom is not possessed autonomously but participatively, drawing us into relation with the Son Who identifies Himself with the least. Christophe describes this in terms of "becom[ing] an accomplice of the Innocent. And to receive from [Jesus] the attitude, the gesture, and even the words, adjusted as all these are to the precise measure of our listening ability, of our availability, of our obedience. I am learning freedom in the SPIRIT."[40] Listening and solidarity become modes of our participation in Christ's freedom, Who is the enfleshed Word generated by the Father, radically committed to solidarity with all human beings. Christophe's *lectio divina* opens a dialogue with Christ, whose "I love you" echoes throughout the words of Scripture, inviting Christophe to enter a conversation with ever-deepening significance, even to the foot of the cross. Such a conversation can alter the unfree values of our world.

In response to Andrew Prevot's invitation, Christophe Lebreton offers a model for how prayer and poetry enflesh a challenging and prophetic witness for spiritual freedom today. With the nineteen Algerian martyrs, Christophe calls us to a stable form of deep listening which can free us for liberative solidarity in Christ. He shows how the practice of *lectio divina* proves invaluable as a "practice for a spiritual abolitionist movement." Though the contemporary American experience of unfreedom proves significantly different from Algeria's, Christophe reveals how praying with

---

38. For instance, Christophe recognizes that it may become *more* dangerous for the townspeople of Tibhirine for the monks to stay, which would shift their choice to remain: "Perhaps it's not enough to say that we don't have to choose between the powers that be and the terrorists. As a matter of fact, every day we already make the concrete choice in favor of those Jean-Pierre calls 'the little people.' We cannot stay if we cut ourselves off from them. That makes us depend, in part, on their choice concerning us. We could become troublesome to them tomorrow or later on" (Lebreton, *Born*, 145).

39. In this way, *lectio divina* on Scripture may be seen analogously to the believer's perception of the Eucharist: what appears to be a normal human word can be revealed to the ears of faith as the enfleshed Word of God to me now. Just as the Eucharist encourages the recognition of the "hidden Christ" in what appears to be bread and wine, so too *lectio divina* draws attention to Christ speaking from the least likely person.

40. Lebreton, *Born*, 109 (emphasis original).

Scripture can empower the struggle for elusive freedom. May we make our own the attitude of freedom which opens the pages of Christophe's final journal: "I shall say what comes to me from you and writes itself in me[;] this writing detaches me from the world[.] Who will teach me how to write on earth as it is in heaven?"[41]

REFERENCES

Benedict. *The Rule of Saint Benedict in English*. Edited by Timothy Fry. Collegeville, MN: Liturgical, 1981.

Benedict XVI. "*Verbum Domini*: Post-Synodal Apostolic Exhortation on the Word of God in the Life and Mission of the Church." Post-Synodal Apostolic Exhortation given September 30, 2010. https://www.vatican.va/content/benedict-xvi/en/apost_exhortations/documents/hf_ben-xvi_exh_20100930_verbum-domini.html.

Georgeon, Thomas, and François Vayne. *Simply Christians: The Lives and Message of the Blessed Martyrs of Tibhirine*. Translated by Daniel B. Gallagher. Huntington, IN: Our Sunday Visitor, 2020.

Guigo II. *The Ladder of Monks: A Letter on the Contemplative Life and Twelve Meditations*. Translated by Edmund Colledge and James Walsh. Kalamazoo, MI: Cistercian, 1981.

Kiser, John W. *The Monks of Tibhirine: Faith, Love, and Terror in Algeria*. New York: St. Martin's, 2002.

Lebreton, Christophe. *Born from the Gaze of God: The Tibhirine Journal of a Martyr Monk (1993–1996)*. Translated by Mette Louise Nygård and Edith Scholl. Collegeville, MN: Cistercian, 2014.

Lebreton, Christophe, and Dominique Minassian. "Frère Christophe Lebreton (1950–1996)." In *Moines de Tibhirine: heureux ceux qui espèrent: autobiographies spirituelles*, edited by Dominique Minassian, 489–688. Paris: Les Éditions de Cerf, 2018.

Leclercq, Jean. *The Love of Learning and the Desire for God: A Study of Monastic Culture*. Translated by Catherine Misrahi. 3rd ed. New York: Fordham University Press, 1983.

Olivera, Bernardo. "Behold Your Mother: The Experience of a Contemporary Martyr, Christophe Lebreton (1950–1996)." *Cistercian Studies Quarterly* 41.2 (2006) 217–34.

———. *How Far to Follow? The Martyrs of Atlas*. Kalamazoo, MI: Cistercian, 1997.

Polan, Gregory J. "*Lectio Divina*: Opening to God's Word." In *The Oxford Handbook of Christian Monasticism*, edited by Bernice M. Kaczynski, 645–57. Oxford: Oxford University Press, 2020.

Prevot, Andrew. "Elusive Freedom: The Struggle Continues." *Proceedings of the Catholic Theological Society of America* 77 (2023) 1–17.

41. Lebreton, *Born*, 6.

Schumacher, Jean-Pierre. "Foreword." In *Born from the Gaze of God: The Tibhirine Journal of a Martyr Monk (1993–1996)*, by Christophe Lebreton, xxiii–xxiv. Translated by Mette Louise Nygård and Edith Scholl. Collegeville, MN: Cistercian, 2014.

Studzinski, Raymond. *Reading to Live: The Evolving Practice of* Lectio Divina. Trappist, KY: Cistercian; Collegeville, MN: Liturgical, 2009.